WELLINGTON'S SMALLEST VICTORY

Peter Hofschröer, a specialist in Napoleonic history, is the author of the critically acclaimed and award-winning two-volume study *1815 – The Waterloo Campaign* (Greenhill Books).

Further praise for *Wellington's Smallest Victory*:

'A work of remarkably skilful historical investigation, and its findings may well dismay the Duke of Wellington's many admirers . . . It is often the footnotes of history which provide the most absorbing reading. Almost two hundred years after Waterloo, this long-overlooked and lamentable story has at last been unravelled.' Peter Weston, *Literary Review*

'[Hofschröer's] knowledge is great, his research formidable and his evidence impressive . . . This is an engaging and informed account of Siborne and his wonderful model, now displayed in the National Army Museum. It's a fascinating footnote to history, and essential reading for students of the battle.' Alan Judd, *Daily Telegraph*

'The mesmerizing story of a lieutenant whose research revealed that the glorious victory of 1815 wasn't all it seemed. Fascinating.' *Good Book Guide*

'Mightily impressive. I remain a fan of the Duke of Wellington. But, as this well-researched book demonstrates, he was jealous of his reputation, and brought his weight to bear on accounts that conflicted with his own.' Richard Holmes, author of *Redcoat*

'[Siborne] was the only human casualty of – as Hofschröer's brilliant title suggests – the Duke of Wellington's smallest victory. Hofschröer's allegory works on many levels. It is a tale of arrogance and conceit, and contempt for verisimilitude. It portrays the age-old ruthlessness of politicians on the make. It is relevant to our twenty-first-century attempts to disentangle the battlefield facts from battlefield spin. But it is mostly a memorable story of two men who, under vastly different pressures, had identical petty human frailties.' Roger Hutchinson, *Scotsman*

'Fascinating . . . A quirky cautionary tale for those who would mess with the establishment.' Nick Smith, *Geographical*

'What a brilliant idea for a book and, surely, one of the wittiest and best titles for a recent volume of military history! Siborne did his job to reveal the truth, but Wellington did his job to make history work for him – and Britain. Hurrah for them both – and hurrah for this book!' Tim Newark, *Military Illustrated*

Wellington's Smallest Victory

THE DUKE, THE MODEL MAKER
AND THE SECRET OF WATERLOO

Peter Hofschröer

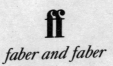

faber and faber

First published in 2004
by Faber and Faber Limited
3 Queen Square London WC1N 3AU
This paperback edition first published in 2005

Typeset by Faber and Faber Limited
Printed in England by Mackays of Chatham, plc

A CIP record for this book
is available from the British Library

ISBN 0–571–21769–9

2 4 6 8 10 9 7 5 3 1

To Frederick White (1914–2003), my history teacher

Contents

Additional documents of interest can be found on the Faber website:

William Siborne: A Chronology
Wellington's *Waterloo Despatch*
The Waterloo Campaign – Timetable of Events
Reasons Why 40,000 Prussians were Removed from the Model

www.faber.co.uk

List of Illustrations

ILLUSTRATIONS IN THE TEXT

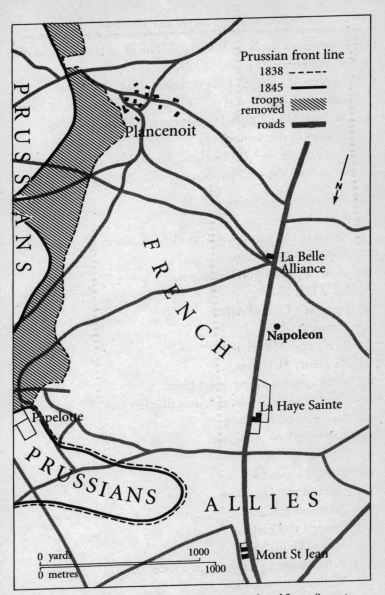

Prussian front line
1838 – – – –
1845 ⎯⎯⎯
troops
removed ▨▨▨
roads ▬▬▬

PRUSSIANS

Plancenoit

N

FRENCH

La Belle
Alliance

Napoleon

La Haye Sainte

Papelotte

PRUSSIANS   ALLIES

0 yards   1000
0 metres   1000

Mont St Jean

The number of Prussian soldiers represented was reduced from 48,000 to
8,000 when the Large Model was refurbished after its first exhibition in 1838.

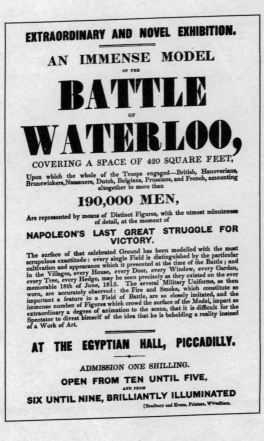

EXTRAORDINARY AND NOVEL EXHIBITION.

AN IMMENSE MODEL

OF THE

BATTLE

OF

WATERLOO,

COVERING A SPACE OF 420 SQUARE FEET,

Upon which the whole of the Troops engaged—British, Hanoverians, Brunswickers, Nassauers, Dutch, Belgians, Prussians, and French, amounting altogether to more than

190,000 MEN,

Are represented by means of Distinct Figures, with the utmost minuteness of detail, at the moment of

NAPOLEON'S LAST GREAT STRUGGLE FOR VICTORY.

The surface of that celebrated Ground has been modelled with the most scrupulous exactitude: every single Field is distinguished by the particular cultivation and appearance which it presented at the time of the Battle; and in the Villages, every House, every Door, every Window, every Garden, every Tree, every Hedge, may be seen precisely as they existed on the ever memorable 18th of June, 1815. The several Military Uniforms, as then worn, are accurately observed: the Fire and Smoke, which constitute so important a feature in a Field of Battle, are so closely imitated, and the immense number of Figures which crowd the surface of the Model, impart so extraordinary a degree of animation to the scene, that it is difficult for the Spectator to divest himself of the idea that he is beholding a reality instead of a Work of Art.

AT THE EGYPTIAN HALL, PICCADILLY.

ADMISSION ONE SHILLING.

OPEN FROM TEN UNTIL FIVE,

AND FROM

SIX UNTIL NINE, BRILLIANTLY ILLUMINATED

[Bradbury and Evans, Printers, Whitefriars.

'Extraordinary and Novel' Model exhibition advertisement

'On Thursday last we had the gratification of attending the private view of this consummate exercise of skill and ingenuity; and have no hesitation in pronouncing it the most perfect model that has ever yet fallen under our notice.'

United Service Gazette, 6 October 1838

Visitors to the National Army Museum in London cannot fail to be impressed by the enormous, beautifully detailed diorama displayed there, the Large Waterloo Model. Comprising some four hundred and twenty square feet of miniature farmland (the scale is nine feet to the mile), it is peopled by some 75,000 tin–lead soldiers, each one 10 mm high and hand-painted with absolute regimental accuracy.

On closer inspection, one might suppose that there has been an embarrassing mishap – perhaps the sleeve of a clumsy museum official has knocked over many of these tiny antique soldiers, spoiling their neat ranks, scattering them about the diminutive crops and farm buildings. And then, of course, you realize that there has been no accident, but that a master crafts-man has deliberately composed everything. This scene, with all its terrible carnage, has simply been frozen in time. The rolling landscape before you is that of the countryside near Brussels on a Sunday evening in June 1815. Here, as if viewed through the wrong end of the telescope, stretches the bloody battlefield that was Waterloo.

Waterloo aficionados will have heard of its maker, Captain William Siborne. Some will have read his classic *History of the War in France and Belgium in 1815*, first published in 1844 and still in print today. Others will be aware that his son, Major-General Herbert Taylor Siborne, edited and published a selection of the many letters his father obtained from Waterloo veterans, producing a work known as the *Waterloo Letters*. That was first published in 1891 and also remains in print.

Although Siborne's model is the greatest monument of the Battle of Waterloo ever made and celebrates an important turning point in modern history, scant attention has been paid to the full story of its construction or of its maker. The little that has been said has concentrated on the financial problems the project caused, not on the man. It is not generally known what a labour of love this work was or how much attention to detail he paid to it. What is also not known is how close Siborne's model came to being confined to the dustbin of history. It was a central exhibit at the former United Service Museum in Whitehall for more than a century. Removed from public display in 1963, it was then put into storage and almost forgotten. But for the efforts of a small group of dedicated people, it may well have ended up being destroyed.

At the time of the first exhibition of the model in 1838 and the publication of his *History* in 1844, Siborne's work attracted a considerable amount of controversy. Since then, he has continued to be Waterloo's most disputed historian. Some have lauded his achievements, while others question not only his judgement, but also his integrity. This controversy has continued into recent years.

This amazing work of art, a unique monument to Britain's greatest commander, should have assured Captain Siborne both fame and fortune. Instead, he died an impoverished and broken man. The extraordinary saga of what happened to

Siborne and why the Duke of Wellington, the victor of Waterloo, turned against him has never before been told. Despite copious amounts of documentation, the Duke's biographers and Waterloo historians have all overlooked this episode, one that tells us much about how Wellington controlled his public image. The subsequent effect of this affair on perceptions of the great battle is now, nearly two hundred years later, finally coming to light. My aim then is simply to tell Siborne's story – the story of one man's dogged if naive determination to create a perfect representation of that evening in 1815.

2 A Nation of Show-Keepers

Napoleon medallion

'Well might the great Napoleon say, we trafficked in every thing; but he was little aware that to "a nation of shopkeepers," he might have added, of show-keepers.'

Letter to the Examiner, 7 March 1824

The first Duke of Wellington was the most celebrated Englishman of his era. Born in 1769 in Dublin to an impoverished family of the nobility, and not being the most academically gifted student, he chose a military career. Arthur Wesley, as he was then known, first saw action in the Revolutionary Wars in 1794 as part of the unsuccessful British expedition to the Netherlands, where he marched up and down with the Duke of York. Wesley's first opportunity for fame and fortune came when he was posted to India in 1796. It was in the subcontinent that he learned both the art of war and of politics, graduating with honours from the university of life.

Returning to Britain in 1805, Major-General Sir Arthur Wellesley, as he had become, was well positioned to play a role in the war against Emperor Napoleon of France. The first chance came in Denmark in 1807, where he captured the port city of Copenhagen. This was one of the few successes on a continent of Europe that Napoleon now dominated. The real challenge came in 1808 when Wellesley was sent to the Iberian Peninsula, where he opened the 'Spanish Ulcer' that plagued the French until Napoleon's first abdication in 1814. Appointed the Duke of Wellington during this long campaign, he was the one commander with an unbroken record of success against the French. This made him a popular figure, and he became highly respected throughout Europe.

By 1815, Wellington was no longer a man with a reputation to gain; he now had one to lose, which may go some way to explaining his caution at the beginning of the Waterloo campaign. Nevertheless, he returned to Britain sporting the victor's laurels yet again. Like many a successful general before and after him, now that peace was established, Wellington went on to pursue a career in politics. Very much a conservative, he held the office of Prime Minister from 1828 to 1830. He then served as Foreign Secretary under Sir Robert Peel from 1834 to 1835, and later as cabinet minister without office in Peel's next administration from 1841 to 1846. The Duke also held various other posts in both the administration and the army. He was one of the most powerful men in Britain.

The morning after the great battle, Wellington wrote his *Waterloo Despatch*, the official report of the events of the previous few days. Destined for Lord Bathurst, the Secretary for War and Colonies, in London, it began: 'Buonaparte [*sic*], having collected the 1st, 2nd, 3rd, 4th and 6th corps of the French army, and the Imperial Guards, and nearly all the cavalry, on the Sambre, and between that river and the Meuse, between the 10th and the 14th of the month, advanced on the 15th and attacked the Prussian posts at Thuin and Lobbes, on the Sambre, at day-light in the morning.'¹ He added, 'I did not hear of these events till in the evening of the 15th.' Napoleon's attack had evidently taken the Duke by surprise and his advance continued along the Charleroi to Brussels highway, reaching the strategic crossroads at Quatre Bras that evening. The Prussian

Army of the Lower Rhine, under the command of Field Marshal General Prince Blücher von Wahlstadt, fell back from the frontier and concentrated in the Sombreffe position, where it was to fight the Battle of Ligny the next day, 16 June 1815.

'In the mean time,' Wellington's *Despatch* continued, 'I had directed the whole army to march upon Les Quatre Bras.' The next day, Marshal Michel Ney's wing of the *armée du nord* attacked the Duke's army there with large bodies of infantry and cavalry, and with heavy artillery support. Ney's cavalry staged several charges on Wellington's infantry, but all were repulsed in the steadiest manner. The thin red line did its job.

The lines in Prussian blue had not been so successful. After a bitter struggle for the village of Ligny, Napoleon eventually imposed his will, driving back the Prussians with a last charge at the end of the day's fighting. Their defeat was partly due to a foul-up with their staff work, which resulted in General von Bülow's IV Army Corps not arriving. Nevertheless, Wellington was magnanimous in praising his ally, adding, 'I was not able to assist them as I wished, as I was attacked myself, and the troops, the cavalry in particular, which had a long distance to march, had not arrived.' The Prussians lost at Ligny due to their own incompetence, while Wellington's intention to support them directly did not quite come off.

Despite heavy losses, Wellington was in a position to continue the battle the next day. However, the Prussians had fallen back in the night and were rallying at Wavre, a town north-east of Wellington's position. As the Duke was now out on a limb, he decided to fall back. His army passed through Genappe, where the narrow bridge formed a bottleneck. The steep river banks offered a good defensive position, and Wellington's

General Bülow von Dennewitz

cavalry expertly covered the withdrawal to the Mont St Jean position. Wellington set up his headquarters in the village of Waterloo and made ready to accept battle after Blücher had assured him of his direct support with at least part of his army.

That night, the larger part of Napoleon's army assembled on the range of heights south of Wellington's position. The rest had been sent off in pursuit of the beaten Prussians. Late the following morning, the battle commenced with the assault by Marshal Reille's corps on a complex of buildings named Hougoumont. This great farmhouse was to the right centre of Wellington's position and was one of the three strongpoints of his front line. It had been well prepared for the defence, the perimeter walls being loop-holed and firing platforms built behind them. This fortress-like position was manned by a detachment of General Byng's Brigade of Guards. By placing crack troops here, Wellington was leaving little to chance. He could be sure that any attempt to storm these buildings would be met by fierce resistance. He was right. His redcoats held this position the whole day despite a murderous bombardment and several ferocious attempts to storm it. Hougoumont was all but destroyed in the battle.

The central strongpoint of Wellington's line was the farmhouse of La Haye Sainte. Here too the Duke had posted élite troops – men of the King's German Legion, a body of German soldiers in British pay. Numbering just a few hundred, they spent several hours fighting off several determined French assaults from an entire army corps, that of the Count d'Erlon, before running out of ammunition and falling back. Wellington's line was subjected to an intense artillery bombardment, and d'Erlon's men staged a number of assaults on the Duke's centre, but each was driven off, if only just. The French cavalry also joined in, but Wellington's infantry held firm. The solid British squares, a defensive formation used against cavalry where the line of infantry folded back on itself to form a hollow box, became the stuff of later legend.

Wellington's cavalry occasionally took the opportunity to charge, driving back the infantry assaults, giving the hard-pressed squares the occasional respite, taking many prisoners and two eagles, as the colours carried by the French infantry were known. Their valiant actions did much to stabilize a precarious situation. Wellington, who was surely the greatest tactical general of the era, if not of history, held on.

'These attacks were repeated till about seven in the evening,' reported the *Despatch*, 'when the enemy made a desperate effort with cavalry and infantry, supported by the fire of artillery, to force our left centre, near the farm of La Haye Sainte, which, after a severe contest, was defeated.' Not only had the Duke maintained his position against the odds, he drove off Napoleon's last desperate attack, made with the Imperial Guard. These veterans of so many campaigns were regarded as invincible – that is, until they met Wellington. The *Despatch* continued, 'Having observed that the troops retired from this attack in great confusion, and that the march of General Bülow's corps, by Frischermont, upon Planchenois [*sic*] and La Belle Alliance, had begun to take effect, and as I could perceive the fire of his cannon, and as Marshal Prince Blücher had joined in person with a corps of his army to the left of our line by Ohain, I determined to attack the enemy.' The Prussians evidently arrived late and deserved no mention

in the *Despatch* until this point, for it was only after the final
defeat of Napoleon's last reserve that they played any significant role in the battle. As Wellington commented in the conclusion to the *Despatch*, it was his attack 'which produced the
final result'.

With the Imperial Guard recoiling, Wellington now ordered
his battered line to go on the offensive. The infantry advanced
along the entire front, supported by artillery fire. The cavalry
moved up to turn the pursuit into a rout. The French not only
fell back to their starting position on the opposite ridge, they
fled with the utmost confusion, leaving behind the bulk of
their artillery and ammunition trains. The rout was total, and
Wellington's victory was complete.

After the symbolic shaking of hands with Blücher at the inn on
La Belle Alliance shortly after 9 p.m. on 18 June 1815, the close
of the Battle of Waterloo, Wellington rode back the five miles
to his headquarters at the inn of Jean de Nivelles in the soon to
be famous village of Waterloo. On his way, he passed by the
mounds of dead and dying lying on the field of battle, which
was now in darkness. The Duke took a slow ride through this
mournful scene, reaching his headquarters at about 11 p.m. He
gave up his bed to his aide-de-camp, Sir Alexander Gordon,
who was having a smashed leg amputated. Wellington then had
supper at a table laid for his companions, of whom only one,
his old friend the Spanish General Alava, joined him. At about
midnight, the Prussian Major-General von Müffling came in
with news of the pursuit of Napoleon's beaten army. Swallow-
ing a draught of wine, the exhausted Duke lay down on a pallet
before dropping into a deep sleep.

Three hours later, Wellington's personal surgeon, Dr John Hume, woke him and informed the Duke that Gordon had just died. The doctor then read out the long list of casualties, causing tears to run down a face from which the grime and dirt of the battle had not yet been washed away. Now that he was awake, Wellington started to pen the *Waterloo Despatch*. He sat at a small wooden desk near an open window, but disturbed by passing wagons and the moans of the wounded, found it difficult to concentrate on the task at hand. After an hour or two, he decided to get away from the detritus of war and return to his headquarters in the Rue Royale in Brussels, where he hoped to complete his *Despatch* undisturbed. There, he went up to his room and continued to write, sitting by an open window while a curious crowd gathered, hoping to catch a glimpse of the hero.

Wellington gave this document considerable thought, making many alterations before deciding on the final draft. He was aware that his every word could have implications throughout Europe, so he chose them with care. He was not over-generous with the praise of his companions-in-arms, but gave nearly all due credit for their role that day. With regard to his Prussian allies, he had to be careful not to give them ammunition to fuel their aggressive territorial demands, but at the same time, he could not underplay their role so much that they would be upset. After all, Napoleon was still at large, and Paris had yet to fall, a burden that would fall largely on Prussian arms. The Duke would also have to acknowledge the role of his other allies and put the right gloss on his own role in the affair. At 11 a.m., he was still writing, but an hour later he had selected the man who would carry the fair copy to London. Wellington had not only made history, he had now recorded it.

*

On the evening of 21 June 1815, three days after the Battle of
Waterloo, Major the Hon. Henry Percy of the 14th Light Dragoons arrived in London bearing Wellington's *Waterloo
Despatch* and trophies from the battle.[2] This was the first official news of the decisive defeat of Napoleon to arrive. As Percy
was the only one of the Duke's ADCs that was apparently
unscathed – all the others had been either killed or wounded –
he had been selected to carry the news to London. At about
midday on 19 June, Percy took a post-chaise-and-four from
Brussels to Ostend, carrying with him two French infantry
colours crowned with a gold eagle as proof of the French
defeat, one from the 45th Line and the other from the 105th. He
paused at Ghent to give the French king-in-exile, Louis XVIII,
the news before continuing to Ostend, where he boarded
HMS *Peruvian*, a 200-ton brig sloop of sixteen guns, for the
six- or seven-hour crossing to Dover.

Becalmed in mid-Channel, Percy despaired of getting his
news to London rapidly. However, Captain White, the sloop's
commander and a man who took the bit between the teeth,
lowered the gig, chose four stalwart men from his crew, took an
oar himself and handed one to Percy, who had learned to row
at Eton. With the two French eagles lying in the stern, this
determined group of men rowed hard for the Kent coast.
Around 3 p.m. on 21 June, they arrived somewhere near Broad-
stairs, where Percy and White immediately took a post-chaise-
and-four bound for London. The chaise raced through the
Kent countryside, the French standards streaming out of each
window, with one officer clad in scarlet and the other in navy
blue, causing a stir in each village it passed. It reached London

at about 10 p.m., as dusk was falling, and clattered over Westminster Bridge before wheeling into Whitehall and turning abruptly into Downing Street, followed by a cheering crowd.

The chaise came to a halt outside Bathurst's office, next to the Treasury in Downing Street. As he was not there, Charles Arbuthnot, then a secretary of the Treasury, redirected the messenger to the Earl of Harrowby's house at 44 Grosvenor Square. Arbuthnot was somewhat relieved that it was not another radical demonstration causing the tumult. Harrowby was hosting the Wednesday cabinet dinner, which Bathurst was attending. The sound of cheering woke Harrowby's children, Frederick and fourteen-year-old Mary. Mary recalled seeing a dishevelled officer wearing a gold-embroidered scarlet tunic enter the house brandishing the *Despatch*. He was followed by two other men, presumably White and Arbuthnot, all asking for Bathurst and crying, 'Victory! Victory! Bonaparte has been beaten!' On entering the dining room, they were greeted with cheers from the guests. Harrowby then went outside to announce the news to the jubilant crowd.

Percy was exhausted and close to collapse. His coatee, which he had not taken off for six days, was torn, dirty and bloodstained. He had hardly slept since the Duchess of Richmond's ball in Brussels on 15 June and was suffering from the strains of having rowed halfway across the Channel. Nevertheless, Percy had one last commission to perform. As instructed, he then went on to deliver the two captured French eagles to the Prince Regent, who was dining in St James's Square at the home of the wealthy Boehm family. Clutching the two standards, one in each hand, Percy climbed the steps to the ballroom, where the guests were assembled, before bending down on one knee in front of the Prince Regent and announcing the news. Percy then retired to his family home at 8 Portman Square, on the corner of Baker Street, where he fell into a deep slumber, oblivious to the curious crowds outside. The news of the victory had reached London, initiating jubilant celebrations on the street. Some would soon turn the euphoria into hard cash.

The reports reached Henry Aston Barker (1774–1856), a Glaswegian panorama painter. Panoramas were a popular form of entertainment, and it was common for major events to be portrayed in this way, a sort of early form of newsreels. As he was also an astute businessman, Barker was not slow to realize the potential of a Waterloo panorama. Indeed, he was in the first wave of artists to reach Waterloo after the battle. Barker sketched the site before going on to army headquarters to interview the officers and draw portraits of the commanders. He was particular as to the time of the representation, wanting to reproduce one moment or episode as accurately as possible. The canvas he painted was displayed at the rotunda in the Strand.

As well as charging one shilling (5p) for admission, Barker also encouraged the visitors to purchase printed descriptions of the whole battle from him, so that they could experience the panorama in the context of the whole event. He expected that Waterloo, 'in the course of nine eventful hours . . . would furnish subjects for many Panoramas'.[3] This panorama, however, represented the triumphant conclusion of the contest, 'about eight o'clock in the evening, when the British and their Allies, having finally repulsed all the attacks of the French, are attacking and routing them in their own position'.[4] The climactic end of the

battle proved a popular attraction. To add to the realism, returning soldiers of the 42nd Highlanders were admitted free for two
nights when the *Panorama* was later displayed on the Mound of
Edinburgh. Unlike in the theatre, the viewer of a panorama
stood within the scene, so those viewing the *Waterloo Panorama*
occupied a position equivalent to that of no less a person than
the Duke of Wellington at that moment of the battle. By
merely turning their heads to view the 360° display, they could
observe in detail everything Wellington had seen.

The *Panorama* drew huge crowds and was one of the
biggest box-office successes of its time, making its owner a
profit of £10,000 within a few months. Barker was soon able to
buy out his backers. It then toured all the major cities of England and Scotland before it was shipped to North America,
where it was exhibited in Boston. The *Panorama* was so successful that, in 1822, Barker sold out to John Burford and his
son Robert, also a panorama painter, and retired on the proceeds. A few years later, it was hung at the Leicester Square
rotunda and continued to prove highly popular. It was left on
display until it literally fell to pieces.

Barker's was not the only Waterloo panorama. A group of
artists under the direction of a man by the name of Marshall
(though not the famous panoramist Charles Marshall) also
headed for Waterloo once news of the victory had arrived in
London.[5] Apparently assisted by the Adjutant-General's
Office in Paris, Lord James Henry FitzRoy Somerset, Wellington's Military Secretary, and Colonel Francis Ponsonby, they
produced *Marshall's Grand Historical Peristrephic Panorama
of the Ever-memorable Battles of Ligny, Les Quatre Bras and
Waterloo*. This type of panorama was highly elaborate, the

canvas being on rollers. This allowed the paintings to move, revealing various scenes. A full military band, accompanying the show with the appropriate airs and battle pieces, added to the grandeur of the show. It is likely that the first performance took place in 1816, and Marshall's panorama toured Britain and Ireland for at least the next ten years, visiting Bristol, Manchester, Dublin and other places in Britain. It was also exhibited in the USA.

Waterloo was no flash in the pan. Nearly thirty years after the event, Barker remade the original *Waterloo Panorama*. A report in *The Times* of 22 March 1842 recommended visiting it:

> The new panoramic picture now opened to the public, and of which a private view was yesterday afforded to many of the nobility, to the friends of the artist, and to many persons immediately connected with art and literature, represents the battle of Waterloo, a subject which will never lose its interest with Englishmen, and which, though nearly 27 years have elapsed since the event took place, still possesses attractions to draw the British public to view a well painted picture of the incidents and circumstances by which it was distinguished. A panoramic picture of this battle was exhibited in 1815, at the same place, Leicester-square, at which the present picture is now being exhibited, and at that time attracted multitudes of spectators. That picture has, unfortunately, perished from damp and other causes, but the loss of it is the less to be regretted, because the present picture is so similar to it, that anyone who has seen the former picture would, at a first glance, mistake the present picture for it . . . It is one everybody should see.[6]

Thousands did go to see it and even that did not satiate the enthusiasm of the public. As late as April 1852, the scene painters William Telbin and John Burnett opened their *Grand National and Historical Diorama, Illustrating the Wellington Campaigns, in India, Portugal, and Spain; Concluding with the Battle of Waterloo* at the Gallery of Illustration at 14 Regent Street, London. As luck would have it, Wellington died at Walmer Castle, one of his residences, on 14 September. Not wasting a moment, the exhibitors renamed the show *The Life of Wellington*, adding further scenes. Hardly was the Duke buried when, on 17 November, another panorama of Waterloo was opened at Leicester Square.

The Battle of Waterloo continued to draw the crowds even after Wellington's death. In 1890, yet another Waterloo panorama was exhibited, this time just behind the Army and Navy Stores in Victoria Street, London. Colonel Maurice commented, 'the crowds of all classes which continually visit it show the deep interest still felt in the great battle by all Englishmen'.[7]

Barker was among the first of many who would soon flock to Waterloo, creating a mini-boom in the local economy. Members of the British community in Brussels visited the battlefield, and Waterloo became one of the musts on European tours undertaken largely by the wealthy at this time. The local inns flourished and native guides were employed to escort the visitors around the battlefield, bringing welcome additional income for many a poor farmer.

John Scott, a London-based journalist, was an early visitor to the battlefield. He recalled, '. . . behind our carriage, was an

English sociable with a party of our countrymen and women on the same errand with ourselves: – before it was an English tandem; and, at the doors of the small inns, belonging to one or two hamlets, several English equipages were standing. The people of this foreign land seemed all to look as if they expected us, when we met them on the road. They nodded their heads to each other when they passed us, – as if saying, – "More of the English for Waterloo!"'[8]

A certain J. S. Noldwritt, Honorary Secretary of the Walworth Literary and Scientific Institution, frequently availed himself of the services of the local guides. He recalled that 'Soon after the battle, there sprang up among the peasants of the locality a new and lucrative trade of guides, relic-venders [sic], and stick-cutters; all noisy and wrangling rivals, and all able and but too willing to expose and cry down the pretensions of any one of their number who should set up an unfounded claim for the purpose of securing an undue and a more highly-paid share of the gains.'[9]

Scott noted that from 'almost every house in the hamlet of Mont St. Jean, poured forth women and old men, to every fresh arrival of visitors, – who eagerly offered relics of the battle for sale. From the complete cuirass, the valuable sabre, carbine, and case of pistols, down to the buttons that had been torn from the jackets of the slain, all the wreck of the field had been industriously collected, and each article found ready purchasers. Letters taken from the pockets of the dead, were frequently offered, and were always eagerly bought . . .'[10]

Commercially astute Waterloo veterans, the best known of whom was Sergeant-Major Edward Cotton, soon joined the Belgians in making some extra cash this way.[11] Cotton 'resided more than fourteen years on the field, as Guide, and Describer of the battle',[12] and Noldwritt is known to have used his services. The first edition of his book *A Voice from Waterloo* was published in 1846. In the Preface to the third edition (1849) Cotton stated, 'In the first instance this little volume was originally intended for sale on the battlefield and in Belgium, but from the quick sale of the first and second editions, I have been induced to put it into the hands of a London publisher.'[13] This is an indication of the level of battlefield tourism from Britain. This cottage industry is still active today.

For those who did not go to Waterloo, Waterloo was brought to them. After his father's death in 1814, Philip Astley Junior took over the Royal Amphitheatre of Arts. A type of circus, Astley staged a re-enactment of the battle. It was a grand affair, replete with cavalry charges, bugle calls and cannon fire. It ran for 144 consecutive performances before going into repertory and became the Amphitheatre's second most frequently performed show. Astley also wrote one of the first popular histories of the campaign.[14]

At the time, Vauxhall Gardens was the favoured location for Londoners' *al fresco* entertainments. In 1827, a space was cleared for an open-air theatre to accommodate 1,200 spectators on rows of benches forty feet high. A re-enactment of the Battle of Waterloo was billed as the opening attraction. Prior to parting the huge red curtains, a cannon discharged and the band of the 2nd Guards Regiment struck up. The farmhouse of Hougoumont was revealed. Napoleon's guards advanced, led by bearded sappers, with the actor portraying Napoleon riding past in review, greeted by a multitude of voices crying '*Vive l'Empereur!*' Firing was heard in the distance, and the French retired. The actor playing Wellington then entered accompanied by his staff, and the battle began. One spectator described the scene:

> Whole columns then advance upon each other, and charged with the bayonet; the French cuirassiers charge the Scotch Grays; and as there are a thousand men and two hundred horses in action, and no spare of gunpowder, it is, for a moment, very like a real battle. The storming of Houguemont [*sic*], which is set on fire by several shells, was particularly well done; the combatants were for a time hidden by the thick smoke of real fire, or only rendered partially visible by the flashes of musquetry, while the foreground was strewed with the dead and dying. As the smoke cleared off, Houguemont was seen in flames, – the English as conquerors, the French as captives: in the distance was Napoleon on horseback, and behind him his carriage-and-four hurrying across the scene. The victorious Wellington was greeted with loud cheers mingled with the thunder of the distant cannon.[15]

This epic show went on for two hours, employing hundreds of soldiers as actors. So impressive was this re-enactment that its location became known as the Waterloo Grounds.

Astley's popular history of the Waterloo campaign was, of course, not the only one to appear in that year. The British Library's catalogue lists seventy items on Waterloo dating from 1815 alone. A number of these went into several editions that same year, indicating their popularity. Obviously, such books were put together with some haste and their contents reflected that. However, most included the official dispatches from various headquarters, and some contained lists of officers killed and wounded and the numbers of men lost by the British regiments, as well as the various awards won.

Among the works published in 1815 was *An Account of the Battle of Waterloo, Fought on the 18th of June 1815, by the English and Allied Forces, Commanded by the Duke of Wellington, and the Prussian Army, under the Orders of Prince Blucher, against the Army of France, Commanded by Napoleon Bonaparte*. A British staff officer wrote it, but as was common at the time, did not reveal his name. The book came with 'an appendix containing the British, French, Prussian and Spanish official details'. Although there were no Spanish troops involved in the affair, Spain was one of the several friendly governments that had an observer present. James Ridgway, a bookseller of Piccadilly, London, was the publisher and it was reprinted several times in 1815 alone. Ridgway's premises were located next door to the London Museum, or Egyptian Hall, as it was better known, where Napoleon's carriage was soon to go on display, attracting enormous crowds and no doubt ensuring lively business for Ridgway.

A 'Near Observer' wrote *The Battle of Waterloo, Containing the Accounts Published by Authority, British and Foreign, and other Relative Documents, with Circumstantial Details, Previous and After the Battle, from a Variety of Authentic and Original Sources*. Messrs John Booth, a bookseller of Duke Street, Portland Place and T. Egerton of the Military Library, Whitehall, were the publishers. This work too ran into several editions, the fourth containing the Hanoverian, Spanish and Dutch accounts.

More works appeared over the following years, including translations of various non-British accounts. Two of the better known were those written by Major-General von Müffling, the Prussian liaison officer in Wellington's headquarters in 1815, and the Netherlands engineer W. B. Craan.

A number of publishers and authors contacted Wellington seeking his approval for their work. The Duke declined all such invitations on principle: he did not want his name associated with written works on Waterloo, as he entertained 'no hopes of ever seeing an account of all its details which shall be true'.[16] Furthermore, he was 'really disgusted with and ashamed of all I have seen of the battle of Waterloo'.[17] To one author, he wrote, 'I can refer you only to my own despatches published in the "London Gazette".'[18] Wellington had made his one public statement on the subject and that was that.

One of London's more popular attractions of the nineteenth century was William Bullock's Egyptian Hall located at 22 Piccadilly. Bullock, originally a jeweller and goldsmith in Sheffield, intended it to house his London Museum of Natural History. His collection, including items brought back from the South Seas by Captain Cook, had until then been on display in Liverpool. A traveller, naturalist, and antiquarian, Bullock paid £16,000 for the museum's construction. Demolished in 1905, the Egyptian Hall stood facing the end of Bond Street. Visitors went along a passage that led to the main exhibition hall and from there through a basaltic cavern similar to the Giant's Causeway in Ireland into an Indian hut situated in a tropical forest, where models of various exotic plants and animals were to be seen. Admission was one shilling (5p).

To supplement the Museum of Natural History, whose collection was valued at £30,000, exhibitions were held in other rooms. Napoleon was a topical and popular subject, so Bullock took in Lefèvre and David's huge portrait of the fallen emperor. Fifteen feet by six feet in size, it was advertised as 'the only natural likeness now publicly exhibiting in Europe' and had already attracted large crowds when shown at rooms at 53 Leicester Square, the Adelphi and the Waterloo Museum.

Located at 97 Pall Mall, London, at the St James's Street end, the newly founded Waterloo Museum was the speculation of a cutler named Palmer. Founded in 1815, his collection included four French eagles (that is, the finials that crowned the flagpoles of Napoleon's regiments) and an array of weapons and armour, and a collection of paintings. These included Robert Lefèvre's painting of Napoleon in his coronation robes, a portrait of his great cavalry commander Joachim Murat and a scene from the Battle of Waterloo with Wellington in the foreground. The Cuirassier's Hall contained a vast number of French cuirasses, helmets, sabres, muskets and bayonets. In 1823, Napoleon's famous white Barb charger Marengo, or at least a horse that its owner *claimed* had been Napoleon's, could be seen here. The battle-scarred animal had five visible wounds and apparently still had a musket ball in its tail. The imperial crown and monogram were branded on its hindquarters. Admission was one shilling for ladies and gentlemen, sixpence for children and servants. The famous portrait painter Benjamin Robert Haydon, who visited the exhibition on New Year's Day, 1824, expressed a yearning, evidently unrealized, of riding the mount of a person he had painted forty times. Marengo's mortal remains – the beast died in 1832 – are now on display in the National Army Museum in London, only a few feet away from Siborne's model.

These exhibitions were, however, overshadowed by the most lucrative of them all, the one that took Waterloo curiosity into the realms of Waterloo-mania. In January 1816, the Prussian officer Major von Keller, captor of Napoleon's luxurious, bullet-proof travelling coach at Waterloo, accompanied it to London, along with the coachman taken prisoner with it. This carriage had provided transport for Napoleon on the ill-fated Russian campaign in 1812 and on his return from Elba in March 1815. Napoleon had planned to use it to enter Brussels after Waterloo, but he abandoned it in Genappe to the pursuing Prussians: Keller's fusiliers (light infantry) of the 15th Regiment and the Brandenburg Uhlans (lancers). Keller duly handed over this rich prize to his commander Blücher, although part of its valuable contents – a million francs' worth of diamonds – apparently went missing. Blücher had the coach sent to England and presented to the Prince Regent. The Prince, strapped for cash, sold it to Bullock for £2,500. At its peak, this exhibition attracted 10,000 people a day – more than any previous London exhibition. In all, 220,000 visitors paid one shilling each to see this vehicle, painted dark blue and gilt, with vermilion wheels, two horses, Napoleon's folding camp-bed and the contents of his travelling case, much of which was in solid gold. Once the show closed on 24 August 1816, it then went on tour around Britain. A total of 800,000 people visited it, bringing Bullock revenues of £35,000 – not bad for an outlay of £2,500.

Having made a veritable fortune, Bullock later disposed of the carriage for £168 to a coach-maker. In 1843, Madame Tussaud

& Sons purchased it to include with their new waxwork display *The Shrine of Napoleon, or Golden Chamber*. This waxwork was the most durable of all the Tussaud exhibits, running for over three quarters of a century. The elderly Wellington was among its visitors. In fact, he came so often to gloat at the effigy of Napoleon that Sir George Hayter was commissioned to paint the scene. The picture was finished after Wellington's death in 1852, but was destroyed in the fire that gutted the building in 1925. Fittingly, the same fire destroyed Napoleon's carriage, symbolically ending their conflict.

The Duke of Wellington attended all these Waterloo entertainments. He repeatedly visited and approved of the several Waterloo panoramas displayed at Leicester Square.[19] He was a spectator of the re-enactment in Vauxhall Gardens in 1827, and again at the revival in 1849. He was a frequent visitor to the Egyptian Hall, attending a private viewing of Catlin's Indian paintings, and was seen at demonstrations of Professor Faber's speaking automaton and at performances of the celebrated American midget Tom Thumb, whose impersonation of Napoleon was said to have particularly amused the Duke. In fact, there was to be only one such entertainment that Wellington did not grace with his presence.

3 Fame and Fortune

Lord Hill

'We are at a loss for fitting terms to praise this beautiful work in . . . The figures at last all but move. You fancy that you see even the scattered sharp-shooters, who are thrown out in clouds in advance of the heavier masses, availing themselves of bush or hillock to take securer aim; and the smoke from the heavier firing, whether of extended line, artillery, or rising in eddying volumes from the yet *glowing* embers of the fired *Hougoumont*, seems to float on the air.'

John Bull, 14 October 1838

Ironically, the vanquished appeared to think more of its armed forces than the victor. While in Les Invalides in Paris, the visitor could enjoy the spectacle of its collection, the world's leading military museum, and admire its substantial collection of militaria. Post-Waterloo London could offer no equivalent institution, a situation that cried out to be addressed.

When Queen Victoria ascended to the throne in 1837, the great museums of modern London had yet to be built. In 1823, work had indeed started on the construction of Sir Robert Smirke's neo-classical building housing the British Museum, but it would take thirty years to complete. The museums of South Kensington were added to London's places of interest later in the nineteenth century. However, there was nothing commemorating the most recent European conflict, the Napoleonic Wars, which were still very much in living memory. Great popular support for adding a military museum to the growing capital's offerings of entertainment could be counted on.

It was not long before the idea of the founding of a naval and military museum in London was mooted in military circles. A discussion took place in the *United Service Journal* (*USJ*), the recently founded professional periodical published for officers of the army and navy.[1] The idea of founding a museum gained momentum, with several officers writing to the editor of the *USJ*, Captain Thomas Henry Shadwell Clerke,[2] expressing their support. Clerke later edited the final volume of the *Selections from the Wellington Despatches*, after the suicide of the previous editor, Colonel John Gurwood.

The first letter in the *USJ* suggesting the founding of a United Service Museum was published in February 1829 in the second issue of this new journal. It proposed that 'to give a tone of science to the character of both services, it would be a desirable point to set on foot a Museum, to be formed, conducted, and maintained, solely by the military, medical, and civil branches of the Royal Navy, the King's Army, the Hon. East India Company's services, and their connexions: to be called the *United Service Museum*'.[3] Other readers took up the theme in the coming issues.

On 16 December 1829, a preliminary meeting of those favouring the proposed museum took place at 4, Regent Street, with Major-General Sir Howard Douglas in the chair.[4] Among those present were Sir Herbert Taylor, Private Secretary and First Aide-de-Camp to King William IV, who announced that the project would have royal support. Taylor was a friend of Siborne, although it is not quite certain when they first met.[5] The founding of the United Service Museum progressed relatively rapidly. In the March 1830 issue of the *USJ*, the editor announced, 'The pressure of Parliamentary and other engrossing duties on the time of the distinguished individuals, from whose influence the United Services Museum is expected to derive important assistance, has alone retarded the announcement of a General Meeting.'[6] The Duke of Wellington was then Prime Minster. A very distinguished individual indeed had taken a personal interest in this project.

Even before a decision had been made on the location of this museum, plans were put into motion for the construction of its central exhibit – a model of the Battle of Waterloo. The task of finding an officer suitably qualified and skilled to construct this model fell to Lord Rowland Hill.

Born in 1772, Hill first met Lt-General Sir Arthur Wellesley when he was appointed to command a brigade in Wellesley's army in the Iberian Peninsula in 1808. Hill proved to be a reliable commander and rose through the ranks, next commanding a division and later a corps. At Waterloo, he led Wellington's 2nd Corps. In fact, he had been so closely involved in the firefight with Napoleon's Imperial Guard at the close of the battle that he had his horse shot from under him. The poor beast was hit in five places, while Hill himself was knocked over and badly contused. As he went missing for half an hour in the ensuing mêlée, his staff for a time believed him dead. Hill had also commanded the Army of Occupation in France from 1815 to 1818, in which Siborne had served for a while. In Wellington's administration, Hill, who had attained the rank of general on 27 May 1825, was appointed to the command of the army on 16 February 1828, with the title of 'General Commanding-in-Chief'. He held the post for fourteen years.

Hill made enquiries, hoping to be recommended a suitable candidate to construct the proposed model. Among those he consulted was Lt-General Sir George Murray, then Secretary of State for the Colonies in Wellington's administration. While

Commander-in-Chief Ireland, Murray had worked with Siborne, being impressed with his Assistant Military Secretary's ability. In return he gave Siborne much support and encouragement and the two became so close that Siborne dedicated his second book to Murray. This work, entitled *A Practical Treatise on Topographical Surveying and Drawing*, soon became a standard text on the subject. At some stage in his early years, Siborne had constructed a model of the Battle of Borodino, which had taken place at the gates of Moscow in 1812. Murray, knowing of Siborne's skills, did not hesitate to recommend him for the task.

The decision to construct a model of Waterloo for the United Service Museum was going to change Siborne's life. In the spring of 1830, Hill contacted Siborne to enquire if he was interested in constructing the model.[7] After the meeting, Hill notified Major-General Sir Henry Hardinge, then Secretary at War, to secure funding for the design and construction of the model, as he '. . . considered very desirable that a Survey should be obtained of the Field of Waterloo, with a view to the Construction of a Model of the Ground,' and that 'Lieut. Siborn of the 47 Reg. had been selected for the Service'.[8]

Hardinge was also a close associate of Wellington and yet another Waterloo veteran. He too had first come across the Duke in the Peninsular War, where he had spend much of his time on the staff of the Portuguese army that fought alongside the British. In 1815, Hardinge had been attached to Blücher's headquarters as liaison officer. At the Battle of Ligny on 16 June, the impact of a cannonball threw up a stone that shattered Hardinge's left hand, which was then amputated. Under the Duke's patronage, Hardinge too returned home to pursue a career in politics. In the following years, he held various offices, including Secretary at War in various governments. From 1846–8, he served as Governor-General of India, before being transferred to an unruly Ireland. Shortly before Wellington's death in 1852, he was made Master-General of the Ordnance, one of the senior military appointments. Hardinge was one of the few select people in Wellington's closest circles that the Duke could trust absolutely for his discretion. He was totally loyal to his benefactor, even acting as Wellington's second in a duel with Lord Winchelsea.

Hardinge was no doubt aware that this model was to be a tribute to the Great Duke, as Wellington was referred to at this time, and, as such, would enjoy pride of place in the proposed Waterloo Room of the planned United Service Museum. That being the case, he would not have hesitated to authorize the funding. Reference is made in other correspondence to an Authority of 15 May 1830, but it has not been possible to locate this document. It does not appear that Siborne was given a copy of it or any other written instructions.[9]

Major George Lennox Davis once wrote, 'Of Captain Siborne it will suffice to say that he was a perfect gentleman and a most able officer. A man of fine intellect and judgement, truly unpretending in his manner and very well informed. Pity that the British Army was so constituted as to condemn a man like Siborne to an utterly subordinate and inadequate sphere of duty.'[10] Although he was well educated, intelligent, respected and liked by all who came into contact with him, Siborne had not advanced beyond the rank of lieutenant obtained over a decade earlier. As a counterbalance to his mundane and routine duties, he spent his free time with Dublin's intelligentsia.

Siborne

Siborne's Coat of Arms

He also met William Makepeace Thackeray, the famous novelist, who toured Ireland in 1842. Thackeray's novel *Vanity Fair*, published in 1847–8, was set in Napoleonic Britain. It included scenes from the Battle of Waterloo, and the two men are known to have discussed the subject. One wonders if Thackeray based his Captain Macmurdo, 'a veteran officer and a Waterloo man, greatly liked by his regiment, in which want of money prevented him from attaining the highest ranks', in any way on Siborne.

As a married man bringing up a family on a subaltern's pay in a job he could not be certain would last, Siborne needed greater financial security and very much wanted to make his mark on life. He jumped at the opportunity Hill offered him. At last he had been offered an intellectual challenge, an escape from the daily routine of the Commander-in-Chief's office in Kilmainham and a chance to prove himself. Fame and fortune seemed to be within his grasp.

William Siborn – the final 'e' was added later in his life – was born on 15 October 1797 in Greenwich, which was then in Kent. His father Benjamin was an officer serving in the West Kent Militia who transferred to the 9th (East Norfolk) Regiment of Foot in 1799.[11] At this time – in the middle of the war with France – militia officers could join the regulars if they persuaded forty men to come with them. Little is known of William's childhood, but he could not have seen much of his father, who spent most of his military career serving overseas. Nevertheless, William decided to follow in his father's footsteps.

On 5 November 1811, a month before his fourteenth birthday and just five feet tall, William entered the Royal Military

College (RMC) as a Gentleman Cadet, as aspirant officers were known. Although the new building at Sandhurst had been under construction for some time, it was not yet ready, so Siborne spent the first year or so at Great Marlow, where the RMC was then located. He moved to Sandhurst in early 1813.

Siborne was one of the first generation of professionally trained staff officers in the British Army. Today, most of the potential regular officers undergo a course of general and military education as officer cadets at the Royal Military Academy Sandhurst. However, in late eighteenth-century Britain, formal military education was not a requirement for most army officers.[12] The relatively small army was officered largely by the sons of the landowning classes, whose upbringing alone was considered sufficient to lead the 'scum of the earth', as some regarded the ordinary soldier. Prior to the demands caused by the the Napoleonic Wars and an expanding Empire – between 1793 and 1820, Britain's armed forces trebled in size and Britain came to rule 26 per cent of the world's population – it had been common for army officers to purchase their commissions and their promotions.[13] However, the growth in the size of armies required not only a larger number of officers, but also that they should be trained to common systems of drill, tactics, operations and staff work. Young men of ability were given the opportunity to prove themselves by passing sufficient examinations to gain their first commission. Siborne proved to be one of the more able officers to graduate from here.

As his family does not appear to have been particularly wealthy, Siborne may well have obtained one of the twenty places at the junior department reserved for the sons of serving officers, who paid only £40 per annum instead of the normal £90. Siborne was one of the roughly 4 per cent of officers the RMC produced for the army at this time. Many of these men later received staff appointments.

Two men had independently recognized the need for a formal education of all army officers. One was the Frenchman Général Jarry;[14] the other was Colonel Le Marchant, commander of the 16th Light Dragoons.[15] The two men met and joined forces, founding, organizing and running the RMC at High Wycombe in 1799. Jarry, in his time as Director of Instruction at the RMC, had brought with him the French tradition of using models of various fortifications for the purposes of instruction in both their construction and the methods needed to besiege them and stage a successful assault. These models later formed the most graphic part of the teaching Siborne received, and the memory of their use for educational purposes appears to have fixed itself in his young mind. It would, however, be some years before he came up with the idea of a model made for mass entertainment.

Thanks to the standards established by enlightened teachers such as Jarry and Le Marchant, the young Siborne, a studious fellow, received a good education. To pass the examination needed to obtain his commission, he was required to have a thorough knowledge of Books 1 to 6 of Euclid, the ancient Greek mathematician; to be well versed in the classics of history, or German, or French; to know the first and third systems of fortification as laid down by the great Vauban;[16] and to be proficient in military drawing. We know that he learned both French and German, although his French was better. He excelled in military drawing.

While at Sandhurst, he was commissioned, 'without purchase', ensign in his father's regiment, the 9th Foot, on 9
September 1813.[17] His first step on the ladder of the military
hierarchy was most likely accomplished with paternal assistance.

The seventeen-year-old Ensign Siborne passed out from the
RMC on Christmas Eve 1814, having obtained his Military
College Certificate with distinction on 13 June 1814, at the end
of his three-year course. His euphoria must have been deflated
by the events in France. After inflicting war on Europe for a
generation, Napoleon Bonaparte, erstwhile Emperor of France,
had been brought to bay. Napoleon abdicated on 6 April 1814,
just weeks before Siborne graduated. With the former emperor
now exiled to the Mediterranean island of Elba, it seemed as if
peace had broken out at last. Siborne's three years of study
seemed pointless for a time.

It must have been all the more frustrating for Siborne when
his regiment missed the Waterloo Campaign, the culmination
of the Hundred Days after Napoleon's escape from exile.
Unlike his father, Siborne was never to experience battle at first
hand. In August 1815, he was transferred from the 2nd to the 1st
Battalion of the 9th Foot, with paternal influence again playing
a role; the 1st Battalion, in which his father was serving, had
just returned from North America. This was the only time that
father and son ever served together. They marched to Paris to
join the post-Waterloo Army of Occupation. From there, the
allied forces moved to the western frontier of France, establishing a zone of occupation and garrisoning a number of the frontier fortresses. The 9th Foot took up their station in the fortress
town of Valenciennes, close to the border with the Kingdom of

the Netherlands, which then included what is now Belgium. Valenciennes was the second largest British base in France at this time and was the headquarters of Sir Charles Colville's 3rd Infantry Division. The 9th Foot was part of the 5th Brigade under Sir Thomas Brisbane.

Siborne's tour of duty in France came to an end with the troop reductions of early 1817. While his regiment remained there until the final withdrawal of the Army of Occupation in 1818, Siborne was sent home on half pay in April 1817. Half pay was insufficient for subalterns to maintain the lifestyle of a gentleman, let alone support a family. His career was going down a cul-de-sac.

The records of Siborne's activities from then until his return to full-pay duties are a little sparse. However, we do know that in September 1820 the Treasury sent him on a special mission to Germany, his knowledge of the language, his intelligence and his trustworthiness playing a role in the decision. He spent a number of days in Karlsruhe, in the Grand Duchy of Baden.[18]

The publication of his first book, *Instructions for Civil and Military Surveyors in Topographical Plan-drawing, Founded upon the System of John George Lehmann*, in London in 1822 is his next recorded activity. Siborne had not remained idle, and judging by his expertise in the subject, he must have studied it intensely.[19] When, on 11 November 1824, he returned to the full-pay list, Siborne had sufficient means to start a family. He had married Helen, daughter of George Aitken of Todhall, near Cupar, in Fifeshire that July. Aitken was a banker and colonel of the Fifeshire Militia. As Siborne needed a full-pay appointment to support a family, it is probable he knew of the forthcoming posting in advance. With Helen he had two children, a son and a daughter.[20]

In March 1826, Siborne was sent to Dublin, where he was employed as the Assistant Military Secretary, a clerk on the staff of the Commander-in-Chief Ireland. Lt-General Sir George Murray held this post from March 1825 to May 1828, and they were based at the Royal Military Asylum in Kilmainham, Dublin.[21] Previously, Murray had served for several years in the Peninsular War as Wellington's Quartermaster-General, as the post of Chief-of-Staff was then known. Murray missed Waterloo as he was in Canada at the time. Considerable responsibility fell on Siborne's shoulders. The Military Secretary, his immediate superior, reported directly to the C-in-C. Most military secretaries held the rank of a colonel, at least. Siborne, as an assistant military secretary, could have expected a promotion to at least captain on merit alone. Let us not forget that Dublin was no backwater either. In the days before the Great Famine, Ireland's population was getting on for eight million while England's was only double that. Siborne was only two steps below the military governor of an entire country and a mere lieutenant did not normally hold so much responsibility.

In 1828, Lt-General Sir John Byng, a veteran of the Waterloo Campaign, replaced Murray, holding the post for three years. In history's most famous battle, Byng had commanded the 2nd Brigade of Cooke's 1st (or Guards) Division, part of which had been heavily involved in the fighting around the fortress-like Hougoumont estate, a key position on the battlefield. Waterloo was Byng's last action.

Siborne resided in a pleasant villa on the banks of the Royal Canal – coincidentally not far from Wellington's place of birth

– but his surroundings could have done little to alleviate the frustration felt by such an able officer. His great intellect was devoted to relatively menial duties, such as administering troop movements, the appointment of officers, the arrangement of escorts, writing reports on riots, affrays and outrages, and on assaults by soldiers on the local police. For the fifteen years before the meeting with Lord Hill, when he was commissioned to construct the model, Siborne had been stuck at the rank of lieutenant. This was all the more exasperating, as he also worked on the lists of promotions in the army.[22] Should he ever find himself being reduced to half pay again – and there was a good chance of that happening at any time – he would find himself in financial difficulty. He needed to secure either a promotion – as a half-pay captain, he could live comfortably – or another source of income.

4 *The Field of Waterloo*

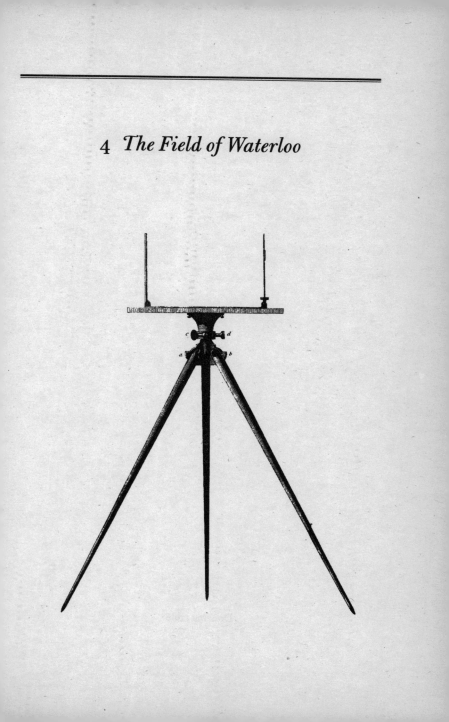

Drawing table

'I have looked over the plan of the ground of the battle of Waterloo, which appears to me to be accurately drawn.'

The Duke of Wellington, October 1836

The Waterloo battlefield suffered its first major alteration between 1824 and 1826, when a large amount of soil was removed from the area around the sunken road on the right centre of Wellington's position. This was used to build the famous Lion Mound, the artificial hill built to display a memorial to the Prince of Orange, who had been wounded in the battle. As more changes could not be discounted, Siborne decided to leave as soon as possible to conduct a survey of the field. It seems he thought that there would be nothing more fitting – and exciting – than to arrange to spend the duration of the survey as a guest in the farmhouse of La Haye Sainte, a group of solid buildings that formed the lynchpin of Wellington's line of defence.[1]

Siborne's journey from Dublin to Waterloo in May 1830 would have taken several days, involving uncomfortable coaches and unpleasant sea crossings, even though his route to London was one of the most modern of its time. Although he travelled a few years too early to take advantage of the coming railway boom, Siborne did benefit from the steam engines that now powered ships. The route he probably took would have been across the Irish Sea from Dublin to Holyhead on the packet, as the ferry was then known. The reconstruction of

Holyhead harbour had been completed by 1824, and it now provided six acres of deepwater harbour at low tide. Work on the world-famous Menai bridge started in 1819 and its opening on 31 January 1826 completed much of the new highway to London. Regular coach services along this route had started in the late eighteenth century and were at first characterized by unreliable service, dishonest innkeepers and highwaymen. However, by 1830, the chaos of coaching's heyday in Britain was over. Technological advances and better organization marked the maturity of this industry, although coaches were still primitive and often overcrowded.

The versatile Scottish civil engineer Thomas Telford (1757–1834) built the new Holyhead road, now known as the A5. Work had started in 1815, using demobilized soldiers and sailors as labour. The Holyhead to London route was one of the fastest in the country, the coaches coming close to averaging ten miles per hour and the journey taking just twenty-seven hours. Fittingly, Siborne travelled down a road constructed in part by Waterloo veterans. As this part of the journey took more than a day, Siborne most likely stayed overnight at one of the many inns on the route before reaching London. He probably spent a night in London before travelling to the coast, either to Dover or Ramsgate, to take another steamer across the Channel.

As well as his personal effects, he also had his surveying equipment and it is possible he took his late father's drawing case, which is still in the family's possession today. From whichever port he landed, Calais or Ostend, Siborne had the option of either taking the fast post-coach to Brussels, the *malle-post*, which ran via Bruges and Ghent, or the passenger boat that serviced the canal from Ostend to Bruges and Ghent, then taking the *malle-post* onwards. He would have needed to change coaches in Brussels, possibly even staying there the night.

Brussels in 1830 was not much different from how it had been fifteen years earlier. The building in the Rue Royale in the centre of Brussels, which housed Wellington's headquarters in the early part of the campaign, is still standing today. The Duke had returned here on 19 June 1815 to finish writing his *Waterloo Despatch*. Opposite this building was the Place Royale, a park where parts of the Brussels garrison had assembled just before dawn on 16 June 1815 before marching off to war. Soldiers had marched here from their billets all over town, departing from their sweethearts, possibly for the last time, their backs bent with their heavy knapsacks containing three days' worth of provisions. One anonymous eyewitness described the assembly of the troops in Brussels that night:

> It was past midnight, and profound repose seemed to reign over Brussels, when suddenly drums beat to arms, and the trumpet's loud call was heard from every part of the city. It is impossible to describe the effect of these sounds, heard in the silence of the night . . . instantly every place resounded with the sound of martial preparations. There was not a house in which military were not quartered, and consequently, the whole town was one universal scene of bustle: the soldiers were seen assembling from all parts in the Place Royale, with their knapsacks upon their backs; some taking leave of their wives and children; others sitting down unconcernedly upon the sharp pavement, waiting for their comrades; others sleeping upon packs of straw, surrounded by all the din of war, baugh horses, and baggage waggons,

artillery, and commissariat trains – carts clattering, hammers knocking, chargers neighing, bugles sounding, drums beating, and colours flying.[2]

This account was one of the many published shortly after the battle and it is likely that Siborne, an educated man and a scholar, had read it. While some went to war that morning, others went to work:

A most laughable contrast to this martial scene was presented by a long procession of carts coming quietly in, as usual, from the country to market, filled with old Flemish women, who looked irresistibly comic, seated among their piles of cabbages, baskets of green peas, early potatoes, totally ignorant of what might be the meaning of all these warlike preparations, and jolting along, one after another, through the Place Royale, amidst the crowds of soldiers, and the confusion of baggage waggons, gazing at the scene before them, with many a look of gaping wonder.[3]

This scene of normality contrasted with a great military pageant that was about to take place:

Yet there was order amidst all this apparent confusion. Regiment after regiment formed with the utmost regularity, and marched out of Brussels. About four o'clock in the morning, the 42nd and 92nd Highland regiments marched through the Place Royale, and the Plaza. One could not but admire their fine appearance; their firm, collected, steady, military demeanour, as they went rejoicing to battle, with their bagpipes playing before them, and the partial gleams of the rising sun shining upon their glittering arms.[4]

Despite the commotion, some men slept in the corners on piles of straw, their fingers wrapped instinctively around their firelocks. A few of the officers' wives were on horses, determined to accompany their loved ones at least part of the way. Local stallholders were hawking their wares. Once the men were assembled, they marched off to the pipes of the 42nd and 92nd Highlanders, the heavy tread of nailed shoes echoing on cobbled stones. Once this great host of men had left Brussels, a hushed void filled the great city. An observer described it: 'Before eight in the morning the streets, which had been filled with busy crowds, were empty and silent; the great square of the Place Royale, which had been filled with armed men, and with all the appurtenances and paraphernalia of war, was now quite deserted.'[5]

This was the silence before the great storm. With foreboding, the Flemish drivers slept in their carts, which were destined to carry the wounded. The heavy baggage wagons were ranged in order and made ready to move when required. The last remaining officers delayed at the Duchess of Richmond's ball were seen riding out to join the army. Of these, many did not return. Siborne had not been there in person, but at least he was now going to make the finest model ever made in honour of these brave men.

On the final stage of his journey, Siborne is likely to have taken the local slow coach service, the *diligence*, which ran from Brussels to Charleroi, passing the Porte de Namur before moving on to the Waterloo highway. This road ran through the village of Uccle and past the Soignes Forest. It was down this road on the morning of 16 June 1815 that Wellington's troops billeted in the Brussels area – General Sir Thomas Picton's 5th

Division and the Brunswick Contingent – had marched on their way to the road junction south of Waterloo.

A few miles south of Brussels, these troops entered the great wood that is still standing there today, the Soignes Forest, where the trees are noted for their height. The trees shaded the great highway that morning, leaving the road wet and soft, and the marching troops often had to veer to the left or right to avoid bad parts. The trees were so wide apart that wheeled transport could pass through, and after having entered the forest, the British troops came across a number of wagons conveying Prussian soldiers who had been wounded the day before. They told Wellington's men that the French were driving all before them, and that the British were greatly needed. The British suspected treachery on the part of the foreigners, and that they would have to retreat. However, the troops continued until they came to the southern skirt of the wood, into which they were marched. Here, they were ordered to lie down and rest for two hours but were not allowed to kindle any fires and on no account to move from their places. Some were sleeping and others breakfasting when the Duke of Wellington and his staff rode by, but they were not called upon to continue their march.

The order to move on Quatre Bras came later, arriving at around midday. Coming out of the wood, they found themselves at the village of Waterloo, where they fell in and marched off. On its way to La Haye Sainte, Siborne's coach would have passed the inn of Jean de Nivelles in the village of Waterloo. Wellington had based his headquarters here for the duration of the battle and he spent the night after the battle there, his sleep disturbed by the groans of the wounded. It was also here that Wellington started to draft his *Waterloo Despatch* on the morning after the battle. The inn is still there today and is now a museum.

The day of 16 June 1815 was oppressively warm, and the road very dusty. The column of marching troops moved slowly on until it reached the village of Genappe, where the inhabitants had large tubs filled with water standing at the doors, ready for the thirsty men. The villagers claimed that a French patrol had been there that morning, but that was unlikely and it is probable they mistook a group of French-speaking Netherlanders for Napoleon's men. Hardly had the column left the village when the sound of cannon was heard, coming from just down the road. It had a stimulating effect on the troops, as they were keen to see action.

The route continued past the left fork at the road junction just south of Waterloo towards Charleroi. The right fork led towards Nivelles and from there to Mons. Wellington too had passed this point when on his way to Quatre Bras. Siborne was following in his footsteps as he journeyed towards La Haye Sainte.

The Prince of Orange's inexperienced troops had been holding their own at Quatre Bras against Napoleon's veterans for an hour or two now and required urgent assistance. '"Forward," was now the word that ran through all the ranks,' noted Sergeant Robertson of the 92nd Foot in his *Journal*, 'but the Colonel had more discretion, and would not allow us to run, lest we should exhaust ourselves before the time. He issued peremptory orders that every man should keep his rank as if on parade, and not to march above three miles an hour. The firing seemed to be coming nearer as we approached a farm and public-house, called Quatre Bras.'[6]

Siborne's route continued past the farmhouse of Mont St Jean and over the ridge that Wellington had so tenaciously defended. The journalist Scott described the view:

> From St. Jean, the road immediately rises up the back of the ridge, – on the height and in the front of which, the infantry of the Duke of Wellington's army was formed in line. The cavalry, at the beginning of the battle, were posted on the St. Jean side of the eminence. The ascent is easy: you reach the top unexpectedly, and the whole field of battle is then at once before the eye. Its sudden burst has the effect of a shock, and few, I believe, are found to put any question for the first five minutes.[7]

From here Siborne would have been able to see the chimneys of the Hougoumont château to the west and the farmhouse of La Haye Sainte, which was downhill and on the right of the road. He was now moving over the ground where the Marquess of Anglesey (the Earl of Uxbridge at Waterloo) had led the Great Cavalry Charge that drove off Napoleon's first major assault on the Allied centre. It was here that the 2nd Life Guards had advanced, riding past the 95th Rifles before charging down the slope towards the French infantry and repulsing the attack on Picton's division.

The farm buildings formed three sides of a square. On the north side stood the farmhouse itself, along with part of the stabling. On the west side were the remainder of the stables and the cowsheds. A large barn stood on the south side. A brick wall extended along the Charleroi highway, linking the north and south buildings and completing the quadrangle. Roughly in the centre of this wall was a lean-to known as the 'piggery', which apparently was a refuge to a solitary calf during the battle. An orchard extended to the south and to the north was a small kitchen garden. The great gate stood directly south of the piggery and next to the barn, and there was a smaller doorway close to the end of the farmhouse at the highway. Another gate could be found at the end of the stables, and on the west side of the barn was a large door. Both opened directly into the fields. A passage led right through the farmhouse from the yard into the kitchen garden. The farm's brickwork had survived the battle relatively intact. The great gate had had to be repaired, with the damaged timbers being replaced, and the barn had a new door, as the original had not survived the battle. The night before, some very wet redcoats had carried it off to make a fire to dry their sodden clothing and to make their bivouac a little less unbearable. All in all, the building had changed little since the battle, and all the damage had been made good.

La Haye Sainte is still standing today, situated on the main road from Brussels to Charleroi. During the Battle of Waterloo, it was one of three strong points to the fore of Wellington's main position. Being the centre of the defence, its possession was to prove key to the battle. A few hundred Hanoverians from the 2nd Light Battalion of the King's German Legion (KGL), a body of German soldiers in British pay, manned it. Their commander was Major Georg Baring.

Baring survived the battle and continued in the service of the Hanoverian army. Indeed, Siborne was later to correspond with him on a number of points. In answer to Siborne's first enquiry of 27 January 1835, Baring, by then a major-general, was so good as to send Siborne a copy of his report on the battalion's role in the battle. This article, published in the

Hannoversches militärisches Journal ('Hanoverian Military Journal') in 1831, gave a full account of the battalion's activities from 16 to 18 June, information that would later be of considerable value to Siborne, who used much of this material in his *History*.[8] Baring had witnessed the start of the battle at shortly after 11 a.m., when the attack against the Hougoumont began. His men then stood to and he went to the orchard, where the first attack was expected. The farmhouse lay in a hollow, so the small ridge to the fore of the orchard hid the advancing enemy. Just after midday, a few skirmishers opened the attack. Baring had his men lay down and ordered them to hold their fire until the French were very close. The first shot from the French tore apart the reins of Baring's horse; the next shot killed Major Bösewiel, the second in command.

After a brief skirmish, two columns of French infantry moved over the ridge. One attacked the buildings, and the other rushed towards the orchard *en masse*, ignoring the fire it was receiving. With just a few men, Baring could not repel the attack. 'We fell back into the barn,' noted Baring in his report, 'to a better position from which to continue the defence. One leg of my horse was shattered and I had to take that of my aide.'[9]

The attacking French were from the I Corps of Count Reille. It was standard practice for an assault to be preceded by an artillery bombardment. A chain of skirmishers would then approach the target in open order, firing and testing the enemy's strength to find his weak point, before the assault columns pressed home the attack. It is interesting to note that this assault was not preceded by artillery fire. Neither did the skirmish fire cause much effect; it would seem that the attackers believed they could carry this strongpoint by sheer weight of numbers.

They were wrong, however. Baring's men held on until re-inforcements arrived in the shape of Lt-Colonel von Klenke, leading the Lüneburg Battalion, one of the units that the German province of Hanover contributed to Wellington's army.

With more men at his disposal, Baring counter-attacked immediately, pushing back the French. A strong line of cuirassiers – French armoured heavy cavalry – then formed up in front of the Hanoverians, to the side of the orchard. Just at that moment, Captain Georg Meyer, the commander of the company in the garden at the rear of the farm, came to report that the French were moving round there, so it would no longer be possible to hold it. Baring ordered him to fall back into the buildings and to help defend them. As the cuirassiers posed a great threat and could break through the flimsy hedge around the orchard, Baring called to his men, who had got mixed up with the advancing Hanoverians during the skir-mishing, to rally around him. He intended to move them into the barn. Although the Lüneburg Battalion was several times the size of Baring's force, it did not prevent the French infantry from taking control of the orchard after attacking it with skir-mishers and a column. The Hanoverians, seeing the cuirassiers on the open field, thought their only chance was to rush back to the main position. Baring called on them to halt, but they did not listen to him. If the attacking cavalry was not enough, the French infantry had gone around to the rear of the orchard, forcing Baring's men to run a gauntlet of fire to get back to their main position in the buildings.[10]

The day had only just begun for Baring. He would have sev-eral horses shot under him. In the frenzied French assaults on the farm buildings, the attackers got so close that they grabbed the Legionnaires' rifles through the loopholes in the walls and tried to disarm them. D'Erlon's men concentrated their efforts on staging a breakthrough at the missing barn door. The fighting was so fierce there that the bodies piled up, blocking the entrance. When all their assaults were driven off, the French then attempted to drive out the defenders by setting light to the farm with incendiary shells. Fortunately, reinforcements arrived in the shape of two hundred Nassau sharpshooters, men from a German duchy on the Rhine that was governed by the House of Orange, the rulers of the Netherlands. Their field kettle was used to transport water to extinguish the fire.

Scott had visited the scene shortly afterwards and described it:

A little way down from this tree, keeping near to the road, is the farm of La Haye Sainte. Here I saw, for the first time in my life, a specimen of what war does to the habitations of the peaceful. The spectacle was one of horror ... The garden was a heap of devastation: hedges were levelled, walls broken down. The door was riddled through and through with all sorts of shot, and furnished a most appalling proof of the fury of the attack, and the determination of the defence ... On entering into the court yard, the aspect of wretchedness and destruction was still more fearful ... the roofs of the dwelling house and offices were knocked into great holes by bombs and cannon balls: the windows were hideous wrecks, – not a pane of glass remaining in the whole range, – the frames all broken, and the fragments hanging most forlornly. The extent of the destruction went beyond all I had ever conceived of such scenes, assisted as one's imagination has of late been by numerous and minute descriptions.[11]

The final French assault on the farm took place between 6 and 7 p.m. Although defended only by a few hundred of Baring's men, later reinforced by various companies of the KGL and Nassauers, the farm held out for most of the day. The French noticed that its defenders' fire was diminishing as ammunition ran out and finally scaled the walls and penetrated the entrances, driving Baring's men out through a back door. With the fall of the keystone of the Allied centre, the Crisis of the Battle was reached. Siborne later decided that this would be the most appropriate moment of the battle to portray on his model.

Across the road from the farm was the famous gravel pit, with its steep sides. During the battle, two companies of the élite 95th Rifles held this position, armed with the latest in small-arms technology, the famous Baker rifle. The 1st Battalion was deployed close to the farmhouse of La Haye Sainte, the lynch-pin of Wellington's centre on the Brussels highway. Two of its companies drew up behind a cut-down hedge, and an abatis was formed from the branches which had been removed and thrown across the highway. Two companies took position in the gravel pit, while the remainder of the battalion remained in reserve, just to their rear. The knoll above the pit offered cover for riflemen to fire while prone before sliding down into the bottom of the pit to reload their pieces while standing. As weapons of this period were muzzle-loaders, it was much quicker and easier to charge them while upright. The rapid drop into the pit meant the French cavalry would avoid it, so the 95th did not have to worry about being ridden over. Their position would only become untenable if the French infantry were to take the farmhouse and press on up the road past it. Should that happen, the Rifles would have to scramble up the far side of the pit and cross the open ground towards the ridge forming the line of Wellington's position. This crack force was to have the opportunity to gain more than its fair share of glory.

Caught up in the maelstrom of the several French assaults on Wellington's centre, the Rifles were thrown back several times, but returned to their original positions after every successful counter-attack. The casualties were horrific and the wounded suffered twice over, once at the hands of the enemy, once at the hands of their own military surgeons, whose treatment for most wounds was amputation without anaesthetic and with unsterilized instruments.

Lieutenant George Simmons was one lucky enough to survive this double dose of butchery. When shot in the back – he claimed that this happened when he was just about to lead his men in a charge against the French – the musket ball broke two of his ribs near the backbone, passing through his liver before lodging in his chest. Knocked unconscious by this blow, he fell into the mud and was trampled over several times, before being rescued and brought to the rear. Here, a surgeon extracted the ball from his chest, which had also ripped one lung apart. The internal bleeding made breathing difficult, so a quart of blood was taken from his arm, supposedly to alleviate his condition. Hardly was this primitive procedure completed when more French musket balls whistled through the house. Sergeant Fairfoot, also being treated for a wound, proceeded to acquire a horse for his officer, who then rode back twelve miles towards

Brussels. The motion of the horse made the blood that was left in him pump out of his wound, and the rough edges of his broken ribs cut his flesh to jelly. Fortunately, Simmons received relatively good treatment from his kindly landlord and landlady, who nevertheless proceeded to extract several more quarts of blood from him in the coming days in an attempt to reduce his fever. Surprisingly, Simmons survived. Siborne is likely to have heard many such tales from Waterloo veterans.

One of the several letters Siborne later received from officers of the 95th was from Lt-Colonel Leach. At Waterloo, he was Brevet-Major in the regiment and commanded the two companies nearest La Haye Sainte. In his letter, Leach described their activities. He gave due praise to Baring's valiant defence of the farmhouse before describing the problems their withdrawal just prior to the Crisis of the Battle caused. 'This, however unavoidable, was highly disastrous to the troops of Picton and Lambert,' he wrote, 'for the French instantly filled the house with swarms of sharpshooters, whose deadly fire precluded the possibility of our holding the knoll and the ground immediately about it, and they established also a strong and numerous line of Infantry, extending along the front of Kempt's brigade. Those Frenchmen, however, *knelt down*, and exposed only their heads and shoulders to our fire, and in this manner the contest was carried on between them and us until the General Advance of the whole of the Duke of Wellington's Army against the French position immediately after the total defeat of the Imperial Guards.'[112]

Leach then went on to describe the next phase of the action:

From the time that La Haye Sainte fell into the hands of the

French until the moment of the General Advance of our
Army, the mode of attack and defence was remarkable for
its *sameness*. But I speak merely of what took place immediately about *our* part of the position.

It consisted of one uninterrupted fire of musketry (the
distance between the hostile lines I imagine to have been
rather more than one hundred yards) between Kempt's and
some of Lambert's Regiments posted along the thorn
hedge, and the French Infantry lining the knoll and the
crest of the hill near it. Several times the French Officers
made desperate attempts to induce their men to charge
Kempt's line, and I saw more than once parties of the
French in our front spring up from their *kneeling position*
and advance some yards towards the thorn hedge, headed
by their Officers with vehement gestures, but our fire was
so very hot and deadly that they almost instantly ran back
behind the crest of the hill, always leaving a great many
killed or disabled behind them.[13]

The veteran Leach considered this the closest and most
protracted musketry contest he had ever witnessed and feared
the French would force their way up the road from where they
could attack his rear and cut off his line of retreat. He did not
have a man to spare to counter that, but hoped that the 27th
Foot, to his rear in square, would hold them off. Fortunately
they did, and 'a very short time (a few minutes only I think)
before Picton's Division joined in the General Advance
against the French position, the French suddenly evacuated
the farmhouse of La Haye Sainte and the ground near it, and
retreated in haste'.[14] This was in consequence of the total

repulse of Napoleon's Imperial Guard and Wellington's forward movement.

Scott described the scene inside La Haye Sainte:

From the farm yard I walked into an enclosed orchard: the combat here had been dreadfully fierce: the paper of the exploded cartridges still lay thickly on the ground, and the caps of the soldiers were strewed about, most of them having holes through them, by which had entered the death of their wearers. The heart exerted itself to discredit the eye, when the latter testified that to some of these decaying bits of felt or leather, the corrupting remains of the heads of human beings were attached. In this orchard the trees were numerous, and in general very slender; but neither my companion nor myself, though we took a regular survey for the purpose, could find one that had escaped being hit by a ball. After observing this, I was only astonished that the number of men destroyed on these dreadful occasions is not greater than it is.[15]

Siborne was lucky enough never to witness such scenes in person, but these stories became fixed in his mind.

Now that he had taken residence in the farmhouse, Siborne could start working on the task to hand. The laborious techniques he used were described in his second book, *A Practical Treatise on Topographical Surveying and Drawing*, published in 1827. They were, in part, ground-breaking. At the time Siborne was conducting his survey of the Waterloo battlefield, Colonel Thomas Frederick Colby was still working on the first series of Ordnance Survey Maps of Great Britain and Ireland. Indeed, he had started work on the survey of Ireland in 1825, the year before Siborne was posted to Dublin.[16]

The instruments then available were too imprecise to give exact measurements of, for instance, the contours. Lines spaced at intervals could not be used to show them, so maps were marked with various types of shading showing the gradients. None of these methods were entirely satisfactory and Siborne had worked on developing improvements. In his *Instructions in Topographical Plan-drawing*, published in 1822, Siborne had advocated the use of a different system, as used by Lehmann. The method Siborne described was based on the principles of vertical illumination, with black strokes of different thickness used to express the quantity of light falling on different declivities. The horizontal plane was represented by perfect white; a slope of 45°, considered the extreme, was represented by solid black. Other slopes were expressed proportionally.

This was an adaptation of the method Colby used in the Ordnance Survey of England, the most thorough cartographical exercise of the time in Europe. What Siborne considered to be the great weakness of the cartography it generated was the presentation of the topographical detail. His system did away with having to rely on a ruler and compasses to estimate small distances, a method that was prone to error. In his second book, Siborne developed on the system described in his first book, advocating a fixed standard for use by all draughtsmen. The system he proposed in 1827 was of great use to the military, as it represented the ground in such a way that it was instantaneously possible to determine the suitability of the terrain for particular troop types and manoeuvres. For instance, when there was more than twice as much light as shade, then the ground allowed manoeuvre. When the quantities of light and shade were equal, or nearly so, then the ground could be ascended or descended by light cavalry. When shade predominated, then the ground was suitable only for light infantry. Furthermore, Siborne's method greatly facilitated the construction of topographical models. In fact, the concepts Siborne outlined are used today in the production of digital terrain models.

Having closely examined the methods of surveying in use in Europe, Siborne had designed an improved plane table (see illustration). A drawing board mounted on adjustable legs, a plane table was suitable for use in the field. The design of tables became ever more sophisticated, and so they became more complicated to use. However, Siborne's table was of simplified design and very easy to use. It consisted of a plain, square board, fixed on a stand by which it could be made to rotate while maintaining a perfectly horizontal position. On it was fixed a measuring device known as an index, with which the surveyor could determine the heights of all points above or below his station.

At this time surveyors were plagued by the poor quality of the paper available, which contracted or expanded according to the atmospheric conditions. To counteract this, Siborne used beaten egg whites to glue the paper to the boards he would be using, preparing his day's requirements in advance. He then marked his measurements on this sheet of paper. Many months of painstaking work would be necessary to complete his survey and would take him over the battlefield footstep by footstep.

Siborne began by selecting and noting the points that offered the most commanding views. These were to become his main stations, the points most advantageous for the survey. From these stations, he endeavoured to complete as much of the survey as he could, because the line of sight was better from the higher and more open ground. He kept the number of stations used in the lower ground to a minimum as the line of sight was not as good and more intersections would be necessary to make an accurate survey. When it came to the villages and farms on the battlefield, Siborne endeavoured to conduct his survey from commanding ground, their boundaries and the most conspicuous objects within them, such as spires, vanes, chimneys, or gable ends of the most outstanding buildings. He had a series of signs for chimneys, gable ends, bends in roads, rivers, canals, high and low trees, etc. Siborne's survey created a unique historical document of the battlefield much as it was on 18 June 1815.

He later used this information in his *History*, writing, 'The field of Waterloo is intersected by two high roads (*chaussées*) conspicuous by their great width and uniformity, as also by the pavement which runs along the centre of each. These two roads, the eastern one leading from Charleroi and Genappe, and the western from Nivelles, form a junction at the village of Mont St Jean, whence the continuance, in one main road, is directed upon the capital of Belgium.'[17] The construction of the road made an impression on Siborne. The paved centre was designed to facilitate the movement of wheeled traffic, whereas the dirt strips running along both sides were for the use of horse-riders, the hooves of their mounts finding the going on soft soil easier.

In the eight months spent surveying the field, Siborne engaged the local farmers in conversation, endeavouring to

discover what crops were growing in which field on the day of
the battle. He carefully marked up a copy of his plan of the battlefield with this information, intending to portray even the
minutest of details on his model. Siborne is believed to have
availed himself of the aid of one Martin Pirson, a resident of the
village of Plancenoit and evidently a cousin of Jean de Costa,
who acted as a somewhat unwilling local guide to Napoleon
during the Battle of Waterloo.[18]

During his survey, Siborne paid close attention to the
château of Hougoumont, drawing a plan of it.[19] François-
Xavier de Robiano was now its owner and he had bought the
ruin a year after the battle for 40,000 francs. The violence of
the French attacks that day was greater even than those against
La Haye Sainte. Large parts of the complex of buildings had
been destroyed or severely damaged in the battle. Siborne later
described the condition of the estate in his *History*:

> There is not, perhaps, at the present day, any single feature
> of the field of Waterloo so well calculated to excite the
> interest of visitors as Hougomont [*sic*], which still contin-
> ues what it was reduced to on the day of battle – a heap of
> ruins. The barn in the courtyard, has, indeed, been again
> roofed, and the gardener's house is now occupied by the
> farmer; but the château itself, and the buildings surround-
> ing the old farmyard, present to the eye nothing more than
> crumbling walls, scattered stones, bricks, and rubbish. A
> portion of the tower, with its winding staircase, still exists.
> But the attention of the visitor is most naturally and
> strongly arrested by the chapel, which, though it immedi-
> ately joined the burning château, survives the wreck

around it . . . The identical loop-holes with the innumer-
able marks of shot indented around them, are still permit-
ted to remain as they were left by the brave defenders of the
place. The wood, however, has altogether vanished, and
the ground on which the beech and elm by their countless
shot-holes told a fearful tale, now yields its surface to the
harrow and the plough. This constitutes the only material
deviation; the orchards, and remaining inclosures [*sic*],
continue unaltered, and retain the self-same aspect.[20]

The ruined buildings were a monument to the tremendous
suffering endured by both attacker and defender. The remaining walls were pocked with bullet and cannonball holes. The
trees, stripped of their branches and foliage, were filled with
musket balls. The fire had made it impossible to evacuate the
wounded, their charred bodies having to be recovered the next
day. Piles of dead had been littered all over the area. To the
south of the farm, a mass grave had been dug, one of several
across the battlefield. Later, the bones were removed and
ground into fertilizer, while the teeth were recovered and recy-
cled: false teeth were known after the battle as 'Waterloo teeth'.

Siborne's time at La Haye Sainte eventually came to an end.
He now had produced a series of drawings of the battlefield, a
unique historical document. He retraced his footsteps to
Dublin, and worked on producing a plan of the battlefield.
The cost of the trip to Belgium, including living expenses and
sundries, came to £62 6s 7d, this amount being refunded by the
War Office as Hill and Hardinge had agreed. All was running
to plan.

5 *The Model of the Battle*

The Large Model, 1838

'No fewer than 160,000 figures are represented, and with so much accuracy that not only the nation, but the very branch of the service to which they belong, is perfectly obvious on the nearer points; while the more distant points are distinctly marked out by the various lines of fire, distinguished as they are by a representation of smoke, as ingenious as it is efficient. The roads and enclosures – nay the different appearance of wood, corn fields, or fallows – are all presented to the eye in the most natural manner.'

Morning Post, 5 October 1838

After returning from his eight-month survey of the Waterloo battlefield, Siborne faced a daunting task. The scale of the project he envisaged was unprecedented. No model of this size, scale and level of detail had ever been constructed. He had experience of making relief maps, but the fine detail of the terrain and manufacturing the figures and buildings were new to him. Also, there were neither specialist model nor figure-making companies to which he could go, obtain a quote and simply award the contract.

Siborne started by drawing a plan or map of the battlefield. He had already developed a system of symbols for marking the terrain features. Standing water was represented by fine lines, the distance between the lines indicating the depth of the water – the closer together, the deeper the water. When the boundary line of the water was distinct and invariable, he marked it as such. When it was not, the boundary line was unmarked. He designated rivers by fine lines to show the direction of flow, with the distance between the lines again indicating the depth. Lines also indicated the speed of the current, the more curved the lines, the more rapid the current. The river banks, if distinct and invariable, were represented as such. If not, the outermost lines indicated their furthest extent. Sand was represented by small dots; stones and sand mixed together, such as the gravel pit near the farm of La Haye Sainte, by dots of unequal size. Pasture was represented by very small strokes, arranged to give the appearance of tufts of grass. Small dots arranged two by two were used to represent meadows. Tufts of grass with a few shrubs or bushes represented heaths. Parallel lines were used to represent cornfields. Appropriate marks indicated swamps, marshes and morasses. Siborne preferred using different signs for different types of tree. Woods were represented by groups of trees at irregular distances from one another, depending on their real appearance. Parallel lines were generally used to show roads, a high road being indicated by thicker lines. Thick single lines were used to show lanes; thinner single lines to show field-ways; and dotted single lines to show footpaths. Stone buildings were drawn in such a way as to show their proportionate horizontal extent on the plan. The appropriate mixture of markings for buildings and gardens indicated towns and villages, with different marking for stone and wooden buildings. Specialist buildings such as churches, windmills and watermills were shown by appropriate symbols. Solid lines represented stone or brick walls; a solid line with dots along one edge represented paling; hurdle and field hedges were distinguished individually.

As Siborne had some experience of the construction of relief maps – he was, after all, a published authority on the subject – he knew what problems he would have to face when planning the model. The first decisions he had to make regarded the questions of size and scale and what proportion to take for the necessary differences between the horizontal and vertical scales. To explain, in topographical modelling, if the same scale is used both horizontally and vertically, things will appear out of proportion. This is because of the great disparity between the view obtained when crossing terrain and that presented by a model of it. When crossing terrain, the eye is only five or six feet above the ground and it sees all objects in profile, or nearly so, and consequently in their greatest apparent magnitude. However, when viewing a model, the perspective is as if the eye is several miles above the ground, as if floating in a balloon. In choosing the size of the vertical scale for a model, both the horizontal scale and the character of the terrain had to be taken into account to give a realistic impression to the viewer.

Siborne's earlier work on the subject had shown that horizontal scales of six inches or more to a mile were best suited to produce the effect desired. One third had to be added to the horizontal scale if the terrain were mountainous, one half if hilly and two thirds if composed of gentle undulations. If the horizontal scale were less than six inches to a mile, these additions for the vertical scale would be increased in proportion. Siborne chose a horizontal scale of nine feet, or 108 inches, to the mile, roughly 1:600, which was a much larger scale than he had used for his previous work. His vertical scale was roughly 1:180, this combination of scales giving a good feel for the terrain. Siborne must have undertaken considerable experimentation to establish this.

Each figure displayed on the Large Model represented two actual soldiers. These figures were disproportionately large when compared to the terrain features, but the units occupy the correct area on the model. This too was a compromise between accurate realism and aesthetics. The final result was 'the most perfect model'. It looked right and conveyed a most realistic impression of the battle.

Having decided on the optimal scales to use, Siborne was able to calculate the size of base needed: 21 feet 4 inches by 19 feet 9 inches. As he was located in Dublin, the work would have to be undertaken there, but as the model was to be exhibited in London, it would have to be relatively easy to transport. The obvious solution was to construct the model in such a way that it consisted of a number of parts, which could then be easily transported and then assembled at the place of exhibition. From his previous experience of making models, Siborne was aware the parts preferably should not exceed three or four feet square. However, on a model of this scale, that would have meant making too many parts. The model actually consists of thirty-five sections that vary in size from the smallest at 1 foot $8\frac{1}{2}$ inches by 2 feet $9\frac{1}{2}$ inches to larger sections several times that size. However, none of the sections were so big that a craftsman working on them could not reach the centre with ease.

Siborne made an outline plan of the ground of each part. He then obtained pins of a sufficient length and fixed them with a small hammer at the principal bends of the horizontal lines, as well as their intersections with roads, rivers and other boundaries. Starting at the highest point, he trimmed them with a small wire-cutter to the appropriate length. After having hammered in a pin or wire, he took the horizontal section with a set of compasses, placed one point at the part where the pin was driven into the board or plaster and made a scratch upon the pin with the other to show where he was to cut the wire or pin. He then took fine clay and filled up the space below the pins until the tops of them were almost covered. This way he obtained the general form of the ground, making it easier to model the more minute features between the horizontal sections that corresponded to the horizontal lines upon the plan. For this part of the work, he used pieces of pencil-sized boxwood or ivory with variously shaped extremities. Some had been slightly turned and flattened, others squared or pointed, etc. With these, he moulded the clay into the most intricate forms. Whenever he left the work for any length of time, Siborne placed a slab of plaster of Paris on it. Under this slab was a damp cloth that kept the clay he was using for the finer work moist.

To make the mould, he made a wooden frame about an inch thick and an inch higher than the highest point of the model. The frame was exactly equal in size to that part of the model and was fixed to the clay in such a manner that its inner sides pressed closely to the outer sides of the model. With a camelhair brush, he then covered the whole surface of the model with what he described as 'sweet oil', leaving the sides of the frame perfectly dry. 'Sweet oil' is today known as olive oil, although according to the family's oral history, Siborne used palm oil as this kept the plaster malleable. He then poured plaster of Paris, mixed with water to a proper consistency, over the clay, until it was level with the top of the frame. It took fifteen or twenty minutes for the heat of the plaster to subside. He then removed the mould formed and set it aside to dry, either by the heat of the sun or very gradually before a fire. When perfectly dry, he gave the mould two or three coats of linseed oil and let it stand for a couple of days.

To make the cast, he brushed more oil over the surface of the mould and the inner sides of its frame, and then poured the plaster into it, as he had done for the mould. When it was time to remove the plaster or cast, he began by striking the upper sides of the frame all round the mould with a hammer, loosening the cast sufficiently from the mould to enable him to remove it. He glued back any smaller pieces that broke off the cast during its removal. He replaced larger pieces with appropriately shaped *papier mâché*, gluing them in place. When the cast was perfectly dry and still quite hot, he gave it a coat or two of a solution of isinglass, a gelatinous clarifying agent made from the bladders of freshwater fish. This prepared the surface for painting. The solution was of such strength that when the cast dried, its surface shone a little.

To represent and fix the detail on the casts, Siborne made a wooden frame, the inner extent of which was the same size as the cast. He then placed the cast on a smooth surface and put the frame over it, fixing it in place. Next, he divided the plan of the construction of the model into a number of squares, using a ruler to mark off the respective lengths on the upper surface of the frame. He then drew the corresponding number of squares on the surface of the model. Using these squares and the layout of the terrain, he marked the position and orientation of the various objects that were going to be represented on the cast.

Once that was done, the objects themselves were made and fixed on the model. Green interwoven silk chenille, a type of yarn used in embroidery, was used to represent hedges. Wool chenille was not used, as moths are partial to wool. The hedges were laid along their corresponding pencilled lines, and held in place with strong gum-water or isinglass, mixed with green paint. Narrow strips of thick white card were used to make the walls. These were glued in place in the same way as the hedges. Siborne made the trees from small bunches of chenille fastened with fine wire, which was twisted with a small wire-cutter to form a stem and cut off at a proper length. The ends of the loops of the bunch were cut, and the chenille was then trimmed to the appropriate size. The trees were then fixed into narrow holes made in the model with a finely pointed instrument and firmly attached to it with gum.

The buildings were cut out of cork or wood, appropriately painted and stuck on the model with gum or glue. The scale of the model allowed the more minute detail to be represented. Smoke and fire from the burning buildings was represented by appropriately painted cotton wool. The streams were coloured pale blue and painted in gloss oil colours. The roads, lanes and paths were a drab dusty colour. The main roads were not simply dark streaks painted on the surface of the model; such was Siborne's attention to detail that he had the paving stones cast in lead. Fine towelling was used to simulate the fields and crops, appropriately trampled and devastated by the raging battle. The smooth earth fields were reinforced with scrim. When painting the fields, Siborne took care to avoid monotony, using shades of green, brown and yellow, according to what was growing in the particular field on the day in question. He painted the terrain with body colours, that is, applied the paint thickly, the powder being dissolved in very thin gum-water. Once it had dried, he coated it with shellac, a varnish made by dissolving the yellowish resin secreted by the lac insect in ethanol. The casts had to be covered to prevent dust making them dirty, and as the colours faded if exposed to the sun, Siborne kept them out of direct light.

Sergeant Starr of the Royal Artillery apparently assisted him.[1] This part of the work took two years to complete.

Once this stage had been completed, a triumphant Siborne informed the readership of the *USJ* of the results of his endeavours. His notice began:

MODEL OF WATERLOO. BY LIEUTENANT SIBORN.

It will be gratifying to our military friends, and indeed to Englishmen in general, to hear that a model of a very considerable size is being constructed of the ever-memorable Battle and Field of Waterloo. This extensive work, which promises to be a most interesting monument of Britain's prowess, is undertaken by Lieutenant Siborn, under the immediate sanction and authority of the General commanding in Chief . . .[2]

With the base nearing completion, Siborne then concentrated on obtaining the figures to place on it. Only the best would do. Later imitations of his work have been pale in comparison, lacking both the detail and the artistic skill. Siborne's Large Waterloo Model was the first ever made and has never been outdone. However, work of this quality did not come cheap.

6 *Money Matters*

Sir Henry Hardinge

'I hope he will not be allowed any longer to remain under
pecuniary difficulties, but that the means he proposes may be taken
to supply him with the sum requisite to finish the Model.'

Sir Hussey Vivian, 20 August 1833

So far, all seemed to be going well, but events in London ended
Siborne's run of good luck. Wellington's ministry had ended in
November 1830, and Earl Grey became the Whig Prime Minister, holding office until July 1834. Edward Ellice, a radical, was
appointed Secretary at War in April 1833. The War Office was
under civilian control and run by a government minister, so
there was a conflict of interests between it and the Horse
Guards, the headquarters of the Commander-in-Chief Britain,
Lord Hill, a soldier. Ellice's tenure of the office was a difficult
time for the conservatives in the army, particularly as he
endeavoured to wrest control of the appointment of officers
from the Commander-in-Chief in the face of considerable
resistance. The expenditure of public funds on a model hon-
ouring the Great Duke, who opposed Ellice on a number of
issues, would no doubt be anathema to him.

On 8 March 1833, Sir Hussey Vivian forwarded Siborne's
statement of expenses for 1832 to the Horse Guards, claiming a
total of £217 12s 6d. Vivian had got to know and appreciate
Siborne when, from 1831–5, he served as Commander-in-Chief
Ireland, one of several governmental and military posts he was
to hold after Waterloo. He had commanded a cavalry brigade at
Waterloo, having first seen action in 1794 as an infantry officer

fighting the French in the Netherlands. In August 1798, he had exchanged to a regiment of light dragoons and was posted to the Peninsula in 1808. He conducted himself well during the epic Retreat on Coruña, but did not return to Spain until 1813, when he served under Wellington, was then wounded and sent home to recover. For a time, he commanded the cavalry of Hill's corps.

Frederick Henry Lindsay, the Chief Clerk, replied to Siborne on 4 April, stating that payment was to be 'sent in a few days'.[1] He had processed the paperwork, approved the expense claim and passed it on to the War Office for payment.

When this file was placed on his desk, Ellice initially agreed to the refund but, noting that Siborne apparently had no proper authorization for this expenditure, he decided that closer attention was necessary. The War Office Authority of 15 May 1830 does not appear to have been on file. On 9 April, Ellice replied to the Horse Guards agreeing to an advance of £200, but on the condition that this and the other sums already advanced would have to be repaid from the proceeds of the exhibition of the model. A week later, Lindsay informed Siborne of the situation, who replied immediately, asking why only £200 had been refunded. Siborne also pointed out that if he was to receive no further payments, the project could not be completed, particularly as the main expense, the moulding and casting of the figures, had yet to be incurred.[2] Future funding was now uncertain. As well as conducting his army duties and constructing the model, Siborne would also have to become a fundraiser.

Correspondence between the War Office and the Treasury from September 1833 outlined the sequence of events, pointing out that Hill had directed the work be commenced, 'but, as it would seem, without anticipating the extent of pecuniary aid it would require', and that 'Sir Henry Hardinge however, who would appear to have had some personal communication with Mr Siborne on the subject, objected to a fixed allowance, upon the ground that Mr Siborne was already in receipt of Staff Pay, but consented to the reimbursement of that Officer's actual Expenses to Waterloo and back; reserving the question of further remuneration for consideration upon the completion of the Model . . .'[3] Siborne's recollection of the agreement was different. He claimed Hill had '. . . previously obtained the authority of the then Secretary at War (The Right Honorable [sic] Sir Henry Hardinge) for the reimbursement to your Petitioner, of all expenses attending this national military work'.[4] Siborne was no doubt referring to the War Office Authority of 15 May 1830.

An internal War Office memorandum of 1841 confirmed that Lord Hill had selected Siborne to survey the battlefield and make a model of it; that Hardinge had agreed to pay his travelling expenses, but reserved the question of remuneration to Siborne for his labours until his task was finished; and that sums had been paid to Siborne for 'expenses attendant upon the execution of the Model'.[5] Such payments would not have been made without the agreement of the Secretary at War, a post held by Hardinge at the time in question, which confirms the existence of the Authority in question and the accuracy of Siborne's recollection.

With hindsight, Siborne can be held to blame for not having got a firm, written assurance from Hill and Hardinge.

However, in 1831, the *USJ* had announced: '. . . it is proposed to establish, in London, a NAVAL AND MILITARY MUSEUM, for the use and benefit of the United Service, to contain Models, Plans and Memoirs connected with the Naval and Military Services . . .' The notice continued, '. . . this important undertaking has received the gracious sanction of the King, who has condescended to become its PATRON. His Grace the Duke of Wellington has accepted the office of VICE-PATRON, and the Institution already enrols amongst its Presidents and Vice-Presidents many of the most distinguished names in both arms of the United Service.'[6] The presidents and vice-presidents included both Hill and Hardinge. The publication of this notice clearly indicated – to Siborne at least – that it was the government's intention to fund this work and that the model was commissioned on that understanding.

Despite the uncertainty over the funding, Siborne continued to work on the model. To put pressure on the authorities, he placed an announcement in the June 1833 edition of the *USJ*. While this announcement did little to hasten the decision-making process in government, it did spark off a debate over the events it was to depict. Naturally, poor Siborne was drawn into this as well and would soon have to spend a considerable amount of time engaged in correspondence with veterans of the battle. The model was taking over his life.

The issue of funding obviously needed to be resolved. Siborne waited for two months for Ellice to respond, hopefully favourably, to his request for the continuation of the expected financial support. When this did not materialize, Siborne then approached Vivian for advice on how to proceed. Vivian sent him away to write a memorandum on the history of this affair and to give a brief estimate of costs for its continuation. Siborne completed this task on 20 August, handing over the papers to Vivian, who immediately drafted an accompanying letter to go to Ellice at the War Office. In it, Vivian pointed out that the General Commanding-in-Chief had authorized the work, that Siborne now had financial difficulties through no fault of his own and asked that his application be given favourable consideration.[7]

Siborne's memorandum commented on his monetary problems, pointing out that pending a reply from the government he had continued to work on the model, financing it out of his own pocket. However, his private funds were now running out and he needed immediate help, as the tradesman employed in moulding and casting the figures would demand payment of about £210 at the beginning of October. About the same time, £60 would be due for the engraving on stone of a very large and detailed plan of the field of battle, copies of which would be sent to various participants in the battle for them to provide Siborne with information on the positions of the troops. Siborne suggested that Messrs. Armit & Borough, the army agents in Ireland, should be authorized to make payments from the War Office to him. Army agents were a sort of bank that dealt with matters pertaining to officers purchasing and selling commissions, drafts sent by the officers' families, accounting for special grants and dealing with clothing payments, as well as other matters. He estimated he needed at least another £1,000.[8]

Vivian's letter, enclosed with Siborne's memorandum, was received at the War Office on 26 August. The next day, a clerk in the War Office went through the existing documentation and then drew up a memorandum for the Secretary at War. This memorandum drew to Ellice's attention the fact that 'There is no record in this Office of the work having undertaken with the sanction of the S. at W. or of any expectation having been held out of assistance from the War Office towards defraying the current Expenses.'[9] It continued by mentioning that Ellice had in fact authorized payment of Siborne's first expense claim for £62 6s 7d in 1830 and that Sir Henry Purnell allowed the second claim of £120 13s 3d in January 1832. The memorandum concluded with the remark, 'No time is now mentioned for the completion of the Work.'[10] On the back of this document, Ellice noted, 'I can give no direction upon this without more information . . . At any rate I cannot authorise the further advance of so large a sum as £1000 without a specific vote of Parlt . . .'

On 21 September, a clerk at the War Office by the name of Sulivan passed the paperwork on to Sir James Stewart at the Treasury, outlining the history of the model and of its funding to date. Sulivan mentioned, 'Mr Ellice feels that, as Secretary at War, he cannot properly authorise the payment thereof without a specific vote of Parliament, and he therefore requests the advice and sanction of their Lordship's [the Lords of the Treasury] with respect to the further steps which may be expedient to take in this matter.'[11] Ellice was most likely aware that a Whig-dominated parliament would not sanction spending such a large sum on a monument to the previous Tory prime minister. By passing the buck, he was at least making sure he would not be criticized personally for this decision.

On 30 September, Stewart wrote to Ellice informing him of the decision of the Lords of the Treasury, who '. . . entirely concur with you in the propriety of suspending any further payments without Parliamentary authority . . .' He continued, 'Before My Lords can sanction the introduction of this item into the Estimates they would require a more specific & authoritative Military recommendation of the works as well as some more conclusive evidence of the maximum of expenses that may be incurred.'[12]

Fame and fortune were now slipping away from Siborne.

On 23 October 1833, Ellice replied to Vivian, the letter arriving in Dublin three days later. Ellice enclosed a copy of the communication he had sent to the Treasury and their reply of 30 September. His letter outlined the history of the model and its funding to date. The reply asked for confirmation of the model's military value and an estimate of its final cost. Vivian broke the news to Siborne, who immediately wrote a circular letter to a number of senior officers in the Dublin garrison. They were no doubt well aware of the project, and he hoped their opinions would carry some weight. In this circular, Siborne informed its recipients that the Lords of the Treasury had refused to consider making any further payments until they had received authoritative recommendations of the merits of the model. He asked them to oblige.[13]

Half the replies came in by return of post, the rest, barring one, within the next two days. They all supported Siborne's application and praised the quality and accuracy of his work.[14] The model had clearly impressed the powers that be in Dublin. One reply, that from Lt-Colonel Augustus Cuyler, arrived too late to be included in the correspondence sent to the War Office. Significantly, Cuyler was the first officer from

Wellington's staff at Waterloo that Siborne contacted. His letter contained an important point: 'Having been employed on the Staff of the Army at that time I can speak with great truth and confidence to this point – and it is very much superior to any [of] the Models of Actions which were to be seen in Paris in 1815, and by which the French set so much store.'[15]

Once he had received these glowing testimonials, Siborne set about drafting an 'Estimate of the Maximum of Expense to be incurred in the Completion of the Model of the Battle of Waterloo, from 30th September 1833' to enclose with his memorandum. It listed the items required and their cost, which came to a total of £1,340.[16] Siborne continued with a list of expenses incurred to date and the payments received. Armed with this documentation, he passed it on to Vivian, who, on 2 November 1833, forwarded it to the Secretary at War, along with a covering letter, again supporting the application. This letter also mentioned 'the Marquis of Anglesey who inspected the Model with me and who in the strongest terms expressed his approbation'.[17] The Marquis had, as the Earl of Uxbridge, commanded the Allied Cavalry at Waterloo.

With such support, references and documentation, Siborne must have felt that his application could only succeed.

Vivian's letter and the supporting documentation arrived at the War Office in London on 5 November, where it was processed. On 7 November, a clerk produced a memorandum outlining the history of this affair to date. Corroboration of the testimonials was sought from a knowledgeable source and his comments were included at the end of the memorandum the next day. Unfortunately, this person was not named, but he too expressed his admiration of the model. Lord Ebury, Comptroller of the Household, and Lord John Russell, the Paymaster-General, had also inspected the model and expressed their high regard of it, finding the great detail particularly noteworthy.[18]

On 23 November, the memorandum was sent to the Treasury, along with a covering letter and copies of the documentation. Vivian was informed of this. Ellice's letter was received on 25 November and the matter was submitted to the Lords of the Treasury for their consideration. On 10 December, they made their decision and on 16 December, Stewart replied to Ellice, informing him that 'I am commanded to inform you that My Lords do not consider that it would be expedient to propose to Parliament a Grant for so large a sum as £1400 for this service – but they are willing that the benefit of the sum already advanced to Lieut. Siborn be made over to that Gentleman if he shall think it fit to complete the work on his own account.'[19]

The War Office clerks again processed the incoming document, drawing up a detailed memorandum, which they then presented to the Secretary at War along with the letter from the Treasury. On 27 December, Ellice instructed them to send a copy of the Treasury's letter to Vivian, which they duly did.

This devastating news arrived in Dublin around New Year. However, Siborne was never one to give up and immediately set about raising funds. The onus to finish the model was now placed on him. The Lords of the Treasury had made it evident they considered the payments already made to Siborne a form of loan, which could be transformed into a non-repayable grant if he completed the model at his own cost. It would seem that Siborne had already considered what to do in such an event and had already discussed the possibility of raising funds by a subscription from senior army officers. He implemented that plan with characteristic energy, having a subscription form printed in January 1834. In it, Siborne asked private individuals for subscriptions of at least £20 in the hope of raising the £1,500 needed to complete the project. Each subscriber was guaranteed the highest rate of interest on their investment and that the original sum would be repaid from the proceeds raised by exhibiting and/or selling the model.[20]

An area was left at the bottom of the form for the interested party to enter his name and the amount he was offering. The money was not to go to Siborne himself but was to be deposited with the army agents in London or Dublin, who would then administer the funds, refunding Siborne against approved receipts of expenses. In view of the great profits that other such exhibitions had made at this time, it was almost certainly a good investment. Siborne remained optimistic that he would now receive the funds necessary to complete the project.

Being a serving army officer, Siborne was required to obtain permission from the Horse Guards before he could send out his proposal, so he forwarded them a copy. He mentioned in the covering letter his intention to send a circular to various surviving officers of the Battle of Waterloo to assist him in placing the figures representing the various regiments on the model. General Sir James Charles Dalbiac, a Peninsula veteran and now Inspector-General of Cavalry, considered the correspondence in the first instance. It was some weeks before Siborne received a reply. Dalbiac wrote to him on 5 March

1834, informing him that FitzRoy Somerset had objected to certain points. He considered the amount of the subscription too high and wanted it to be set at £10, and was opposed to the idea of sending a circular to officers for information on the battle.[21]

FitzRoy Somerset, now a full colonel, had also served under Wellington in the Peninsula. He had soon gained the Duke's confidence, being appointed to his staff in 1808. The two men became very close, and in 1811, FitzRoy Somerset was appointed Wellington's Military Secretary, a post he held throughout that war. As such, he dealt with the Duke's incoming and outgoing correspondence. At Waterloo he suffered a wound to his right arm and had to have the limb amputated. When Wellington was appointed Master-General of the Ordnance in January 1819, FitzRoy Somerset became his secretary, having in the meantime learned to write with his left hand. The two men continued to accompany each other for much of the rest of their lives. When Wellington became Commander-in-Chief of the army in 1827, FitzRoy Somerset was made Military Secretary at the Horse Guards, a post he was to hold for twenty-five years. Wellington trusted him with matters of absolute confidence; there is probably nobody who knew as much about the Duke's most private affairs.

The instant he received Dalbiac's letter, Siborne replied, objecting to these changes and explaining his reasons.[22] Two bones of contention were beginning to develop, which would play a role in the outcome of the affair. First, the Horse Guards expressed concern about the episode of the battle that was to be portrayed. At this stage it was not yet apparent to Siborne why portraying the Crisis of the Battle might be uncomfortable for a certain high authority. Also, there was obviously a disagreement on the future of the title to the model. Siborne certainly wanted it to remain his property after he had repaid the subscriptions, as its continued exhibition was likely to make him a rich man.

Friends advised an exasperated Siborne to go to London to lobby the authorities for a grant. This he did in June 1834, spending the best part of that month in the capital, but to no avail.[23] Although he continued to have financial problems over the summer and beyond, he nevertheless carried on working on the model. It is not certain if he finally got permission to send out the subscription proposal. If he did, his papers do not contain a single reply. It may well be he was not given permission, leaving the future funding of this mammoth project undecided.

An exasperated Vivian wrote to FitzRoy Somerset on 24 July 1834.

> I have a letter from Lt. Siborne this morning, who is at Cheltenham very ill – & his illness has really been brought on by fretting in consequence of the most unpleasant situation in which he has been placed by the Government having withdrawn from him the pecuniary aid he was promised when he undertook the Model of the Battle of Waterloo – I have already written so much & so strongly on the subject that I shall not attempt to add to my former Letters further than by saying that both on publick [sic] & private grounds I do think that this is a case in which it would be wise of the Government to reconsider their decision – & to express a hope that you will do your best to

induce them to do so – I really know not what is to happen unless they do. Is it not possible to introduce the expense into the Army Extraordinaries. –

If the Government will only advance the money to finish the Model, I should not hesitate if it was thought desirable, to guarantee the repayment of the money that will from this time be required, from the receipts of the Exhibition.[24]

There is no record of FitzRoy Somerset's reply, but as the issue of funding was not resolved, it is safe to assume it was negative. Although the financial uncertainty was making poor Siborne ill, he continued to work on the model. The cost of its construction had now reached £2,000. Exactly how this was funded remains a mystery, but at some stage Siborne took out a large bank loan, a further burden he could have done without. The future funding of the model and the hoped for financial support from the government were never far from his mind.

On 18 April 1835, Lord Howick became Secretary at War, which encouraged Siborne to approach FitzRoy Somerset again for both funding and a promotion. With a captain's pay, he would have been able to finance the model with less difficulty. A month later, he wrote in this vein to FitzRoy Somerset, his letter concluding, 'I may take the liberty of adding that my Promotion *now* would be infinitely more acceptable & useful to me than *after* the completion of my Model, & that I should, when the latter takes place, consider my claims in this respect to have been fairly settled.'[25]

Siborne also indicated for the first time that he was preparing to write a history of the Waterloo campaign. On 1 June,

FitzRoy Somerset replied. He rejected Siborne's application for promotion, pointing out that Lord Hill felt that, as a Staff Officer, he already had a privileged position. FitzRoy Somerset did not address the issue of the promised promotion for the construction of the model, but he did not deny Siborne's claim to have been promised his captaincy.

The costs involved in constructing and exhibiting the model had escalated, as is so often the case with prestige projects. Siborne was losing control of his life. One could question his judgement in continuing, but acting on Hill's authority, Siborne had subcontracted much of the work to tradesmen and was obliged to pay them. He was also obliged to reimburse the government for the funding made in the early years of its construction if he did not complete the model. As he did not have the money to repay this amount, he had no real choice but to find a way of finishing and exhibiting it. After all, the model was almost certainly guaranteed to be a financial success, and a substantial one at that. The last great Waterloo exhibition, a panorama, had made its owner £10,000, a massive sum of money in the early nineteenth century. Siborne's model was vastly superior to that series of paintings and he could be fairly certain of becoming a rich man at the end of all his trials and tribulations. That, no doubt, played a significant role in his deliberations. After all, he needed the security of a second income.

Siborne's notice in the June 1833 issue of the *USJ* had sparked off a debate over the events surrounding the Crisis of the Battle of Waterloo that was to continue for several years. The two main protagonists in this dispute were Sir Hussey Vivian and George Gawler.

Vivian was not close to Wellington and was well able to have opinions of his own that conflicted with those of the Duke. Gawler had been a lieutenant in the 52nd Light Infantry, a regiment that had participated in the final defeat of Napoleon's Imperial Guard at the end of the Battle of Waterloo. He had served with the 52nd in the Peninsula, being wounded at Badajoz and San Munos, and in 1815 had led the right company of his regiment. It was his contention that the 52nd, supported by the remainder of Major-General Adam's brigade (95th and 71st Regiments), and not the Guards under Major-General Sir Peregrine Maitland, as was the accepted wisdom, had repelled Napoleon's final attack.

In his contribution to the *USJ* in July 1833, Gawler outlined the role of his regiment in considerable detail, making the case that it played a considerable, but as yet ignored, role in the overthrow of the Imperial Guard. In doing so, he diminished the role of Vivian's brigade. Vivian, in his reply, objected to that, starting a controversy that continued for years afterwards. Gawler's paper, 'The Crisis and Close of the Action at Waterloo, by an Eye-Witness', was reissued as a pamphlet in Dublin in 1833.[26] Siborne would soon be dragged into the dispute.

Two more rounds were fought out in the September and October issues of the *USJ*, with both parties largely repeating their original positions and refuting the counter-arguments brought by the other. Siborne's natural stance on this would have been to support Vivian. Not only was Vivian Siborne's chief, he was also his friend and greatest supporter in the question of funding the model. However, Siborne kept an open mind on this – and the other such disputes that arose – being scrupulously fair in his judgement.

Siborne even approached Gawler, who was also based in Ireland, for further information on the actions of the 52nd during the Crisis. Gawler visited Siborne in Dublin and examined the model. On 24 June 1834, he wrote to Siborne, 'I shall have great pleasure & shall never consider it any trouble to give or promise as far as I am able information that may forward your most interesting undertaking, & to the best of my perception will give it without prejudice.'[27] As well as giving details of the 52nd's activities, Gawler also enclosed a sketch map marking his regiment's positions. Vivian was apparently present at this meeting and he wrote Siborne a long memorandum. Further accusations and refutations followed in the coming weeks and months, taking up more of Siborne's precious free time. He had yet to place any figures on the model, but was already in the middle of a major dispute. There was enough glory for all, but some wanted more than others.

It became clear to Siborne that numerous such disputes would be likely once he added the figures representing the troops on the model. He decided that it would make life easier to print a circular to send to the surviving officers, soliciting the information he needed in an organized fashion, restricting their input to specific points and thereby hopefully reducing any possible points of contention. This circular, another of Siborne's innovations, was one of the earliest known examples of mass polling by post.

Siborne looked for appropriate cartography to accompany the circular. As he would first have to approach the Horse Guards for permission to distribute it, Siborne decided to enquire if this office could assist him in his search. He wrote again to

FitzRoy Somerset, who passed the enquiry on to Colonel Sir Charles Grene Ellicombe of the Royal Engineers and to Sir James Willoughby Gordon. Ellicombe, a Peninsula veteran, was on the staff of the Inspector-General of Fortifications at the Ordnance Office in London. He was well known for his administrative ability and intimate acquaintance with the large range of complicated details connected with military engineering. Gordon was Quartermaster-General at the Horse Guards, that is, its chief-of-staff.

On 29 October 1834, Ellicombe wrote a brief memorandum on Siborne's request, pointing out that his office possessed a copy of two printed sketches and the general plan made by the Netherlands officer Craan which, however, he could not loan except with the Master-General's permission. He also commented, 'I fear the answers to the proposed Circular would only bring a Mass of information that never could be got together with any degree of accuracy.'[28] Gordon replied to FitzRoy Somerset a couple of days later, suggesting that Siborne either copy the Craan map himself or send somebody to do it for him.

Gordon was, however, not as positive about the model as he was about making a map available. He expanded Ellicombe's concern about representing the Crisis of the Battle, as he did not think it possible to obtain reliable information. 'The Commanding Officer of each Regiment could certainly say where his Regiment was posted at any period of the day,' he wrote, 'but to require such information for the purpose of a plan or model, would in my opinion lead to anything but an accurate exposition of the Battle.' This would be due not only to faded memories so many years after the events, but also because

'Two, three, or more Regiments might be, and probably were, posted exactly on the same spot, within a few minutes each after the other.' Finally, he considered it likely that commanding officers would also overplay the role of their unit. He recommended that 'the clearest point of view under which both Armies could be represented on a Model upon a large scale, would be that of their position at the commencement of the action, when each successive movement could best be followed up by an attentive study of the Duke's Despatch.'[29] The 'Duke's Despatch' referred to in this letter was Wellington's *Waterloo Despatch* of 19 June 1815.

While Gordon's point about the reliability of the information Siborne would be soliciting was valid, he had raised an issue that was going to affect the remainder of Siborne's life.

FitzRoy Somerset then had Lindsay write Siborne a covering letter enclosing Gordon's note and telling him that Sir James Kempt, the Master-General of the Ordnance, would allow him access to the cartography Ellicombe mentioned. Siborne responded with an explanation of the reasoning behind his choice of portraying the Crisis of the Battle on the model, pointing out, 'The Model which I am constructing is not merely one of the *Field* but also of the *Battle* of Waterloo.' As such, it was essential to represent the units involved. Dealing with the issue of the reliability of the information, he continued:

> I cannot persuade myself that there are not to be found, among the mass of surviving Waterloo Officers, more particularly among those who held important Commands on that day, many, who even supposing them not to retain a

vivid recollection of *all* the distinguishing features of *the last great action in which they were engaged*, are fully able to answer the simple question – 'What was the formation and position of the Division, Brigade, Regiment or Battery, at the moment the French Imperial Guards reached the crest of the right of our Position' – a moment so definite, so distinct, and so critical. The other question 'What was the formation of the Enemy's Troops opposite the Division' etc. may not be so easily answered, and many an Officer may say 'The smoke was so thick I could not observe them with sufficient distinctness' – Then I must endeavour to procure the information from others who had a better opportunity of observation as also perhaps from the French themselves, but failing in all this I can with the greatest ease represent the thick smoke upon the Model.

Answering the criticisms of his methodology, he stated he did not think it likely that the circular would produce a mass of contradictory information, as his request for information would be specific, pointing out, 'the few answers I have already received justify this opinion'. More importantly, he stated he could not 'conceive how an attempt to illustrate more in detail the main feature of the Battle, "must in a great measure tend to weaken the high authority of the Duke of Wellington's Despatch," for it will contain nothing at variance with one syllable of that document, and moreover, I do not intend to fasten a single figure upon my Model, until I shall have submitted for His Grace's approval and correction, a plan of the action, showing the manner in which I propose to distribute the Troops at the moment in question'. Siborne had no reason to believe for a minute that his model would conflict with the *Waterloo Despatch*.

Siborne concluded by pointing out it would now be impractical to change the juncture in the battle depicted on the model as he had already contacted the French and Prussian armies for information, had constructed the buildings in such a manner that the damage caused by shot and flame was represented and had purchased thousands of figures in positions of action.[30]

Before sending off his reply to the Horse Guards, Siborne took the opportunity of discussing the matter with Vivian. Being of the same opinion as Siborne, Vivian was only too pleased to oblige him by writing a supporting letter, which Siborne enclosed with his. Vivian outlined his reasons, which were sound, before concluding,

> Lastly – and it is of all the most important consideration & which does not appear to have occurred to Sir Willoughby, if you describe the commencement of the Battle or rather the period before the fight commenced – what are you to do with the Prussians? The advance of the Prussians & their attack on Planchenoite [*sic*] and on the right flank & rear of the French was one of the most important features, if not the most important, in the whole day, if your Model has the Troops placed as at the commencement - *the Prussians must be left at Wavre* - this is in my mind conclusive as I am sure will be in Sir Willoughby's & Lord FitzRoy's also.[31]

Siborne sent these two documents to Lindsay at the Horse Guards, who passed them on to FitzRoy Somerset. FitzRoy Somerset gave Siborne permission to send out his circular, writing, 'then let him issue his Circulars and the Lord give him a safe deliverance', on the corner of his letter.[32] The Prussians were not going to be left at Wavre, miles away from the battle.

Once permission was received from the Horse Guards, Siborne had his circular printed immediately, and with his characteristic energy, started sending it out. Blanks were left for him to fill in the date and the name of the regiment in question. He asked the recipients for information on the formation of their regiment at about 7 p.m. on 18 June 1815, the formation of the French troops immediately to their front and enclosed a copy of a plan of the battlefield for them to return with the positions marked. He sent out dozens of these pro formae in the coming days, which must have taken up most of his spare time in that dark, dank Dublin winter. In the six weeks to the end of the year alone, Siborne received nearly seventy answers. Where the information given was clear, he marked the positions given on a map of the battlefield. More answers arrived in the early weeks of 1835. The answers gave rise to more questions, and over the following twelve years, Siborne generated a considerable amount of correspondence, keeping and filing nearly 1,000 items. His records are the most detailed source of information on the Battle of Waterloo ever assembled.

It wasn't just Siborne's records that were incredibly detailed. Today's collector of model soldiers and war-gamer is spoiled by the choice of commercially manufactured figures in numerous scales, but in the 1830s, they weren't available. Siborne had to find tradesmen with the appropriate skills to make the figures, most likely a company of jewellers or silversmiths, as they were apparently modelled using a composition of lead and silver.[33] Only craftsmen would have been able to cast figures around 10 mm tall with almost inconceivable detail. The wheels on the wagons revolve. Their drivers have their own whips. The arms of the infantry were moulded separately, allowing them to be attached in different positions. Very little was cast as a complete entity or glued together. The figures had been cast in strips, and the accoutrements, equipment and weapons were wired or pinned on to them individually. The detail is remarkable. Even today's commercially manufactured figures do not attain this standard and precision.

If this almost microscopic detail were not impressive enough, the individual soldiers were painted to show every aspect of their uniforms and equipment. Every helmet bears a badge; every regimental facing is accurately portrayed; an eagle finial surmounts every French flagpole. One can only imagine the man-hours needed to complete just this part of this massive project.

The exhaustive attention to detail did not stop there. Using the mountain of documentation he had elicited from surviving officers, Siborne ascertained with a considerable degree of accuracy the position and formation of each unit on the battlefield. He placed the figures in such a way as to represent the lines, squares and columns used in a Napoleonic battle. He even portrayed the chaotic rabble of a defeated army, intermingled with burning farms and woodland which were strewn with the dead and dying. In all, around 80,000 figures were manufactured to represent the 160,000 men present at the battle. The scale of this project was – and remains – unprecedented.

Siborne's later research led him to write a *Guide* to the model, explaining in vivid terms what was happening at the particular moment of the battle he had chosen to represent (the positions of the troops indicated below can be seen on the map on p. 71):

The time chosen is that in which Napoleon made his last great struggle for victory; and which may be truly termed the crisis of the battle, for on the success or failure of this effort depended the fate of the Emperor of the French, and the destinies of Europe. The battle had already lasted nearly eight hours, and the result still trembled in the balance. The steady, resolute, and unshaken front presented by the allied army under the Duke of Wellington, notwithstanding the most determined efforts, so frequently repeated, to force its line of battle, and the gradual development of the principal portion of the Prussian army under Prince Blucher Von Wahlstadt, by which so powerful a diversion was effected against the French right, rendered it imperative on Napoleon to resort to one of two alternatives – to commence a retreat, or to make another desperate attempt to break the Duke's line, and establish his left on the allied position, and at the same time, to maintain a firm stand against the Prussian advance upon his right. The only intact reserve which then remained at his disposal consisted of twelve battalions of the infantry of the Imperial Guard, namely, four battalions of the Old, and eight of the Middle Guard, the remainder of that force, comprising the whole of the Young Guard (eight battalions) and four battalions of the Old Guard, being engaged with the Prussians at the village of Planchenoit, with the exception of one battalion of the latter, which was with the Emperor's baggage

at the village of Caillou, in rear of the whole army. It was
with these battalions that Napoleon determined upon once
more endeavouring to force the Duke of Wellington's position, and, having collected them in front of La Belle
Alliance, he made the following disposition: – four battalions of the Middle Guard were formed into one column of
attack in mass of battalions, and destined to advance
against the centre of the right wing of the allied army – the
point occupied by the 1st British brigade of guards. The
four remaining battalions of the Middle Guard, and two
battalions of the Old Guard were formed into a second column of attack, and moved down into the hollow adjoining
the south-eastern angle of the inclosures [sic] of
Hougomont [sic]: it was destined to support the first column, and to direct its advance somewhat more to the left.
The other two battalions of the Old Guard were to continue stationary in front of La Belle Alliance, and these constituted, with the remains of the splendid cavalry force
which had suffered such severe losses during its repeated
attacks in masses upon the allied forces, Napoleon's sole
and last reserve.[34]

Siborne's information had come from various sources that
he used to draw up memoranda on these events. As always, his
research had been thorough and his description largely accurate. There was little that could be disputed here – on the basis
of the facts, at least.

7 *Finding the Facts*

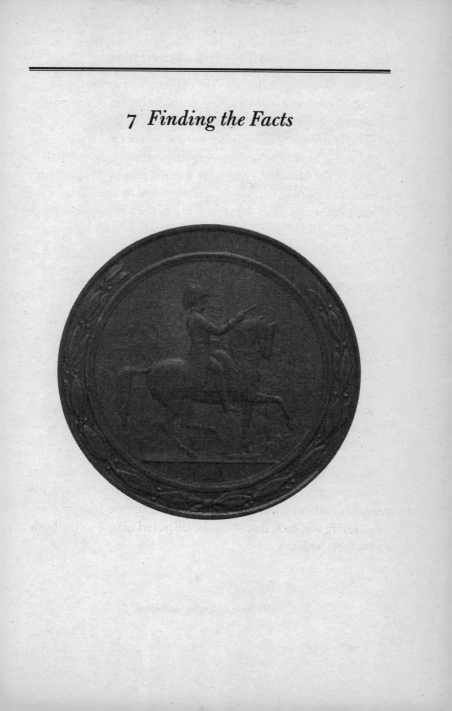

Wellington on horse, medallion

'Perhaps some future day due credit may be given to the conduct of a Brigade which I hesitate not to assert was principally instrumental in occasioning the very sudden & total Rout of the French Army which took place. In one of the Numbers of the Quarterly Review the Conduct of the British Light Cavalry in the Battle of Waterloo is noticed in the most slighting terms.'
Capt. T. W. Taylor of the 10th Hussars

In the winter of 1834–5, Siborne dealt with the correspondence his circular had generated. The Gawler controversy made it clear to Siborne that he had opened a Pandora's box. Rather than face spending years answering charges made by aggrieved parties he would have to spend an inordinate amount of time checking the details of the positions of the figures on the model. The first reply came on 2 November 1834, a somewhat non-committal answer from Sir John Byng, commander of the 2nd Guards Brigade at Waterloo. Captain Barton of the 12th Light Dragoons, whose reply arrived the next day, was more informative. He went into considerable detail and volunteered more information than requested as he described his regiment's role in much of the battle. This wonderfully informative reply was certainly not an exception, merely a harbinger of what was to come. Siborne would soon be suffering from information overload.

Hardly a day went by without at least one letter turning up. On some days, it was as many as six. Many contained snippets of interest on aspects of the battle. For instance, Lt-Colonel Reynell of the 71st Foot provided some fascinating material documenting the ineffectiveness of the French cavalry attacks on Wellington's squares, as well as the destruction caused by the heavy French bombardment. Sir Peregrine Maitland of the 1st Guards Brigade was considerate enough to enclose a highly detailed memorandum. He was, of course, claiming that it was his brigade that played the major part in the defeat of the Imperial Guards, a role that Gawler had claimed for his 52nd Foot. One suspects that this controversy inspired Maitland's memorandum.

Major Winchester of the 92nd Highlanders, who in 1815 was a lieutenant in the same regiment, also went beyond Siborne's request for information, describing the 92nd's role from the beginning of the battle. He was the first to mention the retreat of Bijlandt's brigade of Netherlanders at the start of the battle, which is subject to controversy even today. Siborne did not know this at the time, but he too was later to become involved in an acrimonious dispute with the Netherlanders over this affair.

Four more replies arrived before the end of November 1834, including one from Lt Pringle of Bolton's Battery, Royal Artillery, and one from Lt Kerr Ross of the 92nd Highlanders. Ross mentioned that he would be able to give information on Quatre Bras as well, material that Siborne would use ten years later in his classic *History*. The next day, two more replies arrived, one from Major Dawson Kelly of the 73rd Foot and one from Captain A. C. Mercer, of Dickson's Troop, Royal Horse Artillery. Mercer's reply was the longest Siborne had received to date and went well beyond answering the question posed.[1]

And so it went on, seemingly incessantly, with letter after letter arriving. Some required an answer, others corroboration from a third party. Siborne constantly marked up the positions of troops given on master copies of his plan. His picture of the battle grew in both scale and detail.

*

The one criticism Siborne's detractors made of the model, was the juncture in the battle he had chosen to portray. These critics claimed that, due to conflicting statements, it would be impossible for Siborne to reconstruct these events with acceptable accuracy. Siborne disputed that, and anybody examining his records will see the enormous trouble to which he went to establish the reliability of the information he was given. He was continually marking maps of the battlefield with the positions given and resolved any conflicts by questioning the eyewitnesses in detail. He sent out one undated question-naire to an officer of the 1st (Guards) Brigade, possibly Sir Peregrine Maitland, discussing the final attack of the Old Guard at Waterloo. Siborne listed his questions on the left col-umn of the paper, the answers being entered in the right col-umn. This way, he attempted to establish the time the attack took place, the positions and movements of the British troops in that area, whether the British enjoyed artillery support and if the French deployed skirmishers. The answers he received were detailed.

Siborne did not hesitate to contact high-ranking officers for advice and information, particularly when it came to dealing with any conflicts of evidence. An example of this is the letter to Byng of 31 March 1835, in which he asked for information on the activ-ities of Maitland's brigade during the Crisis. Maitland's Guards were part of Cooke's and Byng's corps, and Siborne was seeking corroboration of Maitland's statements. 'I apprehend that those officers who have placed the brigade so much in advance, have confounded the *last* with the *preceding* attack,' Siborne com-plained, hoping Byng could clarify that problem.[2]

A good example of Siborne's thoroughness in tracking down the facts was in his letter of 17 May 1835 to FitzRoy Somerset:

> The fact stated in the enclosed extract of a letter to me from Lt. Colonel Blair who was Brigade Major to Sir F. Adam at Waterloo is of so interesting a nature that I am anxious to be able to establish it by still stronger testimony, previously to my hazarding a reference to it in my *History* of the Battle and I therefore trust your Lordship will, when a suitable occasion offers, have the kindness, to consult the Duke of Wellington upon this point, with a view to ascertain from His Grace the name of the Foreigner to whom allusion is made, as also, the circumstances under which he became attached to His Grace's Staff.'

From the first paragraph of this letter, we get a further indication of the exhaustive, relentless nature of Siborne's research. Blair had written to Siborne on 1 May regarding the Gawler controversy. In this letter, Blair mentioned an incident involving Wellington towards the end of the battle, writing,

> After the repulse of the Squares of the Old Guard (I do not exactly recollect the spot) Sir Frederick Adam desired me to ride on the prolongation of our right in order to observe if any part of the Enemy seemed to threaten our right Rank – then apparently quite unprotected. Having gone some distance, I met the Duke of Wellington moving at a quick pace, followed by one individual to whom I spoke. His answer was, "*Monsieur, je ne parle pas un seul mot d'Anglais.*" ["Sir, I do not speak a single word of English."] I told him in French the order I had received. He replied,

"*Le Duc lui-même a été voir; il m'y a rien à craindre.*"
["The Duke himself has been to see; there is nothing for
me to fear there."] I rejoined the Brigade. The above circumstance has always appeared to me and to those to
whom I have related it, a very striking proof of the miracu-
lous escape and providential care of that great man on this
eventful day: his Staff, even Orderlies, almost all killed or
wounded, the few that remained untouched carrying messages; his only attendant a French Officer, attached to him
by Louis XVIII!!! If you wish to record it you are quite at
liberty to use my name.[3]

Siborne was seeking to corroborate Blair's story, which was
typical of his approach. He accepted nothing he was told on
face value. Rather, he sought confirmation (or denial) from
other witnesses before determining what would have been the
most likely sequence of events. What is also noteworthy in the
first paragraph of Siborne's letter to FitzRoy Somerset is the
fact that he was endeavouring to contact Wellington. This was
the first of several attempts to seek information from the Duke.
FitzRoy Somerset did discuss the incident with Wellington,
who corrected Blair's error, a matter that Blair raised in his
next letter to Siborne, dated 29 November 1835. In it, Blair
wrote, 'Lord Fitzroy Somerset mentioned to me in town last
spring the mistake I had been led into supposing that the Foreign Officer attending the Duke at the period I referred to was
a Frenchman, he being a Sardinian.'[4]

Ten years later, on 17 May 1845, Siborne wrote to FitzRoy
Somerset requesting him to have Wellington verify this incident. On 1 June, FitzRoy Somerset replied:

Having communicated to the Duke of Wellington the first part of your letter of the 17th Ultimo and the Extract to which it refers, I find that His Grace has no recollection of the circumstance to which Lt Colonel Blair particularly alludes, but certainly at one period of the action it did happen that none of the Staff Officers of the Army were in attendance upon, and that the only Officer who was near him was an Officer attached to his Head Quarters by the King of Sardinia, Monsieur de Salles by name, (I am not certain I spell his name correctly) who did not speak a word of English and who not improbably therefore, was the Individual to whom Lt Colonel Blair addressed himself.[5]

This fact was minute and virtually irrelevant, yet clarifying it had been on Siborne's mind for years.

In December 1834 alone, Siborne received around fifty more replies. There was hardly a regiment or artillery troop that did not provide information. One would have expected Siborne to be so overwhelmed with this flood of correspondence that he would have been snowed under and unable to move on until he had processed it all. However, he painstakingly collated the information, and around the end of 1834, he drew up a memorandum on the positions of the Allied and French armies at Waterloo.

Having obtained so much useful information from British officers, Siborne tried his luck with the French participants. On 31 October 1834, he contacted Marshal Lobau, commander of the French VI Corps at Waterloo.[6] Lobau responded, and Siborne then tried to have a circular sent to the surviving French officers. It would seem that despite an initial positive response

from Lobau, no circular was distributed and no information
was forthcoming.[7] Although there is no direct record of this, it
appears that Siborne also wrote to Marshal Soult as well as to
Generals Flahaut and Exelmans.[8] As he received no response,
Siborne, at the suggestion of a Colonel Stuart (possibly
Colonel Stuart Lennox), contacted Sir Robert Alexander
Chermside, physician to the British Embassy in Paris, to seek
his assistance in getting replies. At Waterloo, Chermside had
been assistant surgeon to the 7th Hussars. On 8 June 1835, in
reply to Siborne's request for support in obtaining information
from Marshals Lobau and Soult, Chermside wrote,

> I regret extremely to learn, by an indirect communication
> from the Honble Colonel Stuart, that you have not yet
> received any information from either of the Marshals, Soult
> or Lobau. I am of opinion that a communication for you
> has miscarried. I can only assure you that I called at least
> five different times on Mar*l* Soult, ascertained the time of
> his return to Paris; left the various parcels addressed to
> him, myself, and was in hope that you had long since heard
> something satisfactory. M*l* Soult did not remain many days
> at Paris, he was, as you are, perhaps, aware, involved in
> political affairs etc. etc.
>
> I did not fail to try to obtain answers to yr different queries
> from Gen*l's* Flahault [*sic*] & Exelmans but they either could
> not or would not furnish the information desired.
>
> I am surprised that M*l* Lobau has not communicated with
> you, as he appeared disposed to do anything in his power,
> indeed said so to myself. With M*l* Soult I never could obtain
> an interview. I sincerely wish I could, in any way, be of use to

you. Could you come here for a week or so, I think you might be able to extract something from M*l* L. or others. I believe Gl. de Flahault will soon accompany his family to Brighton whither they are going very soon for sea bathing.[9]

Siborne does not appear to have gone for an outing to Brighton. Neither did he get any response to his enquiries.

The Earl of Wiltshire, who was also in Paris, then got involved and attempted to get a response from the French Ministry of War. On 7 December 1835, he wrote to Siborne, explaining that he and Chermside had gone to the Bureau de Guerre (War Office) the previous Saturday, where they had met General Pellet's chief secretary. Their enquiry as to the whereabouts of the answers to Siborne's enquiries was met with various excuses. Wiltshire pointed out that, 'The battle of Waterloo is & ever will be a sore subject with the French and as considerable vanity is the leading feature in their Character, particularly as regards leurs faites d'armes [the deeds of their arms], you must make some allowances for their weakness on this point however much interest you may take in your own *Model* & however much *They* may vante [vaunt] their Austerlitz, Wagram, Borodino, Jena, Friedland si ci. It's a subject one never likes to broach here.'[10]

Siborne was particularly eager to confirm the details of the action at Plancenoit, where the Prussians' decisive flanking attack occurred. He wanted, of course, to corroborate their accounts. Chermside did manage to get a verbal reply from General Flahaut on this, and reported, 'Therefore I am inclined to think the last attack on *our right* was made by the *two Columns* in question as a sort [of] dernier [last] effort in a moment of desperation on finding the Prussians arrived *under Blucher* & that it was made *à la hâte* [in haste] without any support *whatever* on reference to the general usage of French Tactics in the advance of Sir Fredk Adam's Brigade proves or he would not have ventured to have wheeled left into line or formed to his left & *exposed his right flank unprotected*. This is the *strongest proof* you can have there was no *support* to the *attacking French Columns*.'[111]

Many of Wiltshire's comments come as little surprise. Waterloo was such a wound to French pride that the first authoritative history of the campaign in French, that by Charras, was published as late as 1857. Even then, the subject was so sensitive that it was first published in Belgium and not in France. This work was even translated into German and Dutch before the sixth and final edition was finally published in France in 1869. Until then, most of the works on the campaign had been those from participants, all of whom engaged in excuse making. It is no wonder that the officers of the Bureau de Guerre were politely unhelpful, and it seems Siborne did not get any further with his endeavours to communicate with surviving French participants.

Having been so successful in obtaining information from British officers and having initiated contact with Marshal Lobau, Siborne's mind now moved on to contacting the German officers involved, particularly those in the Hanoverian Army and the now disbanded King's German Legion. He wrote to Lindsay at the Horse Guards asking for official permission to do so, and Lindsay replied on 5 January 1835,

> In regard to your wish to be allowed to send through Baron Ompteda [Minister of State and of the Cabinet of Hanover at

the British Court] the Letters respecting your Model, my advice is that you should let me send the Packets to my friend Capt. Bené [*sic*] at Hanover, and request him to be the medium of communication with you through me, you writing to Sir James Reynett explaining all you desire. The corresponding as you propose will be liable to delay and all kind of mistakes. – Sir James Reynett is with the D. of Cambridge and is a person who will enter readily into your views.[12]

The Duke of Cambridge was Viceroy of Hanover, which until the accession of Queen Victoria in 1837, was ruled by the King of England. Clearly, Siborne's project was considered so prestigious that doors were being opened for him in the highest places. Lindsay would continue to assist Siborne in his endeavours for years to come and the men became good friends.

On 15 January 1835, Siborne drafted his questionnaire to the Hanoverian officers and for much of the next two months his in-tray was filled with their replies, along with further correspondence from British officers. The energy he put into processing this material was considerable, particularly as the majority of the answers were in German. Siborne certainly had a working knowledge of the language, although he had some difficulty with the Gothic script and never trusted himself to write in German. The first of these replies, from Captain Seeger of the 2nd Light Dragoons, King's German Legion (KGL), was an indication of what was to come. Instead of merely responding to the request to give information on the positions of his men at the Crisis, Seeger wrote a detailed account of the actions of his regiment in the entire campaign, even including a breakdown of the casualties suffered. By the end of March, Siborne had received over forty replies from the Hanoverians. Only one or two were in English and most of this material has never been made available to the general public. Siborne drew extensively on it in his authoritative *History*, although there are those who have accused him of ignoring material in languages other than English.

On 8 November 1834, Siborne first contacted the Prussian Minister of War, sending him a copy of the plan and asking for him to show the positions of the Prussian troops at the Crisis. A reply was finally sent on 8 July 1835. Siborne was also sent a copy of a map of the battle, printed in 1825 to accompany the Prussian official history of the campaign. This was to be the beginning of a long correspondence.

These first two letters were sent directly to Berlin without the knowledge of the Horse Guards. Later correspondence was, for various reasons, sent via the Horse Guards, and as FitzRoy Somerset was Military Secretary there, Wellington became aware of Siborne's dealings with the Prussian General Staff.

Dozens of replies to the circular came in during the coming weeks and months. Siborne also appears to have conducted further correspondence with particular respondents, asking for more detailed information on certain points. In view of Siborne's obvious desire to collect all the information possible from participants on both sides, it is surprising that there is no record of him contacting the Dutch army. Indeed, after the publication of his *History*, Siborne was subjected to severe criticism from them for not having done so. While it is true that

Siborne did not conduct a detailed correspondence with the
Netherlanders, he did obtain a copy of the Prince of Orange's
papers through the offices of his close friend Sir Herbert
Taylor.[13] Furthermore, the Kingdom of the Netherlands as
established at the Congress of Vienna in 1815 had recently
collapsed, a revolution breaking it into its constituent parts –
Belgium, Luxembourg and today's Netherlands – in 1830.
Siborne had got nowhere in his endeavours to obtain information from the French, who were still suffering from post-
Waterloo blues, so it is possible he considered it a waste of time
trying to contact officers of what were now two hostile armies
for information. He had received hundreds of communications
already from British and German officers, a number of which
reported the positions and movements of the Dutch troops. He
certainly indicated in his later reply to the Netherlanders' criticisms that he considered the information he had sufficient. It is
also evident that he did indeed go to some lengths to establish
the facts as to the role of the Netherlanders in the Crisis, as his
memorandum on the issue of 14 August 1837 shows.

As the model neared completion in the autumn and winter of
1837/8, Siborne spent a considerable amount of time sorting out
the final details of the positions of the troops. He corresponded
with former members of the KGL, the Hanoverians, Vivian and
others. Sir Frederick Adam, commander of the 3rd Infantry
Brigade, sent a useful report on the final attack of the Imperial
Guard. General William Halkett wrote on 20 December 1837,
giving an account of the capture of the French General Cambronne at the point of the overthrow of the Imperial Guard.
Cambronne is reputed to have shouted the word '*merde*' in

defiance of calls to surrender. Halkett, however, described the events leading up to Cambronne's surrender rather differently:

> After having received our fire with much effect, the Column left their General with two Officers behind, when I ordered the sharpshooters to dash on, and I made a gallop for the General. When about cutting him down he called out he would surrender, upon which he preceded me [to the rear], but I had not gone many paces before my horse got a shot through his body and fell to the ground. In a few seconds I got him on his legs again, and found my friend, Cambronne, had taken French leave in the direction from where he came. I instantly overtook him, laid hold of him by the aiguillette, and brought him in safety and gave him in charge to a sergeant of the Osnabruckers to deliver to the Duke; I could not spare an Officer for the purpose, many being wounded.[14]

This would not be the only legend to fall victim to Siborne's research.

In a postscript, Halkett added another snippet of information: 'The Knapsacks in possession of the Hanoverian Troops were English, painted yellow. The Luneburg and Bremen Verden had green coats; the latter wore dark blue trousers.'[15]

Siborne was now crossing his t's and dotting his i's.

Somehow Siborne managed to muddle his way through the next year or so, obtaining enough money to keep the project going. While he was adding the finishing touches and planning how he would transport the model to London, where he was planning to exhibit it, Siborne contacted Colonel John Gurwood.

As well as working on the model, Siborne was also writing his *History* and needed some points clarified. Gurwood was editor of *Wellington's Dispatches*, a multi-volumed collection of Wellington's official papers which were then in the process of going to print. The Waterloo volume – clearly of great interest to Siborne – was due later in 1838. There are no copies of his letters to Gurwood in his papers, but he did keep Gurwood's replies, which indicate the information he was seeking.

As Gurwood was working on Wellington's papers, Siborne naturally assumed that the Colonel had been on the Duke's staff at Waterloo and wrote to him on that basis. On 22 February 1838, Gurwood responded that Siborne was mistaken about his appointment in 1815, and that he was actually present and in action with his regiment, the 10th Hussars. This regiment had been part of Sir Hussey Vivian's brigade, so Gurwood referred Siborne to Vivian for information on the Brigade's role at Waterloo. Gurwood also informed Siborne that he had forwarded the enquiry to a friend, W. Slayter Smith of the Yorkshire Hussars, who was a lieutenant in the 10th at Waterloo. Even though Vivian was a close friend, Siborne contacted Smith to check the veracity of Vivian's statements.[16]

Making use of his new contact, Siborne wrote to Gurwood again on 17 March asking for various items of information, including, significantly, the headquarters registers from the Waterloo campaign. The registers were a series of books in which a clerk entered details of all incoming and outgoing correspondence. There were normally columns for details such as time, date, from/to whom and a précis of the document. Siborne also asked Gurwood to obtain certain information from Wellington. Vivian was good enough to send on Siborne's letter with a covering note giving him the necessary authority. Gurwood, who was on a visit to Paris at the time, acknowledged receipt to Vivian, explaining there would be a delay in replying: 'I will thank you to mention to Capt. Siborne my answer to his letter to me on the subject of his request to me. I shall not be able to meet his wishes until after my return to Apsley House next month when I will do all I can in obtaining from the Duke of Wellington the information he requires.'[17]

Gurwood replied to Siborne on 23 March 1838, confirming receipt of his letter of 17 March and informing him that, as he was in Paris, he could not refer to the registers in question. However, he was currently in the process of finishing the eleventh volume of *Wellington's Dispatches* for press and expected to have the twelfth, the Waterloo volume, finished in July or August. Gurwood was confident that this tome would contain the information Siborne was seeking, although he had no immediate recollection of the points in question. Gurwood then advised Siborne that 'the particulars would be best ascertained, that is the orders of movement &c, from the registers of the QMG's dept. which of course were never mislaid, even at the unfortunate moment of Col Delancey's [*sic*] death. I should think that Col Freeth might give you some hint where these are to be found . . . I will however carefully look over them on my arrival at Apsley House after the 15th April & let you know.'[18]

As Sir William Howe De Lancey, Wellington's Quartermaster-General, or chief-of-staff, at Waterloo had been mortally wounded in the battle, Siborne feared his papers might have gone missing. Colonel James Freeth was an officer of the Royal Staff Corps with the post of Assistant Quartermaster-

General at the Horse Guards and was evidently running the archives there.

Gurwood returned to London in April 1838, when he went to Apsley House to seek Wellington's permission to forward Siborne copies of the headquarters registers. He does not appear to have been allowed to do so, as there is no record of Siborne ever having seen these documents. Only a few months later, in November 1838, when the twelfth volume of the *Dispatches* was published, Gurwood entered a footnote on page 474 of the printed text that read, 'The original instructions issued to Colonel De Lancey were lost with that officer's papers.'[19] That summer, the registers, 'which of course were never mislaid', were not available after all. It was clear somebody was hindering Siborne's researches. What was it they did not want him to see?

8 *Father Blücher's Children*

Field Marshal General Prince Blücher von Wahlstadt

'... Too little [is] allowed for the support and assistance of the Prussians on this great occasion. That the British and their allies fought most determinately, and held their position with a degree of obstinacy and courage with which Napoleon had never been before resisted, it must be admitted; but when it is considered how large a Prussian force came to their assistance, attacking the right flank and rear of the French, no military man can refuse to attribute to such assistance a considerable share in the brilliant victory that followed. Without such assistance the British might have held their ground, but the defeat of the enemy never could have been so complete.'

Sir Hussey Vivian writing in the *USJ*, July 1833

Twenty years after Wellington's *Waterloo Despatch* had first been published, Siborne was beavering away at his model of the Crisis of the Battle. He was conducting exhaustive research into the minute details of the battle, down to the type of crops growing that day. There were those questioning his choice of portraying the Crisis rather than the beginning of the battle, as they considered this might weaken the authority of the *Despatch*, which was at that time the main account of the battle used by British historians. Siborne, with Vivian's support, stuck to his choice. He was, however, only too pleased to give Wellington the opportunity of commenting on the plan before the completion and exhibition of the model. Siborne was no doubt aware of what Wellington had written on the Crisis in the *Despatch*. The sequence of events Wellington had given was clear. The great cavalry attacks on his centre continued until about 7 p.m. Then came the final attack led by the Imperial Guard. Wellington drove that off and only at that point had the Prussian involvement begun to take effect. As this was Wellington's first mention of the Prussians' role in the battle in his *Despatch*, the impression he gave was that their intervention was not effective until that point. History often considers that the Prussians arrived late and played an insignificant role until the very end of the battle. However, Wellington's statement conflicts with the facts as established by good historians, following the lead Siborne gave. At the Crisis of the Battle, over 40,000 Prussians were engaged, staging their third attack on Plancenoit. Wellington had started the battle with 68,000 men, a number that had been significantly reduced by 7 p.m. We know that Wellington deliberated for several hours over the wording of the *Despatch*, written the day after the battle when his memory was still fresh. But is it even remotely possible that the Duke was deliberately playing down the role of the Prussian army at the crucial point of the battle?

It is interesting to contrast his public statement with the comments the Duke made in private. The subject was raised in two conversations with Wellington that George William Chad recorded.[1] The first took place in Brussels on 13 August 1821, with Chad asking, 'At what o'clock did the Battle begin?' Wellington replied, 'At about eleven.' Chad continued, 'And at what o'clock did the Prussians come up?' Wellington explained, 'The first person that pointed out the advance of the Prussians to me was Genl. Clinton.[2] The French had sent some Troops, the jeune [Young] Guard, or some such to meet them [it was actually Lobau's VI Corps] & the firing was seen [this happened about 4.30 p.m.] – but at 10 o'clock in the morning, I saw the advanced Guard of the Prussians just out of a Wood to the left, & I am only astonished the French did not see them – I saw them quite plain with my naked Eye, & so did many of

General von Müffling

my Officers. We had been in communication with them upon that Line.'[3]

In the second conversation, three years later at Wellington's country residence Stratfield Saye, Chad sought confirmation of this: 'I asked the Duke, whether what he had several times at other periods told me was correct as to his having seen the Prussians so early on the Morng. of the Battle of Waterloo; he quite confirmed his previous statement.'[4]

The time of the arrival of the Prussians and the effects of their intervention were so crucial to Wellington's battle plan that he ensured he was fully informed of their every move. This was done through a line of couriers between the two head-quarters which Major-General von Müffling set up and ran all that day. Indeed, the Duke's staff had held a conference with their Prussian counterparts a little before midday. When, at 4.30 p.m., the Prussians became actively involved in the battle, the noise of their cannonfire could be heard. In other words, Wellington knew very well the true role of the Prussians in the battle and was aware that his *Despatch* did not give them the credit they deserved. What is more, many of his officers present at the battle shared his knowledge.

Siborne continued to work on completing his plan of the field of Waterloo, establishing the positions of the troops and corre-sponding with numerous officers. Later in 1835, he again wrote to FitzRoy Somerset, this time regarding a map of Waterloo prepared by Sir George Murray. On 12 November, FitzRoy Somerset replied,

> I have reminded the Duke of Wellington to let you have a sight of the plan of the Battle of Waterloo which you say was prepared under the directions of Sir Geo Murray during the time of the Army of Occupation, and delivered by him to His Grace, and I am sorry to say that he has no recollection of having such a plan in his possession. On his return how-ever to Town in a few days he will look for it and if he should be so fortunate as to find it he will let me have it.
>
> I was afraid that your difficulties would be rather increased than diminished by a general reference to Officers in Command of Divisions Brigades & Regiments.

It is no easy task to reconcile contradictions and these I apprehend must abound in the statements which have been sent to you.[5]

This is an interesting reply. FitzRoy Somerset had consulted Wellington regarding the map in question, so the Duke had been informed of Siborne's request for information. Wellington appears less than helpful, even though the object of the model was to create a record of his greatest achievement. FitzRoy Somerset also took Siborne to task for having chosen to portray the Crisis of the Battle. Siborne, still unaware he was treading in a most sensitive area, did not take the hint.

Instead, he continued to press the Prussian Ministry of War for further information. On 3 March 1836, he wrote asking for information on the patterns of colours carried by the Prussian infantry in 1815, along with other details. Siborne was fortunate indeed that this enquiry was passed on to Colonel Wagner of the Prussian General Staff. Wagner was the author of the *Official History of the Wars of Liberation*, as the campaigns of 1813 to 1815 were known in Germany. This work had been published between 1825 and 1831. He provided Siborne with detailed information not only on the flags carried, but also on the position of the colour party in the infantry battalions when on the field of battle.

Siborne appears to have impressed the Prussian military hierarchy with his efforts to be accurate in every detail about their participation in the Battle of Waterloo. A friendly relationship started that was to continue for years. It was not long before Wellington found out about this.

*

When Siborne had first mentioned his intention to portray the Crisis at the end of 1834, the response from the Horse Guards had been to suggest he instead show the opening of the battle and allow the viewer of the model then to use Wellington's *Despatch* to follow its course. Siborne, supported by Vivian, disagreed with this, and, despite hints from FitzRoy Somerset to change his mind, continued to work on depicting the Crisis. He thought he had done the decent thing when he said that, once his plan had reached completion, he would send Wellington a copy for his perusal and approval before completing the model by attaching the figures to it. Siborne, an honourable man, kept his word. On 6 September 1836, he sent FitzRoy Somerset a copy of the plan, together with a series of questions directed towards Wellington.[6]

FitzRoy Somerset duly presented this communication to Wellington for comment. The Duke then wrote a memorandum, in which he remarked, 'I have looked over the plan of the ground of the battle of Waterloo, which appears to me to be accurately drawn. It is very difficult for me to judge of the particular position of each body of the troops under my command, much less of the Prussian army, at any particular hour.'[7] Furthermore, he was not in the slightest way critical of the plan. However, Siborne was never sent a copy of this memorandum.[8]

Meanwhile, Siborne was no doubt hoping that the plan would so impress Wellington that the chances of him getting his long-coveted promotion would improve. With this in mind, he sent an application to Lord Hill at the Horse Guards on 16 September 1836. He asked Sir Herbert Taylor to forward it to FitzRoy Somerset, the Military Secretary there, hoping Taylor's support would give it additional weight. On 1 October, FitzRoy

Somerset replied to Siborne, declining the application, but pointing out that 'Lord Hill continues to entertain the most favourable opinion of you, and will I am sure be glad of an opportunity to mark his sense of your Services.' He added a PS: 'The Duke of Wellington has not yet returned me your plan.'[9]

Siborne was bitterly disappointed at the news, which added to his general discomfort caused by the burden of funding the model from his own pocket. On 4 October, he wrote in this vein to FitzRoy Somerset.[10] He also wrote to Taylor that day. After twenty-three years stuck at the rank of lieutenant, Siborne felt he was not getting the recognition he deserved for his responsibilities.[11] Was there a reason for the constant rejections? A letter marked 'confidential' and sent by Lindsay at the Horse Guards to Siborne on 26 October may well help us to answer that question. He wrote,

> Lord FitzRoy Somerset appears to have placed your Papers in the hands of the D. of W. – and from what I can gather it is clear he (Lord FRS) is solicitous to converse with you upon some points which are very material to the perfect accuracy of your Plan – especially touching the share the Prussians actually had in deciding the Battle – I therefore write – *earnestly* – to press your coming here – and as it may lead to your having an interview with the D. it will be as well that you should be prepared accordingly.
>
> Let me hear by return of Post that it is convenient for you to come – and the sooner the better as you may catch the Duke either on his way through Town – or at Walmer [Castle][12] where you might have the assistance & advice of Lord FitzRoy before hand.

Keep the object of your Journey quiet but believe me you will do well to come.[13]

Suddenly, Wellington was summoning Siborne to a secret meeting to discuss the apparent inaccuracies in the positions of the Prussian troops on the plan. Only a few days earlier, the Duke had commented he could recall nothing about that. Evidently something had caused him to remember.

One wonders what went through Siborne's mind when he got this summons to urgently attend a private audience with the Great Duke. Did he consider this to be recognition of the importance of his work? Or did he feel threatened by the demand to keep this meeting secret? What would FitzRoy Somerset's advice have been? And what would Wellington have said to him? Siborne's curiosity could only have been satisfied by going to England, but amazingly he did not make the journey. It was probably the greatest mistake he made in his life. His one opportunity of coming to an agreement with Wellington was missed. And why? Siborne replied to Lindsay on 29 October, outlining the financial problems the construction of the model was causing him – 'The truth is I am so completely *ruined* by my undertaking' – complaining that the Government had not kept its word – 'so much for my having to complete a work commenced under the authority & sanction of Govt., without which *I* should never have ventured to have undertaken it *in the first instance*' – and adding that the stress had caused 'such havoc with my health', before concluding,

Although my going to London is quite out of the question, I think it right to remark that I am most ready to supply answers to any questions respecting the proposed disposition of the Troops on the Model. With respect to the Prussians, I may observe *en passant* that the distribution of their 4th & 2nd Corps coincides generally with the best French accounts, & that the disposal of the 1st Corps (Ziethen) more especially as regards the most advanced Prussian Cavalry Regts *in [the] rear* of the British left wing, *before* the general advance of our line is strongly confirmed by the corroborative evidence in my possession.[14]

Had he attended this meeting, Siborne's life may well have taken a radically different course. Was it pride that stopped him from wanting to listen to Wellington? Was he so obsessed with the model that he had now lost touch with reality? Was he so naive that the penny still had not dropped? Did he really think that his differences with Wellington could be resolved by means of discussion? Although he was certain he had got his facts right, was it not clear to him that matters weightier than the positions of some lead soldiers on a table were at stake here?

Siborne's desire for fame and fortune conflicted with Wellington's wish to maintain his power and glory. Now, on top of the severe financial problems caused by the model, the lack of recognition for his services and his deteriorating health, Siborne was on course for a conflict with one of the most powerful men in Britain.

In February 1837, a month after another unsuccessful attempt to get government funding, Siborne returned to the issue of the positions of the Prussian troops on the field of battle at the time of the Crisis. Not surprisingly, he discussed this with his old friend Vivian, who, as we know, had commanded a cavalry brigade at the battle. Vivian was able to assist Siborne, and on 6 February, sent him some information, including a sketch map showing the Prussian positions and movements as he had observed them. The next week, Vivian again wrote to Siborne giving a very interesting account of those events just preceding the Crisis. He mentioned that De Lancey, Wellington's Quartermaster-General, was aware of the effect of the Prussian intervention, and that had he survived, he would have been able to confirm the sequence of events.

Vivian's account makes it clear that the Prussian Corps under Lt-General Hans von Zieten had linked up with Wellington's left before the Crisis. As De Lancey was aware of this, then Wellington must have been as well. Not only De Lancey but also the Marquis of Anglesey recognized that, thanks to the Prussian advance, troops could now be moved to reinforce Wellington's crumbling centre. At Waterloo, Anglesey commanded the cavalry and had ordered Vivian to move to bolster Wellington's battered positions before the French staged their final attack. It was now beginning to dawn on Siborne that Wellington's *Waterloo Despatch* misrepresented the role of the Prussians in the battle.

Rumours started to circulate that the Prussian General Staff had plotted to mislead Siborne and that he was, albeit unintentionally, their dupe. However, emboldened by the support and information various British officers gave him, Siborne felt confident enough to approach FitzRoy Somerset and refute this accusation. On 23 February 1837, he sent him a memorandum with an accompanying letter. The letter shows that he was aware FitzRoy Somerset had discussed the issue of the positions of the Prussian troops with Wellington, although the

Duke had been unable to recollect them when writing his memorandum of October 1836. Siborne was at last beginning to notice he was dealing with a sensitive issue here and indicated that he had made some retrospective adjustments to the positions of the Prussian troops. As there is no file copy of his memorandum in existence, it is not possible to check exactly what adjustments he made. However, Siborne's indication that he was prepared to reduce the role of the Prussians at the time of the Crisis was immediately followed by a request for funding.[15] It may or may not have been mere coincidence that these two issues were directly linked in the letter.

On 7 March, FitzRoy Somerset replied to Siborne,

Knowing how much time and labour you have bestowed on the Model of Waterloo, how ably you have executed the Work and how important it is to your interests that no time should be lost in exposing it to view I feel great reluctance in acknowledging to you that I continue of the opinion I before expressed and that I still think that the position you have given to the Prussian Troops is not the correct one as regards the moment you wish to represent, and that those who see the work will deduce from it that the result of the Battle was not so much owing to British Valour, and the great Generalship of the Chief of the English Army, as to the flank Movements of the Prussians . . . Colonel Egerton will write to you or Colonel D'Aguilar on the subject of Lord Hill's subscription. I regret to say that it would be very inconvenient to me to subscribe at this moment and I am therefore obliged to relinquish the idea of assisting in the completion of the work.[16]

FitzRoy could not have made the situation much clearer to Siborne. The accuracy of the model was not the real issue here. Rather, by embodying this particular moment in time, Siborne's model would conflict with Wellington's authority and question his integrity. Not surprisingly, FitzRoy Somerset refused to do anything to help Siborne out of his financial dilemma. However, Siborne, ever a stickler for accuracy, held firm. He replied to FitzRoy Somerset on 18 March 1837, stating his position, as confirmed by Vivian, the Prussians and the French authorities, in more detail. He wrote, 'I see no reasonable ground for doubting the general accuracy of the *Prussian* statement . . . So far from being able to dispute this by opposing facts & counter statements, I find strong presumptive evidence of our own Officers in support of it.'[17]

Siborne dug in his heels. He continued with an outline of the sequence of events regarding the Prussian intervention and the various troop movements before adding a postscript that summed up the crux of the matter: Vivian had been aware of the Prussians linking up with Wellington's left at 5.15 p.m., two hours before the Crisis and well before the Duke had mentioned their effect in his *Despatch*. Furthermore, Vivian had witnessed the first Prussian assault on the village of Plancenoit, and the noise of the cannonfire from 4.30 p.m. onwards had made it clear to Wellington and other British officers that the Prussian advance was now taking effect.[18]

The first Prussian intervention in the battle took place when General von Bülow's corps assaulted the French positions in and around Plancenoit at Napoleon's right rear. This village was the most sensitive point in Napoleon's position because its loss would prevent his remaining reserves from supporting his front line. As such, the combat for Plancenoit was probably the most vicious of the battle, with neither side giving quarter to the other. The Duke was simply not giving the Prussians the credit they deserved and his senior officers knew it. Siborne, blithely unaware that he was now playing with fire, contacted the Prussians again for more information to confirm his view. He was determined to prove himself right, without pausing to reflect on the likely consequences of such a line of action.

On 22 March 1837, Lt-General Karl von Witzleben, the Prussian Minister of War, forwarded a letter from Colonel Wagner dated 15 March. Wagner suggested that Siborne should read his published account, as this was the most comprehensive then available.[19] Unlike the British army of the period, all Prussian officers commanding a unit in battle were required to write a report on their unit's actions. These reports were then sent to the Historical Section of the General Staff, where they were used as a basis for writing the official histories of the campaigns in question. Wagner had written his account of the campaign of 1815 by drawing on this rich seam of first-hand information.

Siborne discussed this material in greater detail with Vivian, seeking confirmation of the Prussian account. On 19 April, Vivian replied to Siborne pointing out that '. . . had not the Prussians carried Planchenoit [sic] & had not the Enemy in consequence begun to waver & send some part of their Force towards the Rear which was observed by the D of Wellington (I apprehend) before he gave the order to move.'[20] Vivian added sarcastically, 'I know not what high authority may object to giving due credit to the Prussians – certainly not the D of W. I should think.' He then outlined the effect of the Prussian assault on Plancenoit, before mentioning, 'The Duke's Despatch however speaks for itself & shows what were his feelings on the subject.' Vivian clearly understood what was going on and drew Siborne's attention to the Duke's deliberate misrepresentation of the facts in his *Despatch*. Vivian was not the only Waterloo veteran and senior officer in the British army that was aware of this. A dispute was beginning that would last several years and become very bitter.

The next twist in this affair came on 13 May. Until then, Siborne had been corresponding with the Prussians directly. Wellington would have presumed that Siborne was merely drawing his information from published works. That day, Baron Bülow of the Prussian Embassy in London presented a parcel of information to Lindsay at the Horse Guards, asking him to forward it to Siborne in Dublin. It had just arrived from the War Ministry in Berlin.[21] The Commander-in-Chief, Lord Hill, was no doubt informed, and he was always in close contact with Wellington. The Duke now realized that Siborne was being sent copies of documents held by the Prussian General Staff.

On 28 August 1837, FitzRoy Somerset's reply to Siborne's latest enquiry for information from Wellington was negative. Wellington was not prepared to co-operate. The door was shut firmly in Siborne's face and would never be opened again.[22]

From the Duke's point of view, attempts to find some sort of compromise with Siborne and work out a solution to their differences had not been taken up. Siborne was sticking to his guns and showed no inclination whatsoever to even consider toning down his view on the effectiveness of the Prussians. Also, he was showing no respect to the *Waterloo Despatch*, and to make matters worse, he was obtaining information direct from the Prussian General Staff.

Wellington had made his position on certain crucial events clear in the *Waterloo Despatch*. Regarding the outbreak of hostilities at the beginning of the Campaign, he wrote, 'Bonaparte . . . attacked the Prussian posts at Thuin and Lobbes, on the Sambre, at day-light in the morning. I did not hear of these events till in the evening of the 15th; and I immediately ordered the troops to prepare to march.' But did he? In the following twenty or so years, there had been no reason to doubt this, and British accounts obviously followed the Duke. However, Major-General von Müffling's account, published in translation in 1816, stated that the information had arrived at 4.30 p.m., which could hardly be classified as evening on a bright June day. What could explain this conflict of information?

Let us return to the beginning of the Waterloo campaign. The build-up of Napoleon's troops on the northern border of France had not gone unnoticed. On 9 June, the Allied troops facing the French army were placed on alert. All eyes were on Paris, with Napoleon's movements being closely observed, as his departure for the front would be considered a strong indication that a military confrontation was about to commence. The build-up of large French forces facing the Prussians in and around the area of Charleroi was noted. No other substantial French forces were located, so it seemed evident that the Prussians were to be the first target. That being the case, the

Prussian commander at the front, Lt-General Hans von Zieten, sought assurances of Wellington's support in such an event. The Duke agreed to this, confirming to both Blücher and Zieten in writing that he would have his entire army concentrated at Nivelles or Quatre Bras in less than twenty-four hours after the commencement of hostilities.

Rumours were rife as to Napoleon's whereabouts, but on 14 June, the Allies were convinced he was at the front. That evening, Hardinge wrote to Wellington from Blücher's headquarters in Namur, informing his master that, 'The prevalent opinion here seems to be that Bonaparte intends to commence offensive operations.'[23] That being the case, the Prussians were expecting Wellington to move his forces the next morning as he had promised.

Napoleon's offensive began in the early hours of 15 June 1815. His advance guard clashed with the Prussian outposts from 3 a.m. onwards. The Prussians fired their alarm cannon to alert the surrounding area. This alerted Zieten in Charleroi, who leapt out of bed. He had retired the previous evening fully dressed, as he was anticipating having to spring into action at a moment's notice. Zieten waited a while just to be sure this was not a minor clash. When he heard the noise of large amounts of musketry, he knew things were serious. At about 4.30 a.m., he called two aides into his room, dictated one letter in German to go to Blücher, and wrote the other in French for Wellington. Minutes later, the two riders raced off with the news. Zieten's brigade commander at the front, Major-General von Steinmetz, saw that this intelligence was imparted to the Allied troops deployed nearest his. The Prussians were expecting Wellington to be on his way in a matter of hours.

Blücher received the report at 8.30 a.m. He reacted immediately by ordering the remainder of his army to the Sombreffe position, where he was intending to confront Napoleon the next day. Steinmetz's message arrived in Major-General van Merlen's headquarters in St Symphorien at 8 a.m. He forwarded the message to Major-General von Dörnberg at Mons, who received it at 9.30 a.m. Dörnberg passed the information up the line to the headquarters in Braine-le-Comte. Here, Wellington's representative, Lt-Colonel Sir George Berkeley, sat on this vital intelligence for two hours before finally forwarding it to Brussels, where it arrived at 6 p.m. Fortunately, Major-General von Behr, the commandant of Mons, had had sufficient presence of mind to forward this news directly to his commander, the Prince of Orange, in Brussels. He did so at 10.30 a.m., and his report arrived at 3 p.m.

Thanks to entries in various letter books – the logs of all incoming and outgoing messages kept by clerks at military headquarters – and eyewitness accounts, it is possible to reconstruct this series of events with a considerable degree of accuracy. The letter books kept by the Prussians are missing, believed destroyed during the bombing of Potsdam in 1945, but fortunately German historians had published much of this information long before. Those kept by the Dutch are still in existence and it is possible to get copies of the relevant pages.

As the movements of all these messages can be monitored precisely, then it is somewhat of a surprise that there is confusion about the timing of the arrival of Zieten's message to Wellington in Brussels. What is more, Wellington's letter books were subsequently lost. His *Despatch* gave the time of the arrival of the news as being that evening, so why did it take so long for this message to arrive? After all, Charleroi was no more than four or five hours' ride from Brussels, yet this courier would appear to have taken over twice as long. Historians have grappled with this issue for many years now. Few consider the time of evening to be correct, particularly as, some years later, Wellington wrote an internal memorandum to his advisors admitting that he witnessed the arrival of Behr's message to the Prince of Orange at 3 p.m.

The information Wellington had on the morning of 15 June was that the Prussians were expecting Napoleon to launch his offensive that day. He was also aware that to keep his promises of support to them, he would have to move immediately and rapidly, although many of his troops were a long way from the Prussian positions, covering the western sector of the frontier. Being an experienced soldier, the Duke knew the French assault was likely to commence at dawn, which at that time of the year was around 4 a.m. He was also more than capable of working out that a dispatch rider would need four to five hours to reach him, so he should have heard this news by 9 a.m. at the latest. Knowing speed was of the essence for the defence of the Netherlands to be successful, if Wellington had heard nothing that morning, the logical course of action for him would have been to have enquired about the situation from his outposts, yet he did no such thing. That begs the question as to why. Had he in fact heard the news much earlier than he both claimed in his *Despatch* and later grudgingly admitted in private?

Wellington finally started issuing his orders from 6 p.m. that day. This was after receiving confirmation of Zieten's original message from Blücher at 5 p.m. and from Berkeley at 6 p.m. By then, it was too late to move a single man, let alone his entire army. He had lost twenty-four vital hours in a situation where speed was of the essence to ensure the successful outcome of the campaign. This error of judgement contributed to the defeat of the Prussians at Ligny the next day. It was not, however, how the Duke recorded it in the *Despatch*.

Siborne was clearly willing to contradict the *Despatch* on the issue of the time of the Prussian intervention in the battle. What would he say if he found out that the news of the commencement of the French offensive had arrived much earlier than had been stated?

Faced with a dilemma, Wellington had to consider how he could avoid taking any responsibility for his role in the Prussian defeat at Ligny on 16 June 1815. The path he chose was to spread stories in influential circles that this was the result of the incompetence of the Prussians. It would seem Wellington discussed the situation with Sir Henry Hardinge, who had been his liaison officer in Blücher's headquarters in the campaign, and they agreed on a story. On 26 October 1837, the Duke and Hardinge met with Philip Henry Stanhope, the fifth Earl Stanhope. During the course of the day, they discussed several matters, and Stanhope recorded parts of their conversation, including the Battle of Ligny.

'It is a curious thing,' said Hardinge, 'that those who have written about Waterloo in poetry or prose, don't seem to be aware that the Duke came over before the battle to Quatre Bras and examined the Prussian position ... When you had examined the Prussian position, I remember you much disapproved of it, and said to me, if they fight here they will be damnably mauled.' Wellington agreed, 'I told them so myself, but of course in different terms. I said to them, everybody knows their own army best; but if I were to fight with mine here, I should expect to be beat.' Hardinge continued, 'Turning to me, and marking the back of one hand with the fingers of the other, he [Wellington] added: – "They were dotted in this way – all their bodies along the slope of a hill, so that no cannon-ball missed its effect upon them; they had also undertaken to defend two villages that were too far off; only within reach of cannon-shot."' [24]

To be certain this story would spread, Wellington told it to others, including William, the 20th Baron de Ros, who recorded the Duke stating that

I told the Prussian officers, in presence of Hardinge, that, according to my judgement, the exposure of the advanced columns and, indeed, of the whole army to cannonade, standing as they did displayed to the aim of the enemy's fire, was not prudent . . . It all fell out exactly as I had feared – the French overwhelmed them, as they stood, by a prodigious fire of artillery, and I myself could distinguish with my glass from Quatre Bras a general charge of the French cavalry on their confused columns, in which charge it was that Blücher was ridden over and near killed. [25]

It is interesting to note that Wellington was now claiming he could see the events at Ligny from Quatre Bras with his telescope.

Waterloo historians do not usually question this story. It does sound plausible, and Wellington and Hardinge were highly regarded authorities on the battle, but it conflicts with the record. One only needs to look at a map of the Prussian deployment at the battle to see that Wellington's comments were inaccurate to say the least.

By reference to various eyewitness accounts, it is possible to trace Wellington's route from Quatre Bras to the Prussian head-quarters at the windmill of Bussy near the village of Brye on the Ligny battlefield. To reach Blücher, Wellington had to ride through the rear echelons of the Prussian forces, which were behind a hill and out of the range of the French artillery. The Duke knew very well he was talking nonsense. Furthermore, visitors to the site of the windmill can observe for themselves exactly what Wellington could see of the Prussian deployment. The 'whole army' was clearly not exposed to cannonade, so how could the Duke possibly have criticized the Prussians for that? These facts demonstrate very clearly that Wellington and Hardinge were consciously spreading false information. They were to continue to do so for several more years.

Not only were the Prussians the target of this campaign of dis-information. Somebody started spreading a malicious rumour accusing Siborne of neglecting his duties. This whispering campaign was so unnerving for Siborne that he eventually had a notice published in *The Times* of 6 March 1838 denying the charge. It read,

MODEL OF THE FIELD OF WATERLOO. – (From a Correspon-dent.) – The model of the field of Waterloo on which Lieu-tenant Siborn, the Assistant Military Secretary of Ireland, has been for such a length of time employed, is now fast approaching towards completion. This unique specimen of art, when finished, will occupy a space of nearly 420 feet square, and it is said will be ready for exhibition in this metropolis against the ensuing anniversary of the battle, the 18th of June. If anything can add to the credit due to Lieutenant Siborn for the attention which he has bestowed on this elaborate work, it is the fact that it has been accomplished without at all interfering with his official duties, and we are all the more particular in mentioning the circumstance, having heard that a contrary opinion prevailed at headquarters.

This was not the only tall tale that Siborne's detractors were spreading. Colonel Basil Jackson, who had been a lieutenant in the Royal Staff Corps at Waterloo and an assistant to General Sir Hudson Lowe, Napoleon's jailer on St Helena, told his acquaintances that Siborne's pro-Prussian stance was explained by his 'German descent', a story entirely without foundation.[26] An anonymous reviewer of the model in the *USJ* went on to criticize the model for giving the Prussians 'too prominent a share in the battle', echoing Wellington's stance.[27] Ironically, Siborne's endeavours to construct the model had upset not only the Whigs and Radicals, who saw it as a glorification of their opponent Wellington, but also the Duke and his supporters, who considered it a threat to his image. Siborne's quest for the historical truth was clearly leading to him being subjected to tremendous personal pressure. He was a brave man to continue.

9 *Finding the Money*

Lord FitzRoy Somerset

> 'We are exceedingly obliged to Captain Siborne for the labour
> which he has undergone for the purpose of bringing before us the
> details of those great military operations which resulting in the bat-
> tles of Ligny, Quatre-Bras, and Waterloo, gave the final blow to the
> power of Napoleon, and restored peace to Europe.'
> *Fraser's Magazine*, July 1844

By now, Siborne had accumulated a considerable amount of information from participants in the Battle of Waterloo. He had corresponded with certain French marshals as well as the Prussian General Staff and the Staffs of other German states. He had also obtained a copy of the Prince of Orange's papers. Siborne saw the potential of this material and at some stage discussed this with an acquaintance by the name of W. F. Wakeman, who had suggested he write a history of the campaign and offered to put him in touch with the publishers Messrs Boone. On 28 November 1836, Siborne wrote to him to take up his proposal. He made it clear that he very much needed this additional income to continue financing the model.

At this time, it was often the case that the author financed the production of the book – the setting, printing and binding of the text – while the publisher merely acted as a sales agent, taking a commission on the sales achieved and paying the author the balance. Printing costs were very high then, and Siborne was not in a position to fund this project, so he asked 'if Messrs Boone will consent to take upon themselves the expense of publishing my work, including that of the engravings (which must be according to my own views and under my *own* superintendence), advertisements (and allowing me 40 copies for presents), I am willing to come into the terms of half profits with them upon two Editions of 750 copies each, after which they should continue to publish my Book, but upon the usual publishing terms'.[1]

Siborne also pointed out the need for producing a guide to the forthcoming exhibition of the model and that the set of maps required to accompany the *History* would require additional expenditure.

Siborne's publishers-to-be wrote to him, agreeing to finance the production of his *History*. The original letter is not in Siborne's records, but on 25 January 1837, Messrs Boone wrote to him again, confirming '. . . our former letter expressing our willingness to undertake the publication of your work, in two Editions of 1000 copies each, you to receive 50 of the 1st Edn as part of the expense of publication. The profits on which two editions to be equally divided, we agree also to publish any & all agreed editions on your account, charging you a commission of 10% upon the price at which the Book may be sold to the trade.'[2]

As Siborne's latest attempt to get government funding for his project had been rejected just days earlier, any additional income came as most welcome news. He hoped to have his *History* finished in time to take advantage of the sales opportunity the exhibition of the model, which was planned for June 1837, would bring. As always, his plans never seemed to work out. Further problems with the funding made him put back the date of the exhibition by more than a year, and other matters so diverted his attention that the *History* was not ready for publication until June 1844.

*

As the few hundred pounds Siborne had secured for writing a *History* was not enough to complete the construction of the model, he decided to make a further effort to get the government to honour its promise. On 2 January 1837, he wrote a second time to Lord Howick, the Secretary at War, reminding him of the history of the affair and its funding. He then mentioned that the loan of £1,500 was costing him £10 a month to finance, a substantial part of his income. Complaining about the effects the worry was having on his health and of the drain on his finances, he wrote, 'I would beg most respectfully though most urgently to submit to your Lordship my present application for your assistance in enabling me to complete the work by the advance of the sum of money I require for that purpose, not in the shape of a *Grant* as was proposed on a former occasion, but by way of a Loan the Interest on which should be paid in advance out of my Pay, until the whole amount shall be repaid out of the proceeds of the Public Exhibition of the Model.'[3]

Siborne estimated that he needed another £400 to be able to transport the model to London and £300 to erect a temporary building in which to exhibit it, a total of £700. Ever a good friend, Vivian wrote a covering letter to Lord Howick on 3 January 1837, pointing out, 'I think there can be little or no doubt that the Receipts from exhibition will be sent on to enable him in a very short time to repay the loan he requests. At all events as he pledges his pay for repayment. I sincerely hope you will feel yourself at liberty to assist him as he solicits. If but to use his own explanation in a note that accompanied this letter, "ruin stares him in the face" – & that because he undertook a work in compliance with the Military Authorities.'[4]

On 9 January, a clerk at the War Office annotated the letter, 'This seems to be a subject which has been under the consideratn & finally decided, if so I conceive it to be impossible to make the advance which is requested. – Let me know what is the fact.' Lord Melbourne's Whig administration was still in government. It was most unlikely this ministry would provide funds for a monument to the arch-Tory Wellington. If that were not a consideration, then this government was being typically parsimonious.

A War Office clerk then drew up a report on the history of Siborne's claim, passing that on to Howick along with copies of the supporting documentation. He commented that the Authority of 15 May 1830 expressly reserved the question of reimbursement (excluding travelling expenses) for consideration after the completion of the work.[5] This clerk would not be the only person to misinterpret this document. It's evident that Hardinge did not say to Siborne, 'Make the model and then I'll think about if we are going to pay for it.' Obviously the model was going to require funding *during* its construction. That was not the issue that had been expressly reserved till completion of the work; but the issue of a financial reward or remuneration for Siborne for his work had. What seems likely is that Hardinge simply did not consider how much the construction of the model would cost, and rather than admit he had been so foolish as to give Siborne a blank cheque, acquired a selective memory.

The file was then passed on to the next clerk, who suggested making a loan to Siborne or mortgaging the model. Finally, it was passed on to the Secretary of War, who added, 'I cannot venture a recommendatn if really a work of such merit no doubt private speculators wd be glad to advance the money. – Send an official note to Lt Siborn expressing my regret that I do not consider myself authorised to comply with his request. I will write privately to Sir H. Vivian.'

Public money was not going to be loaned to Siborne to complete this project, even with the security of his future salary. The War Office rejected his application, writing, 'In reply to your letter of the 2nd inst. regarding the advance of a sum of money to enable you to complete the Model undertaken by you of the Field of Waterloo, I am directed to say to you that Lord Howick very much regrets that he does not feel himself approving to comply with you request.'[6]

Howick replied to Vivian indicating he had no authority to comply with his request and recommended he contact the Treasury. Failing that, if it was so certain that the model would produce a good return on investment, he suggested that Siborne should obtain a loan from private individuals.[7]

Vivian passed this letter on to Siborne, who was no doubt greatly disappointed. It is not clear from his records how he managed to continue to fund the model, but work on it did not cease. He somehow muddled his way through, hoping things would work out in the end. The one significant item not present in Siborne's records is his accounts. Despite the kind support of Lloyds Bank archives, it has not been possible to trace all his financial records. However, by bringing together snippets of information from various sources, an almost complete set of accounts can be reassembled.[8] Servicing the loan of £1,500 was costing him £10 a month. Records in Dublin show his annual pay to have been £336 18s 6d, that is, about £28 per month,[9] and just over a third of his income was allocated to funding the model – a nuisance, but not an intolerable burden. Difficult though it was, Siborne was able to keep the project running. He was hoping the exhibition would be a great success and resolve his problems.

In the early months of 1837, it would seem that Siborne devoted a considerable amount of time to issues other than the Crisis of the Battle and the funding of the model. His correspondence contains a whole series of items on the Battle of Quatre Bras. Furthermore, Siborne had instructed two engineers to survey the field of Quatre Bras, maps of which would appear in the *Atlas* accompanying the *History*, for which he was gathering information. Lt-General Sir William Gomm, in 1815 a lieutenant-colonel in the 2nd Foot Guards and Assistant Quarter-Master General to the 5th Division, had already sent Siborne a copy of his journal on 7 December 1836. It covered the campaign from 15 June 1815. As Picton had been mortally wounded at Waterloo, Gomm was the next most senior officer still surviving. Before checking the details, Siborne evidently required an outline of the events, which Gomm's journal described in considerable detail.[10]

With this summary, Siborne set about establishing the finer points. First, on 28 December 1836, he replied to Gomm, asking for clarification of certain matters, to which Gomm responded on 5 January 1837. Siborne then exchanged a series of letters with Captain Robert Winchester, in 1815 a lieutenant in the 92nd Highlanders. Siborne already knew Winchester as a respondent to his circular in 1834. As well as sending Siborne a memorandum dated 27 February 1837 on the activities of the 92nd on 15/16 June 1815, Winchester had included a sketch

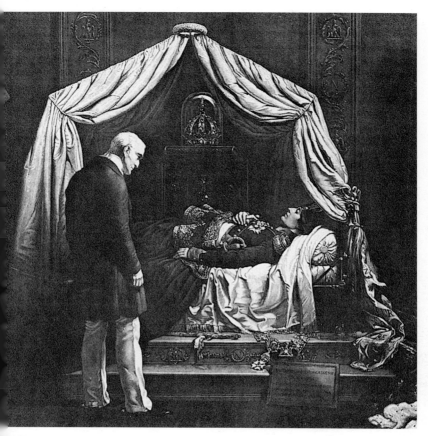

Wellington looking at Napoleon at Madame Tussard's. Wellington, and Wellington alone
t Napoleon at Waterloo and he wanted to make sure nobody ever thought otherwise.
en Napoleon's wax effigy at Madame Tussard's was constantly reminded of this.

2 Prussian Infantry Storming Plancenoit. Possession of this village, in the right rear of Napoleon's position, was the key to victory and was hotly disputed. And not only during the Battle.

3 At the end of the Battle of Waterloo, Wellington and Blücher met at the Inn of La Belle Alliance, which Blücher suggested would make a good name for the battle. Wellington however chose Waterloo, where his headquarters were located.

Wellington writing the *Waterloo Despatch*.
The only known portrait of William Siborne, showing him at the age of thirty-six.
One of a series of drawings Siborne produced to help the artists painting the exquisitely
accurate model figures.

7 The Large Model. The village of Plancenoit on the battlefield of Waterloo is now all but devoid of troops.

8 The Action around Hougoumont. The second wave of the attack of the Imperial Guard's six columns is taking place, with Maitland's British Guards about to receive them.

9 Wellington and his Glass. What could the Duke really see through it?

Blücher's fall at Ligny. This old warhorse led a desperate final cavalry charge at the end of Battle of Ligny, hoping to contain Napoleon's breakthrough. His horse was shot from ̄erneath him and the charge failed.

Scots Greys · Dragoon Guards · Highlander · Life Guards

BRITISH · Royal Artillery · King's German Legion · Infantry · Horse Gua

11 *A Scene at the London Museum, Piccadilly, or – A peep at the spoils of Ambition taken at the Battle of Waterloo* by George Cruikshank. The Egyptian Hall became a madhouse whe Napoleon's coach, captured by the Prussians after Waterloo, was put on display.

12 Figures from the New Model. The details and realism of these figures was unprecedent and a feast to the eyes of the early Victorians that visited these exhibitions.

The New Model. 5th Line Battalion, King's German Legion. This body of infantry is faithfully reproduced down to the last button. They have formed a square, a defensive formation used against cavalry.

The New Model. 79th Highlanders. This battalion, also faithfully reproduced is drawn in line with which it can best hold off the attacking infantry with volley fire.

15 The Large Model. Although Wellington's machinations saw that Siborne's portrayal of the Crisis of the Battle was corrupted, the Large Model survived many trials and tribulatic It is a great monument to the many sacrifices Siborne made.

map of their positions in the Battle of Quatre Bras.[11] His account of Wellington's knowledge of the events at Ligny that day was later to prove significant. Winchester's version of this particular event is largely accurate and corroborated by the accounts of other eyewitnesses.

Characteristically, Siborne sought supporting evidence to Winchester's account, writing on 4 March 1837 to Lieutenant James Kerr Ross of the 92nd to elicit his report of these events, from which comparisons were then drawn. He next went on to contact officers from other regiments in that action, seeking their testimony or their knowledge of specific points. At several stages in this part of his research, Siborne marked up maps of Quatre Bras. Of course, he did not restrict his enquiries merely to the British participants; he also contacted officers of the Hanoverian Army who had served in the King's German Legion. Among these was Lewis Heise, who fought as a lieutenant in Rettberg's battery of the KGL in 1815. Rettberg himself sent Siborne marked plans with a key showing his battery's actions at both Quatre Bras and Waterloo.

Towards the end of 1837 Siborne ceased his research and correspondence for some months. At long last, the exhibition of the model approached.

10 *The First Exhibition*

Sir George Murray

'The surface of that celebrated Ground has been modelled with the most scrupulous exactitude: every single Field is distinguished by the particular cultivation and appearance which it presented at the time of the Battle; and in the Villages, every House, every Door, every Window, every Garden, every Tree, every Hedge, may be seen precisely as they existed on the ever memorable 18th of June, 1815.'
Handbill for the Exhibition of 1838–9

The Egyptian Hall was the main exhibition centre in early nineteenth-century London. In 1819, William Bullock sold it to the bookseller George Lackington, famed for selling tens of thousands of books at the lowest possible price for cash only. Lackington let the hall for miscellaneous exhibitions, so it comes as no surprise that Siborne chose this prime location. Unfortunately, there are no records of when he made this decision and what agreement was reached with the hall's management. However, a notice in *The Times* of 6 March 1838 indicated his intention to exhibit it from the coming Waterloo Day, 18 June 1838. For reasons unknown, he did not manage to do so. Instead, the model finally went on display that October.

Once the model was completed and its exhibition organized, Siborne had the thirty-five sections packed in their specially made cases and shipped from Dublin to London. For ease of transport, it was most likely that a freighter carried the crates directly from Dublin to London. Due to its proximity to central London, it is quite probable that the shipment was landed at St Katharine Docks, built by Thomas Telford and opened in 1828. It would have been fitting that a quest, which started along a route modernized by Telford, would end in a facility con-

structed by him. The unusually large gap in Siborne's records –
from mid-June to December there are only two items of correspondence – can be taken as an indication that the organization
of the exhibition was dominating his life at that point. As
Siborne was a stickler for detail, it is probable he accompanied
it to London and supervised its erection in the Egyptian Hall.

A few days before the exhibition was opened to the public,
selected journalists were given a preview. The press spoke in
the most glowing terms about the model. The first report, in
the *Morning Post* of 5 October, mentioned,

> No fewer than 160,000 figures are represented, and with so
> much accuracy that not only the nation, but the very
> branch of the service to which they belong, is perfectly
> obvious on the nearer points; while the more distant points
> are distinctly marked out by the various lines of fire, distin-
> guished as they are by a representation of smoke, as inge-
> nious as it is efficient. The roads and enclosures – nay the
> different appearance of wood, corn fields, or fallows – are
> all presented to the eye in the most natural manner; and if
> evidence be required of the correctness of this *charte
> vivante*, we can offer that of our own observations made on
> the spot in the last few weeks . . . We strongly urge a visit to
> the Egyptian Hall, where the 'Waterloo Model' will, we
> believe, be this day opened to the public.[1]

The same day *The Times* reported, 'A very ingenious model
of the field of Waterloo has just been opened for exhibition at
the Egyptian-hall, Piccadilly . . . He has executed his task with
great accuracy, and presented to the public a plan of the great
event of the day, which will convey a better notion than a mere

map or the reading of a mere account without auxiliary explanation."[2]

The review in the *United Service Gazette* (*USG*), the official
newsletter of the armed forces, was even more laudatory:

> Nothing can be more perfect than the representation of the
> scene. Not only is every undulation of the ground most
> faithfully represented, but the position of every regiment,
> and its muskets and artillery are most beautifully and inge-
> niously indicated. Moreover, the roads and enclosures,
> even to the various aspects of wood, corn, grass fields and
> potato plots, and ploughed land, are most elaborately
> marked . . . We recognised many distinguished Waterloo
> officers at the private view of Lieut. Siborn's model, all of
> who bore honourable testimony to its admirable correct-
> ness. We cannot, therefore, doubt, that not withstanding
> the lateness of the season, it will become immediately and
> extensively popular.[3]

The weekly magazine *John Bull* had more good things to
say. In the edition of 7 October, it carried an announcement
that read,

> We have little doubt that this unique and national work will
> prove a most attractive exhibition to all classes; and we
> earnestly hope that some portion, at least, of the heavy out-
> lay incurred by the zealous and meritorious officer – its
> indefatigable constructor – may be returned to him in a
> shape which a little becoming and well-bestowed liberality
> on the part of the present Government ought to have saved
> him from having recourse to.[4]

Indeed, in the following week's issue, the long description of the details of the model contained phrases such as, 'We are at a loss for fitting terms to praise this beautiful work in.'[5] This review was not entirely uncritical and it outlined the model's one great weakness – its complexity. It continued, 'If unused to the dots, lines and hieroglyphics of a plan, he [the spectator] grows confused.' Lieutenant James Hope, one of Siborne's many correspondents later echoed this complaint, pointing out in his letter of 3 September 1840 that the detail was overwhelming and difficult for even the initiated to comprehend.[6]

John Bull and James Hope described the problem well. Without a commentary to explain what was going on – and the *Guide* does not appear to have achieved its objective – the spectator can get lost in all the detail. The National Army Museum obviously also recognized this problem and has added an audio-visual accompaniment to the re-exhibition of the model in 1990.

More interesting comments were made in *The Atlas* magazine on 6 October. The *Fine Arts* section carried an article that commented, 'A most accurate and faithful representation of this great battle was opened this week at the Egyptian Hall; and it is, we think likely to rival the popularity of the far-famed panorama.' It continued, '. . . after a labour of seven years, [Siborne] has succeeded in producing a work of the most interesting and *unique* description. In the centre of a room, a platform, breast high, is raised, containing a superficies of about four hundred and twenty square feet, in which the field of battle is shown in the condition it was when the belligerent parties were at their dread work on the afternoon of the 18th

June, 1815.' Towards the end of this review is a passage discussing the future of the model:

> The completion of the model has excited much interest in
> the military circles, and various plans are in embryo as to
> its ultimate destination. It has been proposed that the
> United Service Club should purchase it as an appropriate
> ornament for its celebrated museum of military objects;
> others think a subscription should be announced for its
> purchase, and that those who acquire it by this means
> should present it to the public; while a third, and by far the
> most numerous party, are urgent that it should be pur-
> chased in the same way, but that its destination should be
> different. The latter gentlemen are anxious that it shall be
> deposited in the room which should form the base of the
> monument to be erected from the funds subscribed for the
> *Wellington Memorial*; so that while the summit transmitted
> to posterity the lineaments and effigy of the hero, the inte-
> rior should present an exact counterpart of his greatest
> achievement. There is something felicitous in this idea,
> and, certainly, it is entirely feasible.[7]

Wellington could not have been amused when he read that
suggestion. It may well have been that the 'most numerous party'
thought it fitting to exhibit the model in the base of the Wellington Memorial, but money from the subscription of the memorial
was not made available to purchase the model from Siborne.

The glowing reviews in the press were followed with an
advertising campaign. From 6 October onwards, newspapers
such as *The Courier*, *The Court Gazette*, *The Naval and Military Gazette* and the *Court Journal* carried notices reading,

THE MODEL of the BATTLE OF WATERLOO,
covering a space of 420 square feet, and containing 190,000
figures, IS NOW OPEN for EXHIBITION at the
EGYPTIAN HALL, Piccadilly. Admission One Shilling.
Open from Ten in the morning till Five, and from Six till
Nine in the evening, brilliantly illuminated.

The exhibition actually opened on 8 October and it ran
until at least the end of 1839. Notices advertising it appeared
regularly in the *Court Journal* until August 1839. It certainly
did become 'immediately and extensively popular', with
around 100,000 people each paying one shilling to see it, a total
of £5,000. There was, however, one notable absentee from the
'many distinguished officers at the private view'. Wellington
refused any suggestion that he should join the visiting crowds.
On 23 April 1840, he explained to Lady Wilton, 'I was unwilling to give any Sanction to the truth of such a representation in
this Model, which must have resulted from my visiting it, without protesting against such erroneous representation ... This I
could not bring myself to do on [any] account; and I thought it
best to avail myself of my absence from London, and of Indis-
position, never to visit it at all.'[8]

What could not have improved the Great Duke's mood was
that the Waterloo volume of his *Dispatches* just happened to be
published that autumn. Of course, it included his *Waterloo
Despatch* of 19 June 1815, the reliability of which the model was
calling into question. The initiated would have noted the conflict between Wellington's account and that given by Siborne.
He had produced a written guidebook to the exhibition, the
Guide to the Model of the Battle of Waterloo now Exhibited at

the Egyptian Hall, Piccadilly. This booklet, sixteen pages long with a map of the model, was printed by P. Dixon Hardy and sold to visitors for sixpence.[9] Unfortunately, there is neither a record of the number printed nor of the number sold, but with 100,000 people attending, the numbers must have been substantial. There is also no record of how much revenue this produced for Siborne, but it may well have amounted to a couple of hundred pounds.

The *Guide* started with a mention of Siborne's forthcoming *History*, explaining that it was delayed by difficulties in the production of the accompanying maps. The text then went on to describe the scene represented by the model, pointing out that '. . . the gradual development of the principle portion of the Prussian army under Prince Blucher Von Wahlstadt, by which so powerful a diversion was effected against the French right, rendered it imperative on Napoleon to resort to one of two alternatives – to commence a retreat, or to make another desperate attempt to break the Duke's line, and establish his left on the allied position, and at the same time, to maintain a firm stand against the Prussian advance on his right.'[10]

The *Guide* then went on to list by number all the bodies of troops on the model. Nos 95 to 111 marked the Prussian formations. The last page gave details of the numbers of men involved: 16,546 Prussians with eighty-three guns being given as in action by 4.30 p.m., and 49,886 men with 123 guns by 7 p.m., just before the time shown on the model. The Prussians were being credited with having played a major role in the battle. Wellington could not have enjoyed sharing the limelight.

When the exhibition at the Egyptian Hall finished, the model then went on a tour of Britain. The popular historian

Sir Archibald Alison mentioned visiting it. In a letter to Basil Jackson dated 17 June 1844, he commented, 'I intend in a note (to a new edition of the *History of Europe*) to give the highest praise to his Model, which I saw with the utmost delight in this city (Glasgow) some years ago, and to urge the purchase of it, or a similar one by Government, as a National Monument.'[11]

The first somewhat negative comments published came in an anonymous review in the June 1839 issue of the *USJ*. The reviewer remarked, 'The Prussians, by the way, are generally considered to bear too prominent a share in the battle, as represented in this model.'[12] That was, of course, Wellington's criticism, but not one made by the 'distinguished Waterloo officers at the private view of Lieut. Siborn's model, all of who bore honourable testimony to its admirable correctness'.

Interestingly, when reviewing Siborne's *History* in the *USJ* in May 1844, Jackson, a man of very conservative views and close to Wellington, raised the same complaint about the model, writing, 'Captain Siborne, the author of the work in question, is advantageously known both to the military world, and the public in general, by his admirable model of the battle of Waterloo which was exhibited some years back: it had, indeed but one solitary defect, namely, that of placing the Prussians more forward than they really were at the precise moment of the battle selected for representation . . .'[13] It would seem that the story emanating from a certain high authority was influencing others.

Despite this unfounded criticism, the exhibition of the model was a great success. Siborne's share of the £5,000 in revenues it generated in London alone should have gone a long way towards repaying the construction costs of £3,000 and alleviating his debt. However, it would seem that only a small amount of this money reached his pocket, some £800. He later explained why:

> The cost of its construction amounted to £3,000, and yet, not withstanding its having been visited by so great a number of persons – in London alone, by about 100,000, I have not succeeded in recovering more than a very slight portion of the above outlay. Whether this has arisen from the expensive establishment maintained, from mismanagement, or from the circumstance of my not having been able to devote my personal superintendence to the exhibition, I will not pretend to say, but such, most unfortunately for me, is the result of my labours, in a pecuniary point of view.[14]

It would seem the exhibition manager at the Egyptian Hall might have cheated our unlucky model-maker. Siborne also suspected the agent he had appointed to act on his behalf in London, one of his creditors, may have manipulated the situation so as to be able to seize the model in lieu of non-payment.[15] Indeed, it is difficult to imagine how the exhibitor could possibly have incurred costs totalling £4,200. A few years earlier, in 1820, the painter Benjamin Robert Haydon hired the Great Room in the Egyptian Hall for a year for £300. Lighting and staffing the exhibition could not have cost appreciably more, so it does seem that Siborne was short-changed by a considerable amount. Despite the model's enormous success, he would now have to try to find a buyer for his beloved work of art.

*

Now that the model had shown itself to be a success with the public and capable of generating large revenues, Siborne decided he should again approach the government. On 19 September 1839, Siborne petitioned the Lords of the Treasury, outlining the history of his case and justifying the use of public funds for the purchase of the model. He pointed out that its exhibition showed how much revenue it could generate. The wheels of bureaucracy moved at a measured pace. Siborne's letter was entered in the register on 30 September and read on 18 October, when the Lords of the Treasury instructed G. J. Pennington at the Treasury Chambers, the clerk handling the file, to write to Siborne declining to comply with his request, which he did on 22 October.[16]

In November 1839, a Mr Thomas of the Egyptian Hall advertised the model for sale as a 'PROFITABLE SPECU-LATION – The MODEL of the BATTLE OF WATER-LOO, which has been visited by nearly 100,000 persons during the last 12 months, at the admission price of 1s. each, is now on SALE by Private Contract, the pursuits and professional duties of the proprietor not admitting of his bestowing the attention required for the exhibition thereof in the provincial towns of Great Britain, throughout the continent, and the United States of America, whence numerous pressing applications for its transmission and exhibition have been received.'[17] There does not appear to have been a buyer.

With his request declined by the Treasury and lacking a private buyer, Siborne turned to the army for support. The Waterloo veterans that had viewed the model were most impressed with it, and it was now more that twenty years since the battle, many officers that had held a field command on that fateful day were now in the upper echelons of the armed forces. Siborne could be certain of a sympathetic hearing and had indeed enjoyed their support on several occasions in the past. Furthermore, the United Service Museum that had been in planning when the model was first commissioned in 1830 had in the meantime been opened, offering a possible permanent location. Siborne, himself a member of the United Service Institution (USI) since at least 1833, had two sponsors, Captain B. M. Wynyard, Deputy Adjutant General for Ireland, and Captain L. M. Maitland of the 52nd Foot. They wrote letters to the Council of the USI proposing the purchase of the model which were read to the meeting of Saturday, 4 December 1839. The proposal was considered and the minutes of the meeting recorded that 'It was ordered that letters be written to Captains Wynyard and Maitland informing them that after due deliberation the council regretted that they were *unable to entertain* the project of becoming the purchasers of the Waterloo Model, on account of the difficulties arising both from the expense and want of room; there not being sufficient space within the walls of the Museum to admit the Model.'[18]

While he was pondering his next move, Siborne obtained his long sought after promotion to captain. His Statement of the Services is a little confusing. It gives the date of his promotion as 31 January 1840, but includes the note, 'Ditto [i.e. without paying the difference] or Purchased.'[19] The memorandum of 27 January 1840 referring to his promotion noted that the 'unattached' Lieutenant Siborn received his 'Unattached Company without purchase'.[20] The reliability of this document is questionable as Siborne was not 'unattached' but a lieutenant in the 47th Foot. Furthermore, it was apparently not possible to be promoted to the unattached list without purchase, so it would seem probable that Siborne bought his captaincy, which would have cost him £1,100. It may well have been that he used his share of the revenue from the exhibition to secure his future income rather than repay his debts. What is clear from his records is that he did not receive his promotion as the promised reward for the construction of the model.

Next, Siborne contacted Vivian in the hope his old friend could provide the funds required. Vivian declined, but expressed his sympathy in a letter to Siborne dated 6 February 1840: 'I am very sorry to find that you are obliged on account of funds failing to curtail your proposed Model. I wish I had not spent so much on my place in Cornwall I would offer to assist you – but I have since I left Ireland in purchases, building & improvements expended above £120,000, which is more than I should have done.'[21]

As Vivian could not help him, and as only parliament could permit the expenditure of such a sum, Siborne sent a petition there on 24 May 1841. Again, he outlined the history of his case and requested a refund of his expenditure on the model. As a postscript, he added,

To the prayer of your Petitioner, he would humbly venture to suggest, that a Committee of Military Officers should be appointed to inspect the Model at the time of its being deposited in the room selected for its reception, in order to ascertain whether any alterations might be advisable as regards the distribution of the troops, with a view to render the representation which it affords of the Battle as accurate as possible, and that your Petitioner should be required to carry any alterations so proposed into effect – and further, that the work should then be thoroughly cleaned, renovated, fitted up, and covered with a glass case, under your Petitioner's immediate superintendence, so as to ensure the due preservation of the work.

Interestingly, Siborne offered to make any alterations to the model demanded of him. It would seem he was again hoping this would be enough to gain Wellington's support for his request. As Siborne made several further attempts to sell the model that year, his request was clearly rejected. The first attempt was to the Royal Dublin Society. On 10 September 1841, he wrote to a Mr Hardman asking him to place his proposal that the society might purchase the model. Outlining the history of its construction and financing, Siborne pointed out, '*It is essentially a work of Irish manufacture*,' hoping this would help his plea. He mentioned, 'With regard to the price which I might be expected to affix to the work, I feel considerable difficulty, and prefer leaving this matter entirely to the decision of the Society.'[22] Again, as there is no reply to this request in Siborne's records and as he made further attempts to dispose of the model, one assumes he either got no reply or, if he did, it was negative.

A potential change of luck came when the Tory Sir Robert Peel formed his second administration in September 1841. Apart from four short months from December 1834, the Whigs had been in government since November 1830. What was more, the new Secretary at War was no less a person than Sir Henry Hardinge, who all those years ago had authorized the funding of the model. Siborne did not waste much time in contacting him. His plight was by now very serious, so to add authority to his application, he enlisted the support of an old friend, Sir George Murray, now Master General of the Ordnance, requesting him to forward the application to Hardinge with a covering letter. Siborne's letter to Murray, dated 16 September 1841, suggested that 'the "Army Extraordinaries" or some other fund, may yet be made available for securing the work as the property of the Nation'. He continued,

> I cannot refrain from mentioning to you a remark lately made by an intelligent French gentleman who paid a long and attentive visit to the Model, and who was greatly surprised to learn that it had not been purchased by the British Government. 'If,' said he, 'the Battle had terminated *the other way*, and this officer had offered such a Model to the *French* Government, he would have been loaded with riches and honors [sic].' I can only say neither riches nor honors are likely to fall to my lot, and my last and only hope of escape from penury rests with the result of my present application to Sir Henry Hardinge.[23]

Murray duly obliged, forwarding Siborne's letter to Hardinge on 18 September with a covering note. The same day, Murray had his ADC Captain Henry Paget write to Siborne acknowledging receipt. Siborne reminded Hardinge what they had discussed in their meeting: 'I need scarcely recall to your recollection that in the year 1830 I was commissioned by the General Commanding in Chief [Lord Hill] to

undertake the construction of a Model of the Battle of Waterloo, His Lordship having previously obtained your authority,
as Secretary at War, for my being reimbursed from time to time
for all expenses attending this national work.'[24] Siborne's letter
then continued by outlining the history of the affair, elucidat-
ing the great efforts he had made in overcoming the various
obstacles placed in his way. He then pointed out the number of
people that had visited it indicated its popularity and that there
was every good reason for the nation acquiring it, before mentioning his immediate problem:

> One of my creditors (who was my agent in London and
> whom my friends strongly suspect of designing to get the
> Model into his own hands) will be empowered on the 1st of
> next December, should I not be prepared to pay him a sum
> of £500, and which I shall be utterly unable to do, to give
> me three months' notice of his intention to proceed to a
> sale of the work, for the purpose of indemnifying himself to
> that amount; and I have no doubt that as a speculator he
> will turn it to good account, and thus deprive me of all pos-
> sibility of retrieving myself or of obtaining the slightest
> remuneration for the toil, the expense, the anxiety, as well
> as injury to my health which I have encountered in conse-
> quence of this unfortunate undertaking.[25]

Siborne's predicament was such that he was prepared to
beg Hardinge for help, before coming to a crucial issue:

> There is another point to which I would wish to allude. I
> am well aware that in the opinion of some of our highest
> military authorities, the Prussian troops occupy too

prominent a position on the Model, an opinion to which I should be sorry to be so presumptuous as to oppose my own impressions, which may very possibly be erroneous, and the moment the work ceases to be *my* property, and I am no longer obligated to adhere to those impressions, I shall be most ready and willing to make any alteration that may be suggested in this or any other respect.[26]

Aware that Wellington disapproved of the positions of the Prussian forces on the model, Siborne was so desperate to prevent his unscrupulous creditor from seizing it that he was prepared to alter their positions to suit the Duke's wishes.

Once the War Office clerk had read and annotated Siborne's letter, he drew up an internal memorandum outlining the facts as he knew them and as could be shown from the War Office records. This memorandum was undated, but was written some time between 18 September 1841, when the latter arrived at the War Office, and 4 November, when Hardinge made the final annotation on it. The style used for such documents was for the paper to be divided into two columns. In the left column, one clerk would write his report, attaching copies of any supporting documentation, denoting it with a number. In the right column, other clerks and, of course, the Secretary would make their comments.

The left-hand column of this document contained a point-by-point history of the affair to date. It concluded with the suggestion that it might be displayed in the British Museum, its new building then under construction, or the Tower, and that £1,800 would be a fair price to offer Siborne. The clerk initialled his report 'J. K.'

Written in different hands in the right-hand column were notes, several of which were favourable to Siborne. One suggested the model should be put on display at the Tower or Woolwich, another at the National Gallery. A third liked that idea, suggesting the vote of parliament, that is, the funds allocated to the National Gallery, could be used to pay Siborne. Another noted that Siborne had indeed been given 'an expectation of a further ultimate grant'. The clerks presented Siborne's case fairly, if not with sympathy, making suggestions for a location for the model and indicating that funds might well be available. However, one comment, in a different hand, was somewhat ominous: 'It has been reported to have been stated on High Authority, that it does not represent the actual Position of the Armies *at any one time of the day* – but this defect might possibly be rectified by Capt. Siborn, who has expressed his readiness to make any corrections that might be required.' This was the one and only negative comment on this memorandum.

Hardinge himself wrote the concluding note on this document, dated 4 November: 'Inform Cap. S. that I much regret the failure he has experienced in the re-imbursement of the expenses he has incurred, in constructing a work of art so interesting to the Public & so creditable to his ability as the model of the Battle of Waterloo undoubtedly is – I cannot originate any proposal for the purchase of the Model – it ought to proceed from the Comdr. in Chief or the Master Genl. Ord. Dept. & be placed as a Record of the Battle in some public Building connected with the Army.'[27]

Being a serving soldier of senior rank, Hardinge was no doubt aware how little support the Commander-in-Chief and the Master of the Ordnance would be able to offer Siborne. In effect, he merely instructed his clerks to fob off Siborne.

The one objection raised bears remarkable similarity to comments Wellington made, but which were never published in his lifetime. The first record of them comes in a letter the Duke wrote to Lady Wilton: 'The Reason for which I have omitted to endeavour to see the Model is that I understood from an Inspection of the Sketches or Drawings that the Model would not give an accurate Representation of the Position of the Troops of either or of both Armies at any particular period of the Day . . . No Drawing or representation as a Model can represent more than one moment of an Action. But this Model tends to represent the whole action; and every Corps and Individual of all Nations is represented in the Position chosen by Himself.'[28] Then, in February 1841, in his capacity as Lord Lieutenant of Hampshire, Wellington entertained a party of thirty-five prominent people, including judges, magistrates and members of parliament at Stratfield Saye, his residence in Berkshire. When one of the assembled judges asked him what he thought of Siborne's model, the Duke replied,

> That is a question which I have often been asked, to which I don't give an answer, because I don't want to injure the man. But if you want to know my opinion, it's all farce, fudge! They went to one gentleman and said, 'What did you do?' 'I did so and so.' To another, 'What did you do?' 'I did such and such a thing.' One did it at ten and another at twelve, and they have mixed up the whole. The fact is, a battle is like a ball; they keep footing it all the day through.[29]

Wellington repeated this story in the years to come. In May 1845, he sent a note to Francis Egerton, who was preparing his review of Siborne's *History*. 'I mentioned Siborne's model only as an illustration of the manner in which he had made up his work. That is to say, he took down every man's story as true and certainly correct, as he had before represented his act and supposed position in his model, of which beautiful work he had made a scene of confusion, such as would be a drawing or representation in one view of all the scenes and acts of a play in five acts.'[30]

These criticisms are, of course, nonsense, and Wellington knew that. After all, he had seen the plan in autumn 1836 and was well aware that it showed the positions during the Crisis. He had praised its accuracy and stated that he could not comment on the positions of the troops, as he could not remember them. Furthermore, he must also have been aware of the press coverage the model received, which made it clear which part of the battle was being represented. Thanks to the ongoing debate in the *USJ* and the massive amount of correspondence Siborne conducted with Waterloo veterans, the whole officer corps of the British Army must have been aware that Wellington's negative comments were motivated by spite. The Duke would appear to have been in a minority of one in his opinion of the model, but nevertheless it was a very influential minority.

Hardinge was a close associate of Wellington and had been actively supporting the Duke's misleading statements about the Waterloo campaign, so he must have been aware of Wellington's view of the model. A reply to Siborne was then drafted.[31] The text was approved, the letter written and signed by L. Sulivan and then sent to Siborne. Dated 20 November

1841, this curt response declined Siborne's application, suggesting he contact either the General Commanding-in-Chief or the Master General of Ordnance for their consideration.[32]

Siborne took this reply at face value, writing immediately to his former chief Murray, who was now Master General of Ordnance. In his letter, dated 22 November 1841, Siborne pointed out that 'The delay in coming to this decision has been production of the most serious inconvenience – The Model still remains packed up at Belfast, and on the *1st of next month* I expect a 3 months' notice from a designing and speculating creditor of his intention to proceed to a sale of the work.' He then made a formal application for Murray to authorize the purchase of the model.[33]

Much though he sympathized with Siborne's plight, as he explained in his letter of 24 November 1841, there was little Murray could do other than give the government a favourable opinion should he be asked. He could not make any funds available, as this matter did not fall into his area of responsibility.[34]

Siborne was beginning to go around in circles. The General Commanding in Chief was Lord Hill, whose office was at the Horse Guards. It was the QMG's department there that first raised an objection to the particular juncture in the battle being shown on the model before it was ever completed. The head of this department was FitzRoy Somerset, who was also Wellington's Military Secretary. Siborne would not achieve his objective there.

Hardinge's scheme to fob Siborne off was working and he wasted more of his time on fruitless correspondence. On 27 November 1841, he drafted a letter to FitzRoy Somerset. He took the opportunity of mentioning 'that my pecuniary affairs have become so distressingly embarrassed by the result of my unfortunate undertaking as to render it most desirable that whatever steps Lord Hill may think proper to take in regard to this question, they may be communicated to me as early as may be compatible with His Lordship's convenience, so as to enable me to avert, if possible, the impending seizure of the Model on the part of certain of my creditors'.[35]

Siborne enclosed a copy of his letter to Hardinge of 16 September, the letter he received from Sulivan on 20 November and a copy of Murray's letter of 24 November. On 7 December, FitzRoy Somerset replied to Siborne, rejecting his application on the grounds that Hill '... does not feel at liberty to propose to Her Majesty's Ministers to buy it off you'.[36] Siborne did not take no for an answer and on 11 December appealed to FitzRoy Somerset. He again expressed his willingness to change the model, if that would assist him in obtaining the necessary funds:

> I should feel greatly obliged by your informing me whether His Lordship's objections be founded upon any inaccuracy which I may have committed, because, as the model of the field itself is mathematically true, and such inaccuracy could therefore only occur in the distribution of the figures, and consequently be very easily corrected, I am most desirous of making any alterations which His Lordship or any officers selected by Him might consider necessary, with a view to render the representation more faithful, and therefore more deserving of His Lordship's patronage and support.[37]

Rather than lose the model, Siborne was prepared to change it, hard though it must have been for him to contemplate such a compromise. However, even that offer was unacceptable. FitzRoy Somerset's final rejection was terse: 'Having submitted to The General Commanding in Chief your Letter of the 11th. instant upon the subject of the purchase of your Model, and His Lordship having observed with regret that you still entertain a hope that he may be induced to recommend the purchase of it to Government, I am directed to acquaint you, that his decision upon that point as communicated to you in my letter of the 7th. instant must be considered final.'[38]

Siborne had kept Vivian informed of developments, and in a letter dated 28 November 1841, Vivian summed the situation up well: '... then comes the Money, then comes the difficulty of disposing of the Model & lastly there comes the D of Wellington, for without him they will not one of them stir one inch'.[39]

Vivian certainly knew the score. The money could have been made available, and several suitable locations for the model were mooted. One in particular, the National Gallery, would have been entirely appropriate for such a work of art. The new building, situated on the north side of Trafalgar Square, opened in 1838, the year of the model's exhibition in the Egyptian Hall. Work started on Nelson's Column in 1839, so having a Waterloo model in the immediate vicinity would have been apposite. However, there was one person behind the scenes pulling the strings, and he was determined to see that Siborne got nowhere. One of his puppets was Francis Egerton, who was a trustee of the National Gallery.

'The answer from the Horse Guards is in one respect just what I anticipated,' Vivian commented to Siborne on 26

December. 'It renders assistance from that quarter hopeless. In another respect it is of value. It acknowledges the ability you have displayed in the execution of the Work – & admits that you might fairly have anticipated a considerable profit from it – this then is at least an official testimony in favor [*sic*] of the Work. – Nothing now I fear remains to be done . . .'[40]

As Siborne's correspondence then ceased mentioning his financial plight, one assumes some sort of solution was found. An unnamed officer of the army is known to have had a mortgage on the Large Model when Siborne died, so it is possible that this was how he eventually prevented it from being seized by his untrustworthy creditor. Siborne went back to researching the details of the campaign for inclusion in his forthcoming *History*. The next great controversy was about to begin.

11 *The* History

Francis Egerton

'The eventful victory which these two splendid volumes are intended to commemorate has had many historians, but none so good or comprehensive as Captain Siborne.'
United Service Gazette, 15 June 1844

By the autumn of 1842, Siborne had made sufficient progress in writing the *History* to feel confident enough to approach various people to subscribe to it; that is, to register their names for a copy prior to publication. From 24 September onwards, he sent several hundred people a printed prospectus. As there is no copy of it in his records, we cannot be sure of the text. However, some of its contents can be determined from the responses of the recipients.

Among the first potential subscribers he approached was FitzRoy Somerset, asking not only for his agreement, but also requesting advice on whether or not he should approach Wellington in this regard. FitzRoy Somerset replied on 28 September,

> I received your letter of the 24th in due course. The Duke of Wellington has been pestered to subscribe to new publications to such an extent that I believe he resolved several years ago never to give his name again on such occasions, and under these circumstances I am inclined to recommend that you should not apply to his Grace for permission to include his name in the list of Subscribers of your forthcoming History of the War in France and Belgium in 1815.[1]

He added, however, 'I shall be happy to add my name to it if you will give me leave.'[2]

It is likely that there was a little more to the Duke's anticipated refusal than mere prudence, because Siborne was not popular in Apsley House. News of the coming subscription also reached two of Wellington's close advisors, Francis Egerton and Charles Arbuthnot. Egerton was not only a politician but also an acknowledged military historian, whose knowledge of the German language was such that he had translated the great soldier-philosopher General Karl von Clausewitz's work on the Russian campaign of 1812 into English. Arbuthnot was such a close advisor to Wellington that he lived with the Duke. On 23 September 1842, Egerton wrote to Arbuthnot,

> I see also that Siborne, the officer who made that curious
> model of the battle, is about to publish a detailed account.
> Under these circumstances I think it probable that a good
> opportunity may present itself of such further use of the
> Duke's memm. as may be required. When I first saw
> Siborne's model I suspected that he had been humbugged
> by the Prussians, & I remember mentioning my opinion to
> Fitzroy [sic] Somerset. I see he advertises something like a
> confession of the fact, & says he has made corrections as to
> the position of their corps. I fully understand the Duke's
> objections, & knowing his position with regard to Prussia,
> I took care to state what I knew were his opinions with
> regard to Ligny in such a qualified form as might avoid
> offence to his allies, & might not commit him.[3]

The Memorandum mentioned was in the process of being written. Indeed, the final draft was in fact finished the very next day. Wellington wrote this note for Egerton, who used it to make negative comments about the 1815 volume of Sir Archibald Alison's *History of Europe* in that month's *Quarterly Review*. Egerton was anticipating doing the same with Siborne's *History*, and in due course Wellington instructed him to do so. What is more interesting is that Siborne had just announced in the prospectus to the *History* that he had been 'wrong' about the positions of the Prussians as shown on the model. He later published a full statement on this issue in the *History*. It is also noteworthy that Egerton considered it necessary to tone down Wellington's hostility towards the Prussians for public consumption.

Despite his promise to subscribe to the *History*, FitzRoy Somerset does not appear to have done so. In all, around five hundred people – half of the first print run – did pre-order a copy. The list of subscribers, printed in the first edition, reads like a *Who's Who* of early Victorian Britain. The young queen herself and her consort Prince Albert headed the list, followed by other prominent members of the royal family. Then came European emperors, kings, princes and dukes, including the King of Prussia. Finally, the numerous army officers and civilians who were eager to possess a copy of what was to be the most thoroughly researched account of the Waterloo campaign yet published in the English language were listed. The absence of Wellington's name could not have gone unnoticed.

The first edition of the *History* was finally published in June 1844. It consisted of two octavo-sized volumes, with beautifully embellished medallion portraits, engraved on steel, of the leading participants in the campaign, and a folio atlas. The *Atlas* contained nine anaglyptographic engravings made on steel, two each of Quatre Bras, Ligny and Wavre, as well as three of Waterloo. Each showed different periods of the action. There were also maps of Belgium and parts of France. The work cost £2 2s (£2.10), which equates to several hundred pounds today, a high price. However, such books were not aimed at the mass market but rather at the wealthier and educated classes.

The first print run of 1,000 copies sold out before any reached the bookshops, so a second edition was produced. It came out in August 1844 and was available in time for the exhibition of the New Model. Siborne, of course, plugged the *History* heavily in the *Guide* to this exhibition. Fortunately, his publishers were located at 29 New Bond Street, just around the corner from the Egyptian Hall. The second edition too soon sold out, and a third was published in 1848. At least one edition was published in the USA, that being in 1845. The print run there amounted to 1,500 copies.[4] Bound in a single volume, it sold for $3.25.[5] Siborne is likely to have earned about £500 or so from the *History*, and he stood to earn a substantial amount from the planned mass-market edition.

Siborne's account drew information from the published Prussian authorities, including Müffling (published in 1816), Plotho (1818), Wagner (1825) and Damitz (1837). Müffling is best known for his role as Prussian liaison officer in Wellington's headquarters in 1815. Like Siborne, he was a staff officer with a leaning towards cartography. His style of representing contours, known as the 'Müffling Method', became one of the standards of the period. His survey of the Rhineland, conducted from 1817 to 1820, was one of the great cartographical exercises of the era. The year after, Müffling was appointed

Chief-of-Staff of the Prussian Army, a post he held for several years. His ability as a historian was also recognized and his account of the 1815 campaign was one of several works on military history from his pen.

Plotho was a lieutenant-colonel in the Prussian Army at the time he wrote his multi-volume work on the campaigns of 1813–15. The final volume was published in 1818. While not an official history, it is clear that Plotho had had access to the archives of the General Staff. What Siborne must have found particularly useful in this book were the extensive appendices, which give highly detailed orders-of-battle of the troops involved and full casualty lists. Wagner, as we know, corresponded with Siborne and provided him with information over and above that given in his official history of the campaigns of 1813–15.

Damitz's work was written with the support of General von Grolman, a senior officer on Blücher's staff in 1815. It provided much valuable information on movements and timings, although it was not entirely reliable.

One Prussian account Siborne does not appear to have read was that by Clausewitz, published posthumously in 1835. The great soldier-philosopher was hardly known outside of Prussia at that time and it would take a world war or two to make him famous internationally.

Siborne made use of all the known published authorities in Prussia. That did not mean, however, that he unquestionably accepted their material or that the Prussians agreed with all he wrote.

One issue that resulted in a long exchange of correspondence between Siborne and the Prussian General Staff concerned exactly when Wellington heard the news of the

General von Grolman

outbreak of hostilities on 15 June 1815. In his *Despatch*, Wellington gave the time as 'evening', a statement that has since given rise to a myth-making industry.[6] In the first edition of his *History*, Siborne stated, 'It was between three and four o'clock in the afternoon of the 15th that the Duke of Wellington received information of the advance of the French army.'[7] Obviously, this time conflicted with Wellington's claim of having first heard in the 'evening', but Siborne's records do not provide an explanation of why he chose this hour. However, in the June 1841 edition of the *USJ*, an anonymous officer of Picton's division, based in Brussels in 1815, gave a most lucid account of the arrival of the news at 3 p.m. at the mess he was sharing with a number of brother officers.[8] It could be that Siborne took his information from that article.

Sound though Siborne's research had been, for a reason he did not explain, in the second edition of the *History* he changed this sentence to read, 'It was about five o'clock in the afternoon of the 15th that the Duke of Wellington, while at dinner, received information of the advance of the French army.'[9] This brought the time closer to Wellington's public statement that he received this information in the 'evening'. It would not be Siborne's last revision to this crucial point.

The model was such a labour of love that one cannot imagine Siborne ever making any significant changes to it without good reason. On page 270 of the second volume of his *History*, Siborne announced that the role the Prussians had played during the Crisis described in his account varied with the model, where he had given them too prominent a role.[10] He mentioned that he had been supplied with information from the Prussian War Ministry,

which they had sent in good faith. He had placed the figures on
the model on that basis, but had now had cause to reconsider its
accuracy. He now apparently considered the Prussians '. . . were
represented in too forward a position', and went on to explain,

It was only subsequently, when collecting that further information which has enabled me in the present work to
describe with such minuteness of detail those brilliant dispositions of the Duke of Wellington, by which he not only
defeated the French imperial guard upon his own position,
but secured the victory, that I discovered the error into
which the Prussian authorities had been unconsciously but
naturally led . . .

Siborne continued by pointing out that the Prussians had
wrongly believed that their final assault on Plancenoit had
coincided with Wellington's defeat of the Imperial Guard,
'whereas, in reality, there was an interval of at least twelve minutes between these two incidents'. He then gave the reasons for
changing his mind, pointing out the final charges made by Sir
Ormsby Vandeleur's and Vivian's cavalry 'could not, from the
configuration of the ground, be observed by the Prussian army;
to which circumstance may be attributed the origin of that mis-
calculation concerning the actual disposition of the Duke of
Wellington's forces at the moment of the general advance of his
line, which induced the Prussian authorities to confound that
advance with the defeat of the imperial guard'.

Plausible though these statements may sound, let us attempt
to establish their veracity. First, the information provided by
the Prussians: Siborne's records show that his earliest contact
with the Prussian Minister of War was on 8 November 1834,

when he wrote in French to the minister to inform him he was acting under instructions from Lord Hill to construct a model of the Battle of Waterloo and would like Prussian officers present at the battle to give him information. He enclosed a copy of his circular and fifty copies of his plan of the field of battle.[11] On 8 July 1835, the minister returned one copy of the map marked up by a 'fully informed officer of the General Staff' with the positions of the Prussian troops as requested.[12]

On 10 February 1837, Siborne again contacted the Prussian General Staff in this regard, asking for more information on the action around Plancenoit. Colonel Wagner informed Siborne that he could send no further information, as the information already made available had been taken verbatim from the after-action reports made by the units involved and deposited in the War Archives.[13]

In the years that followed, no further correspondence with the Prussian General Staff on this issue can be found in Siborne's records, neither before he constructed the model nor, more importantly, afterwards. We know that Siborne consulted the published Prussian authorities on the campaign, but the works of Müffling, Plotho, Wagner and Damitz do not contain anything more specific. What is more, these books were published before the model was made and Siborne used this information to place the Prussians in the original positions. His records from after the exhibition do not contain any correspondence with the Prussians on this issue. No further works of significance were published in Prussia between 1838 and 1844, so there was no new information for Siborne to use.

Not surprisingly, most of the correspondence in Siborne's records after October 1838 is on issues he was investigating as

part of his research for the forthcoming *History*. There are letters on Quatre Bras; on the role of various British, KGL and
Hanoverian units in the battle; there is considerable correspondence with members of various cavalry regiments
involved in the Great Cavalry Charge; the subject of the still-to-
be constructed New Model; there are letters on the attack of
d'Erlon's Corps; there are voluminous missives from Gawler;
there are notes from Vivian discussing his never-ending dispute with Gawler; there is correspondence on the attempts to
sell the model; there are letters on Siborne's endeavours to
locate Wellington's headquarters papers; finally, there is the
paperwork generated by the subscriptions to the *History*.

If Siborne had re-examined this issue, one would have
expected to find one of his detailed memoranda. There are two
memoranda on Whinyates' Troop of the Royal Horse Artillery,
one on the 1st Light Battalion of the KGL, and several on the
Great Cavalry Charge. However, there is absolutely nothing in
Siborne's records from 1838 to 1844 to indicate that he conducted 'a most careful and diligent investigation of the whole
question of the Prussian co-operation', one that led him to the
conclusion that the Prussians 'were represented in too forward
a position', not even a short note or even a letter to his old
friend and confidant Vivian. One would have expected some
sort of record of the reasoning behind as significant an issue as
that which would cause Siborne to remove the figures representing 40,000 Prussian soldiers, one quarter of all the figures
on the model, which had been cast at great expense in minute
detail and individually painted by hand.

There are, however, records of Wellington's disapproval of
the prominence given to the Prussians on the model and of

Siborne's constant attempts to get government funding. Wellington's opinion on the model was common knowledge and Siborne had gone so far as to expressing his willingness to alter it according to the Duke's wishes, if the funds were forthcoming. It is difficult to believe this series of events to be unconnected and mere coincidence. Wellington was well aware of Siborne's concession. The first public announcement of his 'error' had been made a few months after Siborne's unsuccessful attempts at the end of 1841 to get funding for the model, an application that was rejected in part due to the Duke's objections. Was this admission, made in the Prospectus, one final attempt to get Wellington's support for a refund of his costs?

Siborne must have been desperate indeed to carry out this act of vandalism on the 'most perfect model', this great work of art on which he had lavished so much attention for so many years. He had been fanatical about its accuracy and must have been devastated at having to resort to such a deed. He had clearly reached his breaking point. Yet making such a dramatic concession did not achieve the result he intended. Apsley House remained silent on the issue, at least in public. And having announced these changes, there was no going back for Siborne. He had compromised himself in front of his peers and could not do a *volte face* on that without destroying what was left of his good reputation.

As the announcement of the 'error' in 1841 and its repetition in the prospectus of 1842 failed to achieve its objective, the statement in the *History* may have been a double-edged sword. A number of his readers – the list of subscribers was printed in the first edition, so we know who they were – were involved in this affair one way or another. They were well aware of the conflict between Siborne and Wellington and knew what he had suffered at the hands of the Duke. Thanks to various announcements, Siborne's financial difficulties were also public knowledge. The soldiers among them would also have known that certain of the points Siborne made here rung hollow. Any military man of the period would know that it was virtually impossible to be so precise about timings in an affair as confused as the final stages of a battle in the days of inaccurate pocket-watches and before the need for exact timekeeping was necessitated by the yet to be constructed railway system. 'Twelve minutes' – and why not even a round quarter of an hour? – was neither here nor there. It was so insignificant as to be almost comical. It would not be difficult for those versed in these events to add two and two together. Siborne must surely have known that the use of discretion would have been the best way to attempt to repair his relationship with Wellington and get the money he wanted, yet instead he drew his readers' attention to the alterations in the *History*.

Returning to the statement in his *History*, Siborne lavished praise on Wellington, but was this sincere? In the flyer to the 1838 exhibition of the model, Siborne had not even mentioned the Duke, let alone attributed the victory to him. Indeed, he had described the model as 'Napoleon's last great struggle for victory', which must have greatly insulted Wellington. Why now, all of a sudden, was Siborne lauding the man at whose hands he had suffered so much? Can it be that these public announcements – and he made them again for the exhibition of 1845 – were a form of protest?

We cannot be entirely sure what was going through Siborne's mind at this time. While it seems evident that the announcement of his deed may well have been a way to signal his anger at Wellington, could there also have been a degree of self-contempt at having to compromise the high standards he had set himself? Were his proclamations also a form of self-criticism, an attempt to come to terms with doing what he knew to be wrong? Furthermore, was he sending a coded message to his peers to indicate that his concession was not sincere? What is certain is that history was distorted as a result of Wellington's machinations. The most perfect model was now no longer perfect.

Mention was made of the planned *Atlas* volume earlier. Siborne himself had surveyed only the field of Waterloo and later went to the trouble of having a Captain White map the fields of Quatre Bras, Ligny and Wavre. When he wrote to W. F. Wakeman at the end of November 1836 about his plans for the *History*, Siborne also pointed out,

> The work must be accompanied by half a dozen Plans, and these I should require to be engraved in a very superior style – not by professed '*Map*-engravers', but by our first rate *mechanical* engravers, such as Wilson Lowry *was*, and such as his son Joseph Lowry and his pupil Edward Purrell, I believe, now *are*. Mr Edward Kennion, who was also a pupil of Lowry's engraved some plans for me some years ago, and thus became quite familiar with my particular system and style of representing the undulations of ground. What is become of him I know not, but if in existence and still in practice, I am most anxious he should be

employed on this occasion – either partially or altogether as time & circumstances might admit. Foreigners have hitherto excelled us greatly in this branch of engraving, merely because it has not, with us, been sufficiently attended to and encouraged, and I should be glad to prove that we can equal if not surpass them.[14]

Two books by Siborne on topographical surveying were published in the 1820s. That of 1827 included seven illustrative plates engraved by Kennion, which explains Siborne's familiarity with him. However, Kennion does not appear to have been available and instead the highly regarded engraver Alfred Robert Freebairn (1794–1846) produced the maps. Freebairn used John Bate's anaglyptograph, an elaborate machine patented in the early nineteenth century. This machine was specially adapted for reproducing, in engraving, objects with raised surfaces, such as coins, medals, reliefs, etc. It had a pointer that was taken across the three-dimensional object along successive, closely spaced, equidistant lines. A pencil attached to the device made a drawing, which was the guide for the engraver.

Using this process, Siborne's maps were printed in such a way that, when held to the light, they appeared to be three-dimensional. They show a fantastic amount of detail which modern printing methods do not produce. Freebairn's later work was entirely confined to engraving representations made by the anaglyptograph, and Siborne's maps were among the most notable examples of his work. Though there are references to anaglyptography in the 1870s, the early deaths of Siborne and Freebairn combined with the invention of photography seem to have caused a decline in the system.

Siborne's maps are virtually unique. As always, he was on the cutting edge of new technology.[15]

The maps were not just an incredible work of cartography and art; three of them may well contain a hidden message. It is interesting to note that of the maps Siborne used to illustrate the Battle of Waterloo, one showed the situation at the start of the battle at 11.15 a.m., the next showed the situation at 7.45 p.m., and the final map the situation at 8.05 p.m. Major parts of the battle such as the assault on Hougoumont, d'Erlon's assault on Wellington's centre and the Great Cavalry Charge have been ignored, while two out of three maps show the Prussian intervention. It is as if Siborne was emphasizing their role. However, that is not all.

The positions of the troops on the '7.45 p.m.' map correspond with those on the model after the removal of the Prussians, yet the model is supposed to have represented the situation at 7.15 p.m. The '8.05 p.m.' map showed the Prussians assaulting Plancenoit, which actually happened at 7.30 p.m. The times on these maps also conflicted with those given in the *Guide* to the exhibition, so those of Siborne's contemporaries versed in the controversy with Wellington must have noticed the obvious inconsistencies. As Siborne was such a fanatic for detail, it is implausible that this was merely a printing error. Was showing two wrongly timed maps of the Prussian assault on Plancenoit another way of making a coded protest against having been forced to change the model and play down the role of the Prussians?

Shortly before publication, Siborne sent out advance copies of the *History* to various influential publications, including the

United Service Gazette. Its review was published on 8 June 1844 and summed up his great contribution to Waterloo historiography with the words,

> Captain Siborne's facility of access to official documents, both English and foreign, the assistance which he has received from the surviving Waterloo heroes of all ranks, and zeal, energy, and talent, which he has displayed in the construction of his materials, have produced a record, not only of the battle itself, but of the whole Waterloo campaign, which is likely to be as enduring as it is creditable to his talents as a writer, and his reputation as a soldier.[16]

This glowing commentary ended with what were indeed prophetic words, although it is doubtful if the reviewer anticipated the book would still be in print over one hundred and fifty years later.

The *Dublin University Magazine* devoted over forty pages in two consecutive issues in the summer of 1844 to reviewing the *History*. This detailed examination of Siborne's tomes concluded with the words,

> When the work was first announced for publication we conceived great expectations from a history compiled by one, whose access to every source of information was favoured both by interest in the highest quarters and the circumstances of an official appointment on the staff. We looked for a work which should at once and for ever settle the disputed questions of the campaign . . . We were not disappointed. Such are the volumes before us – a military classic.[17]

It was a while before *The Times* published its review. It finally appeared on 27 January 1845, echoing the comments of the *USG*: 'We feel no apology to be requisite for referring again to the subject [of Waterloo], and noticing a work so faithful and excellent as that which has recently been published by Captain Siborne.'[18]

An advance copy of the *History* was also sent to *Colburn's United Service Magazine*, as the *USJ* was now known. Basil Jackson wrote a long review that ran in the May and June issues over a total of thirty pages. He went beyond merely examining Siborne's work, in effect contributing to the Waterloo historiography of the period. He was generous with his praise, making comments such as,

> It is written in a free and impartial manner, is lucid in its descriptions, surprisingly correct in details; and many important features of the campaign, which have hitherto remained either wholly unnoticed, or else kept too much in shadow, are now brought forward into proper relief; whilst the grand military operations of the period are delineated with the pen of an enlightened soldier . . . One of the most lavish supply of excellent plans; besides good general maps of parts of Belgium and France, we have no less than *nine* faithful plans, beautifully executed in the new style of engraving from models, to illustrate different periods of the several actions.[19]

Jackson was, however, not uncritical of Siborne's work. One negative comment he made regarded the model. 'It had', he wrote, 'but one solitary defect, namely, that of placing the Prussians more forward then they really were at the precise moment of the battle selected for representation; the cause of which error, its able and indefatigable constructor explains in a note at page 270, vol. ii of his present work; but I confess that the explanation rather tends to give the reader a favourable notion of his own delicacy and good feeling, than serves to convince him that the error did not originate in a design on the part of the Prussian officers to support, by their *minute detail, and plan drawn upon a large scale, containing a distribution of the troops*, the pretension made on the part of their gallant army, of having saved the Anglo-Allied force from impending defeat at Waterloo.'[20]

Jackson repeated the accusation made by Wellington's close advisor Egerton that Siborne had been 'humbugged' by the Prussians. Jackson, as we know, was also spreading the rumour that Siborne's propensity to side with the Prussians was due to his supposed German origins. Neither story is true. The positions of the Prussian troops on the model in 1838 coincided with historical fact. At 7.15 p.m. on 18 June 1815, the time shown, the Prussians were drawing up before Plancenoit in preparation for their final and successful assault on the village. At 7.30 p.m., the attack commenced, and by 8 p.m., the village had fallen to them, accelerating the collapse of the French army initiated by the headlong retreat of the Imperial Guard. Also, Siborne did not have German ancestry. Was the similarity between Jackson's misleading comments and those emanating from Wellington mere coincidence?

In his article, Jackson also commented on claims made in the published memoirs of Joseph Fouché, the French chief of police in 1815, that he had duped Wellington into delaying his movements on the outbreak of hostilities.[21] He also complained that both Sir Archibald Alison and the Prussian authorities had accepted this story.[22] Egerton's review of the *History* appeared in the *Quarterly Review* of June 1845 and he made several comments similar to those of Jackson: 'Captain Siborne', he wrote, 'judiciously avoids casting any reflection on the Prussians ...'[23] Egerton also criticized Alison for accepting Fouché's story, and condemned the Prussian authority Grolman for believing it.[24] Was it merely a coincidence that both Jackson and Egerton expressed similar views, making the same questionable criticisms?

While one can only make presumptions about the provenance of Jackson's comments, there is a record of the origin of Egerton's. As Egerton noted, 'these proof sheets [of his review] were under the Duke's perusal on the 18th of June 1845, the 30th Anniversary of the Battle of Waterloo. They received his unqualified approbation, and bear evidence of his perusal in one or two pencil corrections under his own hand.'[25] Wellington had written a *Memorandum on the Battle of Waterloo* for Egerton's use. In it, the Duke was highly critical of the model, making his by now familiar claims about the quality of Siborne's research:

> It is curious that the Historian of the Battle of Waterloo, Captain Siborne, having discovered that in his capacity of artist he had failed in producing an accurate, and even intelligible, representation of the Battle of Waterloo, on his beautiful and accurate model of the ground, by having listened to every hero of his own tale, and by having introduced into the model the action represented by each individual to have been performed, without regard to time, order of time, or circumstances, – the consequences of which have been to render ridiculous and useless that

beautiful work, so that it is more like the picture of five (Acts) of a play, and its termination represented on canvas as one scene, than it is to anything else that can be imagined – should in his History of this great military event, have fallen into the same error, so far at least as to have listened to every individual who chose to tell his own tale, to insert into his work as facts, and as operations performed, the reports made by others of what was related to the person who reported, in conversation with third parties; while he lays aside and unnoticed the authentick [*sic*] reports by the General Commanding-in-Chief, and by the Generals and others employed at his Headquarters, made to their respective Sovereigns; the letters written by the General on the morning of that day, and all the well-known circumstances of the Battle, known to all the Officers about the Headquarters, and to all particularly whose duty placed them near the Commander-in-Chief on that day.[26]

It was not just Siborne's alleged failure to rely on the *Waterloo Despatch* that Wellington criticized. The Duke continued, emphasizing the point that 'the perusal of the account of this battle will show where the historian collected the facts which he narrates. But some of the most important facts of the battle are omitted; because the only authorities from whom information was never required were the Commander-in-Chief himself, and the Officers of the General Staff, and those acting under his immediate orders in the Field.'[27]

There was no substance to any of these accusations. Siborne's research into the details of the position of the troops on the model had been exhaustive. His methodology was scientific and what he produced was the most accurate representation of those events possible. In his Memorandum of October 1836, Wellington had confirmed the accuracy of the terrain, though he could not recall the exact positions of the troops. The senior officers present at Waterloo that had a privileged preview of the model in 1838 had confirmed its authenticity. Also, Siborne had corresponded for years with the Horse Guards, with Wellington's Military Secretary FitzRoy Somerset and with numerous senior officers, including several of the General Staff who had participated in the Waterloo campaign. Gurwood and FitzRoy Somerset had consulted the Duke on Siborne's behalf. Moreover, Wellington had passed various messages to Siborne. Wellington knew very well that Siborne required information from the Commander-in-Chief himself. He also knew he was making false statements about Siborne designed to damage severely his reputation as a historian. By repeating what were obviously falsehoods, Egerton was merely acting as Wellington's mouthpiece. Moreover, the timing of the publication of these comments – to coincide with the exhibition of the two models in 1845 – was surely deliberate and designed to damage Siborne's hoped-for success. Wellington was co-ordinating a smear campaign against Siborne, one designed to damage both his reputation and his pocket. At least Egerton had a guilty conscience, noting on the manuscript that he had written a letter to Arbuthnot on 18 May 1845 in which he 'deprecated the Duke's severity towards Siborne'.[28]

Senior army officers were aware that Siborne had contacted both the Commander-in-Chief and officers of the General Staff. One unnamed staff officer published his 'Recollections of Waterloo' in the *USM* in September through November

1847. He commented on Siborne's *History*, writing that it had been 'compiled of materials emanating from very high quarters, if not from the highest authority'.[29] He was surely not the only officer who knew Wellington was criticizing Siborne unfairly.

The implications were clear to Siborne: removing 40,000 Prussians from the model had not sufficed to end the dilemma of his financial plight. The damage to the Duke's reputation had already been done and there would be no forgiveness for that.

Wellington, supported by Hardinge, had been spreading the questionable story regarding the 'exposed' Prussian positions at Ligny. In a conversation with De Ros, he had embellished that story with the claim that he had witnessed the Prussian defeat. In 1845, the Duke repeated that story to Egerton, who noted, 'Arbuthnot sent me back my letter [of 18 May 1845], with the following docqueted [*sic*] upon a corner of it in the Duke's hand . . . "With a glass from Quatre Bras I positively saw the principle events on the field of Ligny. That is to say, the charge and the failure of the charge of the Prussian Cavalry, Blücher's personal situation, and the retreat of the Prussians from the field of battle."'[30]

Egerton repeated these comments almost verbatim in his review of the *History*, writing, 'Till nightfall, moreover, the Duke could see; and, need it be added, did see with his own eyes from Quatre Bras what passed on the Prussian field of battle. With his glass he saw the charge and the failure of the Prussian cavalry, Blucher's disaster, and the retreat of the Prussian army from the field of battle.'[31]

Siborne must have found that comment a little mystifying. He would probably have consulted a map just to check if it were possible. It was not, as there is an intervening ridge, the Heights of Marbais, and a glass that can be used to see through hills has yet to be invented. Always being one to corroborate evidence, Siborne sought confirmation of his suspicions from an eyewitness. On 24 July 1845, he first wrote to Captain White, the surveyor of the fields of Quatre Bras and Ligny, who was travelling through Belgium. Replying to Siborne a week later, White confirmed, 'I may be in error but I nevertheless hold it *physically* impossible for any person *to see* the movement of troops moving round Brie [*sic*], or even Wagnelé, from any spot occupied by the troops during the combat of Quatre Bras.'[32]

As there was a slight element of doubt in White's statement, Siborne made quite sure. He contacted the famous guide, Edward Cotton, who replied on 7 September 1845 from the farmhouse of Mont St Jean. Cotton had recently gone over the ground to double-check. 'No part of the Field or Villages of Sombref [*sic*] or Lingey [*sic*] can be seen from Quatre Bras,' he wrote, 'or can the Mill of Brie be seen from Quatre Bras. The Church Spire and Mill of Marbais can be seen from Quatre Bras, but no portion of the Village. The heights of Marbais and Brie are so elevated as to prevent the Field of Ligney [*sic*] being seen from Quatre Bras. A few Houses called little Marbais can be seen from Quatre Bras along the Namur Road on high ground, about a league distant. No trees has [*sic*] grown up since 1815 between Quatre Bras and Ligney, but the Wood of Dellhutte [*sic*] has been cut down.'[33]

Armed with this devastating evidence, Siborne had a conversation with Rev George Gleig, Chaplain-General of the

Rev George Gleig

British army and a close associate of Wellington. This was before the publication of Gleig's *Story of Waterloo* in 1847, a subject that will be considered in more detail later. Siborne's account of this conversation, published a year later in the third edition of the *History*, was equally damning:

> In a casual conversation which I had with Mr. Gleig, respecting the above article in the 'Quarterly' I mentioned

that - - (naming the writer) [Francis Egerton] had fallen into great error in stating that the Duke of Wellington could, from the field of Quatre Bras, distinctly see that of Ligny. I adverted to the line of argument I intended to adopt for the purpose of refuting the error; and, on my instancing the intervening heights of Marbais, Mr. Gleig remarked, 'Ah! you have him there!' At that time he was preparing his 'Story of Waterloo' for the press, but I was wholly ignorant of the fact, and he did not think proper to disclose it to me. When his book was published, I became curious to see what he had written upon this particular point, and I was not a little amused to find that in his desire to follow in the wake of the writer in the 'Quarterly,' and, at the same time, to overcome the difficulty which I had pointed out, he had represented that 'the fields of action were near enough the one to the other to permit his' (the Duke's) 'seeing, from each height as he ascended it, the smoke of the battle of Ligny rise in thick volumes over the intervening woods.' This is the first time we have heard of the Duke having ascended *each* height on his own field, to see what Blücher was about at Ligny. However, in the third sentence beyond the one above quoted, Mr. Gleig forgets the woods which, as if with a magic wand, he has caused to spring up between the two fields of action, and, borrowing that extraordinary telescope which the writer in the 'Quarterly' puts into the Duke's hands, and which at once levels both woods and heights, and clears away smoke, mist, and even darkness, he actually enables the Duke to see 'the failure of that cavalry-charge which led to Blücher's misfortune, and immediately preceded the general retreat of his army,' – which charge, be it recollected, took place at a distance of seven miles, and after darkness had set in![34]

Siborne's ridicule of Wellington's claims would do him no favours. His already strained relationship with Gleig and Gleig's benefactor was shortly to take a turn for the worst. Surprisingly, even today, certain historians repeat the Duke's implausible tales about the events of that day as Gospel. Siborne was certainly not as gullible, and would continue to draw attention to suspect statements in Wellington's accounts of the campaign. By lambasting Gleig as a plagiarist and pointing out how he supported statements made by Wellington that were obviously not true, Siborne was in effect now calling Wellington a liar.

12 *The Prussians and The* Story

General von Zieten

'Our readers . . . have found Siborne's work to be a detailed and interesting account. A closer look at it will surely be pleasurable and indeed for the Prussian reader of great pleasure, as the author, unlike others of his nation, has troubled to present the truth and to give everybody due credit!'
Militair-Wochenblatt, vol. xxix, 1845, 148

The longest review of Siborne's *History* ever published appeared in the *Militair-Wochenblatt*, the weekly journal produced by the Prussian General Staff for its officer corps. At sixty-eight pages, the review was so long that its parts were published in several of that year's issues. As well as discussing the *History*, largely in a positive manner, the reviewer took the opportunity of providing information taken from the War Archives to elucidate and in places to correct Siborne's text. In fact, this detailed article provides the student of the campaign with much information that is not available elsewhere and as such is a valuable contribution to Waterloo historiography in itself. It started with the words,

There is certainly no lack of works from England on the Campaign of 1815. However, they cannot fully satisfy the Prussian reader because they either treat our participation in the great successes of this war in passing, or reduce or present it in such a way that anybody that does not know the true events will get a false impression. – The causes of this way of treating history lay partly in a limited or even no use at all of our better sources and partly in the egotism that deliberately takes a one-sided view for the sake of national honour. This is not only regarding what happened out of sight, but also regarding what the allied troops in the English ranks achieved.[1]

These words of wisdom could equally apply to most accounts of the campaign, as Siborne's attempt at balance and objectivity was almost unique. Certainly that is how the Prussian General Staff saw it, as the review continued, 'It is thus all the more pleasurable to see a work from this side successfully published that is free of that haughty lack of concern caused by national bias. This work achieves a more worthy point of view of history as it evidently seeks the truth, each part of it thereby being more just.'[2]

A footnote referred to Siborne's original approach to the Prussian General Staff made in 1834 and indeed quoted from his letter of 8 November, a copy of which is in Siborne's records.[3] The anonymous reviewer, evidently a senior staff officer, commented that the highest authority in Prussia had instructed that Siborne be given the utmost support. The points where assistance and information were given were discussed in the review.

The first part of the review concentrated on Siborne's use of Damitz's work. The reviewer, having access to the War Archives, discussed in detail certain errors and omissions in Damitz and their effect on Siborne's *History*. One issue the reviewer raised was the time at which Wellington first heard the news of the outbreak of hostilities in Brussels on 15 June 1815. He wrote,

> With regard to the events in the British–Netherlands Army on 15 June, neither author agrees with the other on the facts

and the verdict. – While Damitz blames the Duke of
Wellington for hesitation and the resulting delays in the
concentration of his army, Siborne attempts to play down
or reject the accusation made by other writers that he had
been surprised and claims that, 'The Duke was fully prepared for this intelligence, thought uncertain how soon it
might arrive. The reports which had been made to him
from the outposts of his own army, especially from those of
the 1st hussars of the King's German legion, stationed in
the vicinity of Mons and Tournai, gave sufficient indication
that the enemy was concentrating his forces.' – that the
Duke was however, 'determined to make no movement
until the real line of attack should become manifest.'

The reviewer continued by noting that whereas Siborne
gave 5 p.m. as the time this news first arrived, Damitz claimed
it was actually 4 p.m. Siborne and the Prussian General Staff
would discuss this issue further.

One thing led to another. Members of the Berlin garrison, and
particularly officers of the General Staff, would no doubt have
availed themselves of the opportunity of viewing the New
Model, which went on display in Berlin in 1846 on Unter den
Linden. This was Berlin's main thoroughfare, running from
the Brandenburg Gate past the New Guardhouse and the
Arsenal to the Royal Palace, a route frequented by the military.
Just as the Berlin exhibition was closing, the German edition of the *History* was published, in two volumes that cost 4
Reichsthaler in total. The English edition, including the atlas
volume, had cost 16 Reichsthaler, so the German rendition was

considerably more attractive to the Prussian reader. The trans-
lator was Lieutenant E. Siber of the 39th Prussian Infantry
Regiment. The publisher was no less than E. S. Mittler, located
at No. 3 Stechbahn in Berlin and publisher by Order to the
King.[4] With official approval from the highest authority,
Siborne's *History* was likely to have become a standard text at
the Military Academy. Now that it was available in German and
at such a reasonable price, it must have been avidly read.
Siborne's name was becoming as familiar in Prussia as it was in
Britain, and the interest generated a further batch of corre-
spondence.

The review of Siborne's *History* in the *Militair-Wochenblatt*
of 1845 discussed the time the news of the outbreak of hostilities arrived at Wellington's headquarters in Brussels on 15 June
1815. On 13 December 1847, Major von Gerwien, of the Historical Section of the Prussian General Staff in Berlin, wrote a
memorandum which Baron von Bunsen at the Prussian Legation in London forwarded to Siborne with an accompanying
letter a month later. Bunsen, aware that while Siborne could
read printed German, he would have difficulty with the script,
summarized the memorandum. Gerwien had provided direct
and indirect proof to show that Wellington had received the
news of the outbreak of hostilities at 9 a.m. on 15 June 1815
from General Zieten, commander of the Prussian I Army
Corps based on the frontier in the area of Charleroi.[5]

Gerwien's line of argument was clear. Zieten sent Wellington a message at 3.45 a.m. on 15 June 1815, which had arrived
by 9 a.m. Wellington had confirmed its arrival in a letter sent
to the Duc de Feltre in Ghent that evening and published in
volume twelve of the *Dispatches*, in which he stated, 'I received

the news that the enemy attacked the Prussian posts this morning at Thuin on the Sambre and is appearing to menace Charleroi. I have received nothing since nine o'clock this morning from Charleroi.'[6] Siborne was no doubt aware that Wellington's statement to Feltre conflicted with the *Despatch*. It also conflicted with his later admission about hearing the news from the Prince of Orange.

Siborne was referred to issues of the *Militair-Wochenblatt* subsequent to those containing the review of his *History*, particularly to an article written by Major Karl Friedrich von Steinmetz. This article examined in detail the events at the front on the outbreak of hostilities in 1815. Also, Lt-General von Hofmann, in 1815 the commander of the brigade on the frontier that suffered the first French attack, commented on Steinmetz's article. Together, they acquainted Siborne with the minutiae of the events early that morning. Siborne analyzed the information sent and annotated Gerwien's memorandum before drafting one of his own.[7] At first, he dismissed Zieten's claim to have sent Wellington news of the outbreak of hostilities at 3.45 a.m. on 15 June, as this was before the fighting had actually started. Siborne's detractors had accused him of having been 'humbugged' by the Prussians, but an examination of his correspondence shows he did not accept what they told him uncritically.

Gerwien's reply to Siborne, dated 29 January 1848, outlined the case for Zieten having sent Wellington a message that morning, but pointed out that the time Zieten gave must have been incorrect because the use of small arms fire that Zieten heard from the front – indicating that large bodies of infantry were engaged in combat – started at 4.30 a.m., so he must have written to Wellington at 4.45 a.m. and not 3.45 a.m. as stated. In his final memorandum on the subject on 7 February 1848, Siborne considered the information provided and came to the conclusion that the evidence and reasoning clearly indicated that Zieten had indeed sent a communication to Wellington at that time.[8] Not only did Siborne alter his text accordingly, he explained his reasoning in a convincing footnote two pages long. Siborne's correction appeared on page 36 of the third edition of his *History*: 'His [Zieten's] report to the Duke of Wellington arrived in Brussels at 9 o'clock in the morning.' Nevertheless, virtually every subsequent Waterloo historian has plumped for 3 p.m. as the time of the arrival of the news of the outbreak of hostilities. They either ignore the conflict in Wellington's statements or explain them away as a lapse of memory.

In the third edition of his *History*, Siborne gave Zieten further support when he refuted the charge of negligence the Rev. George Gleig had made in his recently published *Story of Waterloo*.[9]

Wellington had first come across Gleig in 1826, when John Wilson Croker, then Secretary to the Admiralty, loaned the Duke a copy of Gleig's memoirs of the Peninsular War, *The Subaltern*, first published a year earlier. Wellington was impressed and said, 'He is a clever, observing man, and I shall inquire about him.'[10] He did so, writing to Gleig on 9 November, telling him he admired 'The simplicity and truth with which you related the various events you had witnessed'.[11]

Gleig later approached Wellington in the hope that he would accept a dedication for the second edition of *The Subaltern,* but he did not consent. The Duke explained, 'I have long been under the necessity of declining to give a formal assent to receive the dedication of any work. I conceive that, by such assent, I give a tacit guarantee of the contents of the work so dedicated . . . If, however, you think proper to dedicate your second edition to me, you are at perfect liberty to do so, and you cannot express in too strong language my approbation and admiration of your interesting work."[12] Gleig had gained an influential friend here, even if Wellington was not prepared to change his policy of making no public comment on published works. Gleig's proposal to write his life story, made a few days later, flattered the Duke, but again he declined, pointing out that he would become 'engaged in controversies of a nature most unpleasant, as they will be with the wounded vanity of individuals and nations'.[13] Gleig would later become embroiled in one of these controversies and set about wounding more than just the vanity of a certain individual.

The politician and writer Sir William Augustus Fraser related more of this episode:[14]

The Origin of the well-deserved promotion of Chaplain-General Gleig is interesting. The Duke staying in a country house was, like other great men, reluctant to go to bed early. However, he retired with the rest of the company. Returning to the drawing room for a book, he saw lying on the table 'The Subaltern.' The Duke was pleased with the technical accuracy, and honesty, with which this book was written. He wrote to the publisher; and said that as it was obvious that the author of 'The Subaltern' was an Officer, he would be very glad to assist him. The publisher replied that the author was a Clergyman, who had formerly served in a Regiment of the Line; and that he held a curacy in Kent. On the Duke becoming acquainted with Mr Gleig, the latter said that he had always wished to be made Chaplain to Chelsea Hospital. Later on this was done: and he ultimately developed into Chaplain-General of the Forces.[15]

Gleig was obliged to Wellington and had a favour to return. Their friendship developed over the coming years. On 10 August 1829, Wellington invited Gleig to visit him at Walmer Castle, an opportunity Gleig did not miss, particularly as he lived in Ash, near Wingham, only eight miles away. One member of the dinner party that evening was Charles Arbuthnot, who would play an active role in the denigration of Siborne. Gleig took this opportunity of engaging the Duke in private conversation, gaining his trust. From then until he moved away in 1834, Gleig was a regular guest at Walmer.

As Fraser mentioned, Gleig was offered the position of chaplain of the Royal Military Asylum, Chelsea, in February 1834. Lord John Russell, the Paymaster-General, appointed Gleig after FitzRoy Somerset had given him a glowing reference. It was probably here that Gleig first met Siborne, as he became the Asylum's secretary in 1843. Gleig was made chaplain-general of the forces in 1844, an appointment that ensured him close contact with Wellington. Later, he proposed a plan for promoting the education of soldiers and their children, and in 1846 was appointed inspector-general of military schools. On 30 May of that year, publishers John Murray of London commissioned him to write a book called *The True Story of the Battle of Waterloo*, which was to be written 'in a plain simple style – avoiding all Alison's blunders – without entering into any controversy & incorporating as far as possible parts of the most interesting personal narratives of the Battle'.[16]

So the *Story* was originally planned as a rebuff to Alison. Unfortunately, Siborne then showed his hand, writing to the editor of the *United Service Magazine* on 21 October 1846 to ask for a point of information. Published in the November issue, his letter explained, 'In preparing a third edition of the "History of the War in France and Belgium in 1815," I am very desirous of settling a disputed point connected with the proceedings of Major-General Sir Denis Pack's brigade, (consisting of the 3rd battalion Royal Scots, the 2nd battalion 44th Regiment, and the 42nd and 92nd Highlanders), at the period of the attack made by Count d'Erlon's columns of infantry upon the British left wing . . .'[17]

The original intention of countering Alison was no longer important. In view of the short time available to pre-empt Siborne's third edition of the *History*, Gleig would obviously not be able to do any original research. Instead, he engaged Siborne in conversation, drawing information from him, but without revealing his plans, which Siborne later found particularly objectionable. On Waterloo Day 1847, Gleig's *Story* was first published as part of the Colonial and Home Library series of cheap editions of out-of-copyright works aimed at the popular market. It retailed at a mere 6 shillings (30p), a fraction of the £2 2s that Siborne's *History* cost. It was clearly aimed at the mass market and thousands of copies were sold, the work running into several editions during the course of the nineteenth century.

Adverts appeared in the press prior to the publication of the *Story*. They announced that 'A plain, unbiased narrative of this event, so glorious in our annals, free from all controversial matter, will, it is supposed, not be unacceptable to the rising generation – to Englishmen settled in distant Colonies as well as to those collected round Home firesides."[18]

This work was not based on out-of-copyright material, and Siborne was well aware of Gleig's aim of diminishing the value of his original research with dubious claims. In a sharply written letter to the *United Service Magazine* dated 20 July 1847, Siborne took the opportunity of commenting on a 'mistake' in his *History* that Gleig had referred to in his *Story*. It was regarding Corporal Shaw of the 2nd Life Guards and whether he had died from a carbine shot. 'As far as history is concerned,' commented Siborne, 'it cannot be a matter of the slightest importance whether Corporal Shaw was killed by a carbine-ball or sword-cut, or died from an accumulation of wounds. I considered the incident too trivial to be embodied in my History . . . My informant was an officer of the 2nd Life Guards, to whose troop Shaw belonged. He saw the cuirassier level his carbine in his direction . . . Mr Gleig is certainly incorrect in stating that this is a "common story," and that I have "repeated it." . . . I have never read or heard of it except through the before-mentioned channel."[19]

The dispute did not end there. In the 'Remarks' published in the third edition of his *History*, Siborne did not pull his punches: 'Mr Gleig has found it very convenient to copy nearly all those feats I have described, as well as numerous incidents detailed in my work, into his "Story," merely taking care not to employ precisely the same words, for this would be rather too glaring an act of literary piracy."[20]

Siborne then went on to relate a conversation he had had with Gleig on Egerton's review of the *History* in the June 1845 edition of the *Quarterly Review*. Wellington's memorandum written for Egerton's use here found its way into the review almost verbatim. The issue of Wellington being able to see Ligny with his glass was discussed in their conversation, and Gleig agreed that Wellington's assertion could not be true. Nevertheless, it was repeated as fact and embellished in the *Story*, a clear indication of who had inspired Gleig's work.

If that was not enough to show who was pulling the strings, Gleig went on to describe the arrival of the news of the outbreak of hostilities in Brussels on 15 June, writing, 'The Duke himself sat down to dinner at three o'clock – ignorant that a shot had been fired, or a French column put in motion. It was then that the Prince of Orange, coming in from the outposts to share his Grace's hospitality, made him aware, for the first time, that the Prussians had been attacked at Thuin.'[21] This is the exact story Wellington told Egerton in his memoranda of September 1842 and June 1845. However, these documents first came into the public domain only after the Duke's death in 1852. Knowledge of their content could only originate from Egerton or Wellington, or both. Egerton is hardly likely to have disclosed that confidential information to a third party without permission.

Historical fact was not the issue; Wellington's image was. The motive was also evident to Siborne, who wrote,

> If, with the courtesy usually observable in such matters, Mr Gleig had previously communicated with me, or Mr Murray with my Publishers, either of those gentlemen would have ascertained that it was the intention of the latter to put forth a cheaper edition of my work as soon as arrangements could be made for that purpose. The withholding of any

such communication looks very like 'stealing a march' upon both author and publishers, and tends to the inference that a work which was sold for two guineas a copy, and the fact that its first edition was exhausted within a few weeks of its publication, presented a temptation not easily resisted by individuals who would not scruple to 'get up' the identical subject, embodying all the contents of that work, with perhaps a new head and tail, as well as a new title, and at a low price – in short, with a book at six shillings to drive one at two guineas out of the market.[22]

Siborne then went on to reproduce several columns of Gleig's text, comparing it with his own, just in case there would be any doubt as to the origin of the information. Much of the material Siborne had accumulated on the battle since 1834 was unique. The information in the letters from various eyewitnesses was in his private correspondence and had only been published in his *History*. Siborne then continued,

A greater proof of plagiarism on the part of any writer could scarcely be adduced than the circumstance of his transcribing not merely the substance of an author's statements, but also his errors: for since the publication of the second edition of my History, I have ascertained, partly through discussion in the 'United Service Magazine', and partly through additional correspondence with surviving eye-witnesses, that it contained four or five errors. It is curious that these *identical errors*, which have been rectified in the present edition, should have been faithfully copied by Mr Gleig into his 'Story' – I say *copied*, because it is impossible, in the face of them, to draw any other conclusion.[23]

It is interesting to note that while Gleig later went to the trouble of writing to *The Times* to point out a very minor error in his *Story*, he never answered Siborne's charges against him.[24]

Gleig's book killed two birds with one stone: first, he destroyed any chance of Siborne profiting from a mass-market edition of his *History*. Siborne would now not have this chance of reducing his debts. Gleig received an advance of 200 guineas (£210) for his trouble, money that would now not be available to Siborne.[25] With his popular, condensed editions of Wellington's *Dispatches*, Gurwood made at least £10,000, spread over eight volumes.[26] On that basis, a single-volume edition of Siborne's *History* could have potentially earned him around £1,000, so the damage done was substantial. Secondly, the print run of Gleig's *Story* was considerably larger than that of Siborne's *History*; 5,000 copies of each of the two parts were printed for the release in June 1847, with the same number being generated by three more print runs in the next two years. Gleig saw to it that the masses read Wellington's questionable version of the campaign in preference to Siborne's factually accurate account.

Subsequent historiography has followed the lead given by Gleig. The first account of the campaign so influenced was Cotton's *A Voice from Waterloo*, first published in 1847 and aimed at the battlefield tourist,[27] and most successive accounts have followed Gleig's line.

13 *Charge!*

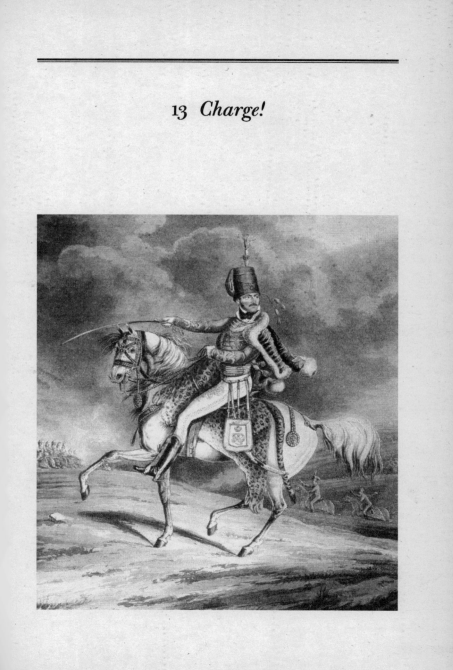

Earl of Uxbridge

'When I was returning to our position I met the Duke of Wellington, surrounded by all the *Corps militaire*, who had from the high ground witnessed the whole affair. The plain appeared to be swept clean, and I never saw so joyous a group as was this *Troupe dorée*. They thought the Battle was over. It is certain that our Squadrons went into and over several Squares of Infantry, and it is not possible to conceive greater confusion and panic than was exhibited at this moment.'

The Marquess of Anglesey, 8 November 1839

Some time after the exhibition of the Large Model in 1838, Siborne decided to make a further model of the Battle of Waterloo. The first mention of this was in a letter to Lt-Colonel Thomas Marten, dated 16 July 1840, in which he mentioned 'Being occupied in constructing another Model, of which the scale is so large that the figures will be nine times the size of those in the former one' and asked him for details of the first charge of the Household Brigade.[1] At Waterloo, Marten had been a cornet in the 2nd Life Guards. A month later, Siborne told Lt James Hope of his plan to make a model of a 'glorious scene'.[2] On 1 August 1842, in a letter to Lord Grennock, Siborne stated he was in the process of constructing a further model.[3] While Siborne's records do not reveal his motives, the circumstances surrounding this event indicate his likely train of thought. The Large Model had first been exhibited in 1838, and the *Guide* issued to coincide with this mentioned the *History*. It had been his original intention to publish the *History* simultaneously with the exhibition, but as always, nothing ever seemed to work out quite right for Siborne.

In 1842, Barker's famous and highly successful *Waterloo Panorama* was exhibited again in Leicester Square, London. While this exhibition was not as successful as the original, its appearance indicated the continuing popularity of the theme of Waterloo. Siborne needed an event to upstage this to get his name back in the limelight to coincide with the publication of his *History*.

Then, on 15 August, ill health forced Lord Hill to resign as Commander-in-Chief, and he died shortly afterwards. When Wellington took over the position, Siborne's hope that one day Hill would honour the promises made in 1830 came to an end. He no longer had that unrealistic dream to cling to, particularly as the Duke was to hold that post for the remainder of his life (outliving Siborne, who was younger, by three years). It was time for Siborne to move on.

That month, Siborne started gathering information for the New Model. He corresponded with Colonel Sir De Lacy Evans, who was an Extra ADC to Sir William Ponsonby at Waterloo. Ponsonby had been mortally wounded leading the 2nd (Union) Brigade of cavalry during the Great Cavalry Charge. Siborne was attempting to establish the details of the movements of d'Erlon's corps, which the Earl of Uxbridge's cavalry had charged. As always, when investigating an issue, Siborne started with the person likely to have the best overview and then checked the details with other eyewitnesses. He now needed to move on and establish the movements of the British cavalry that charged d'Erlon's advancing columns, chasing them back to their starting positions.

After having established the details of d'Erlon's movements, Siborne re-examined a memorandum that Lord Edward Somerset had sent him on 4 April 1835.[4] This document had outlined the role of the Brigade of Household Cavalry that Somerset commanded at Waterloo. Using this memorandum and information obtained from other sources, at some stage Siborne drew up several long memoranda outlining the events. He was probably going to send them to Somerset for comment, but the latter passed away on 1 September 1842, aged seventy-six. Instead, Siborne sent these documents to Henry Paget, the Marquess of Anglesey, in 1815 the Earl of Uxbridge, for his observations.[5]

Wellington and Anglesey had long harboured animosity caused by an earlier family dispute. In 1809, Paget had eloped with Lady Charlotte Wellesley, wife of Wellington's youngest brother, who was also named Henry. This was one of the great scandals of the time, affecting as it did not only Britain's most successful military commander, but also her greatest cavalry leader of the day. Fortunately, both men do not seem to have let their feelings cloud their military judgement and they worked well together on the field of battle.

Siborne had exchanged a few letters over the years with the Marquess. Anglesey was among the first of the subscribers to the *History*, and he gave information on the events of 17 June 1815 in the letter he wrote to Siborne when ordering his copy. Their correspondence continued over the next few weeks, with the subject of the Great Cavalry Charge being discussed. Wellington had not so much as mentioned this significant event in the *Despatch*, but he did praise the role of Anglesey's subordinates Somerset and Ponsonby. When commenting on the withdrawal from Quatre Bras on 17 June 1815, Wellington did not commend him for his expert handling of his cavalry when covering the retreat but did say he was 'well satisfied' with the 1st Life Guards. The only time Wellington mentioned Anglesey's role at Waterloo was when he was wounded at the end of the day and lost a leg. Even then, the Duke did not mention the severity of his injury, though he did give more details of the wounds suffered by other senior officers. On the whole, Wellington was dismissive of Anglesey's role in the battle, and the Marquess bore the Duke a grudge for these snubs. As Anglesey pointed out to Siborne in his letter of 18 October 1842, 'I felt that he [Wellington] had given me *carte blanche*, and I never bothered him with a single question respecting the movements it might be necessary to make.'[6] But where was the due credit? Having a model made of his great deed by the greatest military model-maker of the period would go some way towards recompensing this slight. By collaborating with Anglesey, Siborne would be rubbing salt into an old wound and again doing little to improve his popularity in Apsley House. It would seem that he was taking the opportunity of repaying part of the debt he owed Wellington.

There is no indication in Siborne's records of exactly how he financed this New Model. What is certain is that he could not have done so himself, as he was still in debt from the Large Model. There do not appear to be any records mentioning a subscription being raised or the name of a sponsor. Despite several searches in the archives of Plas Newydd, the home of the Marquess, no correspondence on this issue has been located. However, the available facts give reason to believe it was likely to have been Anglesey himself. After all, he had both the motive and the means and had, at least, aided Siborne's research.

It is not certain where Siborne had the New Model constructed. It may again have been in Dublin, but in autumn 1843,

he moved to London to take up the post of Adjutant and Secretary to the Royal Military Asylum in Chelsea, coincidentally
next door to the building that now houses the Large Model. He
replaced the recently deceased Captain Lugard and had
applied for the post on 18 October.[7] Major-General Brown,
one of the Asylum's commissioners, supported his request.[8]
The appointment was confirmed on 10 November.[9] This post
could be considered as a sinecure for Siborne, now almost
forty-six years old and not in the best of health thanks to the
stress caused by this long drawn out affair. The fact that he got
this position, possibly in the face of opposition from Wellington, is an indication that he enjoyed considerable support from
the army. He was now in a position where he could personally
supervise the exhibition of the New Model.

At 18 feet 4 inches by 7 feet 5 inches, the New Model was
smaller than the Large Model, but it was constructed on a
larger scale – 15 feet to 1 inch, while the figures and buildings
were 6 feet to 1 inch. The terrain was made with Siborne's cus-
tomary attention to detail. The New Model was constructed in
ten sections, six of 40 inches by 45 inches, two of 50 inches by
45 inches and two of 51 inches by 45 inches. This time only
part of the battlefield was represented, namely Wellington's left
centre, the area from the ridge and Wellington's tree down to
the farmhouse of La Haye Sainte, and from there, about half a
mile to the east.

The figures, being bigger than those on the Large Model,
were even more finely detailed. The arms could be moved to
every conceivable position of attack or defence. The flintlock
of the muskets, the claymores in the Highlanders' belts, the
sergeants' pikes, the gunners' sponges and the officers' sabre-

taches were modelled with scrupulous accuracy. The generals' hats, the foot soldiers' knapsacks and the brass cuirasses of the French cavalry were detachable. Every figure was painted in the correct regimental colours, with even the tartans of the 42nd and 79th Highlanders being recognizable. This was a fabulous work of art. According to experts, only the German manufacturers of the period possessed the expertise to make such figures. The 3,000 or so figures, 25 mm tall, represented 5,000 allied infantry and 2,400 cavalry as well as 13,200 French infantry and 1,600 cavalry. The troops represented were parts of Picton's 5th Division and Anglesey's heavy cavalry brigades, under Ponsonby and Somerset, shown engaged against d'Erlon's infantry, which was supported by General Kellermann's cavalry. The French infantry formations were shown dissolving into chaos, pursued by Anglesey's troops, who themselves were breaking down into small groups over which their commanders lost control. Anglesey himself was represented by a single figure shown, of course, at the fore of his troopers and in the thick of the fighting.

Siborne also produced a *Guide* to accompany the New Model, appropriately entitled *Guide to Captain's Siborne's New Waterloo Model Representing the Splendid Charge between One and Two O'Clock by the British Heavy Cavalry under the Marquess of Anglesey and by the British Infantry under Sir Thomas Picton*. As Picton was dead, both Siborne and Anglesey stood to gain the most from the publicity generated.

Siborne intended to make a series of smaller models of various scenes from the battle to be placed on display around the Large Model, thus appearing as satellites to the Crisis, the decisive moment of the battle. As he explained in the *Guide*,

... It occurred to the constructor of the Model that, in order to present a perfect illustration of the battle, the most effectual plan would be to execute a series of additional models, presenting its most prominent and critical features, and that as such models would only comprise those portions of the field which formed the immediate scenes of action intending to be pourtrayed [*sic*], their construction would admit of being undertaken upon a larger scale, thus affording a closer insight not only into the dispositions and movements of the troops engaged, but also into those minutiæ of detail which now characterize the actual battle-field. The new Model, now submitted to view, is the first of the projected series. Whether the remainder will follow must depend on the degree of favour with which this specimen may be received by the public. It need only be further observed, that Captain Siborne's design would be rendered complete by the whole of the Models being ultimately collected and arranged in some public building, so as to constitute a highly instructive, as well as a soul-stirring, national memento of the greatest and most important battle of modern times. This, however, is a question which he leaves to the consideration of the British Government.[10]

Shaming the government into acquiring the models for permanent display to the public did not work, and the construction of the satellite models did not go beyond the earliest stages.

The New Model went on display at the Egyptian Hall in December 1844, and the *Illustrated London News* of 28 December carried an advertisement that read,

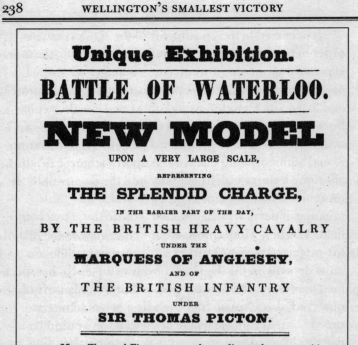

Unique Exhibition.

BATTLE OF WATERLOO.

NEW MODEL

UPON A VERY LARGE SCALE,

REPRESENTING

THE SPLENDID CHARGE,

IN THE EARLIER PART OF THE DAY,

BY THE BRITISH HEAVY CAVALRY

UNDER THE

MARQUESS OF ANGLESEY,

AND OF

THE BRITISH INFANTRY

UNDER

SIR THOMAS PICTON.

Many Thousand Figures, arranged according to the exact position of their respective corps, and in the correct uniforms worn at the time, give to this Model the complete appearance of the Battle Field.

The fields and houses are represented as on the memorable 18th June, 1815, the ground having been most minutely surveyed for this purpose.

The Duke of Wellington with his splendid Staff; the 1st and 2nd Life Guards, Blues, 1st Dragoon Guards, Royal Dragoons, Inniskillings, Scots Greys—Infantry: 1st Royals, 28th, 32nd, 44th, 95th, and 42nd, 79th, 92nd Highlanders, German Legion, Hanoverians, &c. Cavalry charging cavalry, infantry charging infantry, the discharge of cannon—in short, nothing is omitted to give a correct idea to the visitor of this glorious Charge.

EGYPTIAN HALL, PICCADILLY.

Open from Eleven in the Morning to Nine in the Evening.

ADMISSION, ONE SHILLING.

That day, the *Court Journal* carried a short review, mentioning that '. . . The figures are large enough to allow the recognition of the persons most distinguished during the action.'' One distinguished person was prominent at the head of the Splendid Charge of the British Heavy Cavalry, while the figure representing Wellington was to be seen only in the background, not directly involved in the action. This was historically accurate, as Siborne's work always was, but it is not the image that certain circles wished to be presented in public. It is likely Siborne was aware of that.

Waterloo Day 1845 was approaching. The New Model was finished and the Large Model fully restored. Siborne had repainted the figures using brighter colours. He also needed to paint over the areas from where the 40,000 Prussians had been removed. The Egyptian Hall was once again selected as the venue. Now that Siborne lived in London, it would be much easier for him to supervise the arrangements. Adverts announcing the exhibition were placed in the press. That in the *Illustrated London News* of 14 June 1845 read,

CAPTAIN SIBORNE'S WATERLOO MODELS:-
In a few days will be EXHIBITED at the EGYPTIAN HALL, Piccadilly, Captain Siborne's Original LARGE MODEL of the BATTLE OF WATERLOO, representing, on the surface of 420 square feet, the entire Field, with hostile Armies, as they were disposed, and engaged at the moment when the illustrious Wellington, with his British troops, defeated Napoleon's Imperial Guard, and thereby gained one of the most splendid victories on record. This

Model has not only been re-painted, and otherwise renovated and improved, but it has also been corrected, as
regards the Prussian co-operation, so as to make it correspond in every particular with the description of the Battle
given in Captain Siborne's 'History of the Waterloo Campaign.' The other Model, representing the Glorious
CHARGE by the BRITISH CAVALRY, led by the Marquess of Anglesey, and the BRITISH INFANTRY, by Sir
Thomas Picton, in the immediate presence of the immortal
Wellington, will continue as hitherto, that all admirers of
British valour may behold this very faithful representation
of one of the most brilliant actions recorded in history.
Captain Siborne, finding that a desire has been expressed
that those Models should be placed in some public institution, takes this opportunity of stating that he is willing to
dispose of them; and should it be desired, of those also
(partly constructed) which are intended to illustrate the
other prominent parts of the Battle, such as the Grand
Charge on the British Squares, &c.[12]

Similar adverts were run in the *United Service Gazette* and
the *Naval & Military Gazette*. This announcement contrasted
strongly with the ones that advertised the 1838 exhibition and
the 1844 exhibition of the New Model. The earlier advertisements did not mention Wellington's existence, let alone his
apparent brilliance, but the later ones emphasized the point.
On the surface, it would seem that Siborne was now trying to
curry favour with Wellington, but was there more to this than
meets the eye? Siborne must have known their relationship
was beyond repair by now. After all, the announcement of the

'error' on the Large Model in the prospectus for the subscription to the *History* in 1842 had not elicited a positive comment from Apsley House, nor had its publication in the *History* in 1844. What good would repeating the admission of the 'error' achieve? Wellington's mistreatment of Siborne was common knowledge amongst his fellow officers, so this statement must have rung hollow and would surely have sounded insincere to both Wellington and his close associates. It is quite possible that Siborne was aware of that. Was this advertisement ironic, its publication designed to cause Wellington even more embarrassment? If there was an iota of sincerity intended in Siborne's public praise of Wellington, the Duke and his supporters did not see it. Gleig would certainly make that clear.

Anglesey did, however, achieve his objective. At that year's Waterloo Banquet, Wellington made a point of toasting him and praising his role in the battle, snubbing that played by others. 'His Grace,' wrote the *Court Gazette*, 'on rising after the above toast [to the former King's German Legion], claimed the attention of his gallant guests by giving as a toast, "the Cavalry at Waterloo," with which he coupled the name of his gallant friend the Marquis of Anglesea [*sic*]. The toast was responded to with honours.'[13] The two men seemed to warm to each other again, and the next year, Anglesey was appointed Master-General of the Ordnance. He became an enthusiastic supporter of the Duke's campaign to repair and add to Britain's defences against a possible French invasion.

This exhibition ran until the end of December 1845. Certain of the visitors were well known to Siborne, as this report in the *United Service Gazette* shows: 'Last Thursday the boys of the Royal Military Asylum at Chelsea, were taken by Colonel

Brown, Commandant of the Institution, to Suffolk-street Gallery to make their annual visit. On their return through Piccadilly they had the opportunity of seeing Captain Siborne's beautiful model of Waterloo, around which they crowded most eagerly."[14]

Again, Wellington did not join the eager and admiring crowds.

It would seem that nobody responded to Siborne's attempts to dispose of the models during the exhibition of 1845, despite the great public interest on the thirtieth anniversary of the battle. It is not entirely clear what Siborne's financial situation was at this time. Both exhibitions of the models had generated some income for him. Also, the publication of the *History* and its good sales had helped. He still had some outstanding debt to clear though and he needed to see his wife was adequately provided for in the eventuality of his death. He was not in the best of health.

In any case, Siborne had no further use for the models, and as they had not made him the fortune he had hoped, he set about attempting to dispose of them. At the beginning of 1846, he mooted various ideas for their sale before deciding to attempt to raise a subscription for £4,600.[15] Unfortunately, there is no record of exactly how he thought he could achieve this, but he did contact Basil Jackson with his proposals, who replied on 5 January with his comments. They were a little too vague to ascertain what Siborne's suggestions were exactly, but they seem to have consisted of various subscription schemes, including one of prominent people and another of regiments from the British army.[16]

What Siborne's records do show is that on 6 March 1846 he wrote to Prince Albert to enquire if he would be willing to subscribe. Ten days later he was sent a positive reply. Lord Stratford too indicated his willingness, as did Fox Maude, the Secretary at War. However, Sir Robert Peel, then Prime Minister, declined to join what appeared to be a list of prominent people.[7] Nevertheless, this scheme does not seem to have shown enough potential, because by April 1846 Siborne had discussed the possibility of a regimental subscription with various officers from regiments that participated in the battle. Lt Edward Macready mentioned this proposal in a letter to Siborne dated 23 April: 'I scarcely understand how your friend Drummond proposing a subscription to the Guards which would amount to £10 a battalion should think "that every battalion of the Line might well afford to give £25". Surely the wealthy & aristocratic & Waterloo Guards should do more than commonplace mere Waterloo battalions. I think the 30th measure £1 for Captains & 10s for sub's a fair one . . .'[18]

A Waterloo Model Committee had recently been formed to collect the subscriptions, and Macready continued, 'I think the sooner the Committee meet the better'.[19] It met on the next Waterloo Day at 29 New Bond Street, just around the corner from the Egyptian Hall, and issued a statement calling for subscriptions: 'The Executive Committee of the "General Subscription for the purpose of purchasing the Model of the Battle of Waterloo and presenting it to the British Nation", take the liberty of requesting your attention to the accompanying Prospectus of the Plan, and should this meet your approval they will feel much gratified for an *early* intimation of the amount for which you may be disposed to subscribe.'[20] This

subscription raised a total of £847 13s 5d, far short of the
£4,600 Siborne had asked for.[21] Would anything ever work out
for poor Siborne?

As his *History* had received such favourable comments from
the Prussian General Staff, Siborne arranged for the New
Model to be exhibited in Berlin. It was shipped to Hamburg
for transfer to Berlin, and the model remained on display at
No. 26 Unter den Linden from early summer until 28 December 1846.[22]

While the New Model was in Berlin, Siborne took the
opportunity of offering it to the Prussian government for purchase, writing to Baron von Bunsen at the Prussian Legation in
London on 16 September. It was some time before he received
an answer. On 2 February 1847, Bunsen, after having consulted
the King of Prussia, declined the offer. He explained that,
'altho' fully appreciating this praiseworthy undertaking which
is already removed from Berlin, [the King] has declined to purchase it, not considering of such a historical interest for His
Majesty, as if *that moment* of the battle were represented, when
the arrival of the Prussian Army contributed to the Glory of
that day'.[23] There is no record of Siborne having offered the
Prussians the Large Model, with or without the full comple-
ment of Prussian figures. It seems he had other plans for it.

As he was completing the third edition of his *History*, Siborne
made a final attempt to dispose of the Large Model, approaching the United Service Institute (USI) on 15 November 1847.
He proposed that the model should be displayed in a room of
sufficient dimensions and the public be allowed free access.

A subscription was to be raised, the minimum sum being £200. The Council of the USI considered his memorandum at their next meeting on 6 December.[24] A week later, Siborne wrote to Gawler, who was acting as an intermediary, suggesting that if the Council wanted on principle to charge for access to the model, they might make it a nominal sum of say one penny, which would then go towards the subscription. In that event, Siborne would waive the condition of a minimum subscription of £200, or any sum.

The Council, having read both documents, agreed to adopt the proposal, provided there would not be a prospective loss to the USI. A subcommittee consisting of the Chairman Shadwell Clerke, Vice-Chairman Colonel Yorke, Captain Sweny and Major-General Cleveland would execute the arrangements after having taken legal advice. Furthermore, the Secretary was directed to establish which room would be best to exhibit the model in. The same day, the Chairman wrote to Siborne to inform him of their agreement to his terms, subject to legal advice, and that a subcommittee had been formed to manage this project.

For once, it seemed Siborne was making progress with the disposal of the model, but it was not to be. The Meeting of Council on 7 February 1848 noted, 'The Proceedings of the Waterloo Model Committee were read in which they requested, in consequence of the Solicitor's report, that they could not recommend to the Council to proceed any further at present.'[25] The solicitor's report has not been preserved, so one can only speculate as to the reason. The arrangement suggested would seem to have been too vague on the issue of title.

The Waterloo Model Committee met again on 30 March

and reported its recommendations to the Council on 4 April. It was proposed that the members of the institution raise a general subscription of five shillings (25p) each to purchase the model. This was accepted and a circular to that effect drafted and sent to the printers. This arrangement was acceptable to Siborne, who wrote to Clerke on 8 May in confirmation. The minutes of 3 July noted this and instructed Colonels Yorke and Stanhope, and Captains Sweny, Ford and Fraser to recommend the best site. This was discussed and in the minutes of 7 August it was noted that a special room would be constructed to house the model in the proposed extension to the museum.

It would seem that Siborne's dilemma was finally resolved. However, he was on extended sick leave when this decision was made.[26] Aged fifty-one, Siborne died on 13 January 1849 of a disease of the intestines he had suffered from for several years at the Royal Military Asylum, with Dr James Magee in attendance.[27] He was aware that his condition was terminal, as he made his last will and testament just three days before his demise. In it, he left his manuscripts, sword and military accoutrements to his son Herbert and all his remaining estate and effects to his wife Helen. She was executrix and a friend by the name of Thomas Hornby of Saint Swithins Lane, London, Gentleman, was executor. Unfortunately, the will tells us nothing about the model. However, as the will was probated on 9 December 1851, it seems the issue of the model's ownership was not easily resolved.[28]

Siborne was buried alongside his mother in Brompton Cemetery, London. Their gravestone bore the inscription, 'Sacred to the Memory of Charlotte Siborne, widow of Benjamin Siborne, a Captain in Her Majesty's 9th Regiment of

Foot, died 16th January 1845 in the 74th year of her age. Also to that of Capt. William Siborne, son of the above who died on 13 January 1849 in the 51st year of his age. The deceased was Secretary of the Royal Military Asylum Chelsea, Author of the History of the War in France & Belgium in 1815 and Constructor of the Waterloo Models.'

The future location of the model was still unresolved on Siborne's death. The estimate for the cost of the construction of the Waterloo Model Room at the USM came to £1,000. Work started in 1849, and the room was completed and ready for use on 11 February 1850.[29] It would seem that the proposed exposition in London, inspired by Prince Albert, might have led to this planned extension of the USM. The Prince's plans were realized and led to the Great Exhibition of 1851.

At the Nineteenth Anniversary Meeting of the USI, held on 2 March 1850, the membership were informed that 'On the subject of the Waterloo Model the COUNCIL regret that they have no information to communicate to the Meeting. The affairs of the late Captain Siborne being yet unsettled, no negotiation on the subject of the Model has as yet been resumed with the COUNCIL.'[30] The project continued to be discussed at Council meetings and a new subscription was raised in May 1850, netting £280 5s.

On 6 July 1850, a notice was then placed in *The Times* requesting £800 to redeem the model from the mortgage. This would seem to have been successful, because a week later, Colonel Lindsay was able to report to the Council that 'considerable Progress had been made toward obtaining the necessary sum for the purchase of the Model of the Battle of Waterloo'.[31]

The USI's solicitor was instructed to contact the mortgagee's solicitor to arrange its transfer to the possession of the USI. On 5 August, Colonel Lindsay informed the Council that the sum required had indeed been raised and the legal formalities were now being completed. The Council expressed its approbation to him.

Matters are rarely simple when lawyers get involved and there were further delays. At the Twentieth Anniversary Meeting on 1 March 1851, the membership was told that legal problems had led to delays in resolving the issue.[32] These difficulties dragged on for another few months, but on 17 July 1851, Lindsay was able to report to the Council 'the completion of the assignment of the Model of the Battle of Waterloo, to the Institution'.[33] The model left storage, presumably in Belfast, and arrived at the USM a few days later. Its arrival was reported to the Council on 4 August and it was ready for inspection a few days afterwards. A private viewing was held on 7 August for members and their guests, and Prince Albert was requested to honour this event with his presence. Thereafter, it was opened daily to all parties furnished with a ticket of admission signed by a member. Siborne's *Guide* was reprinted with a new plan and sold for sixpence.[34] The version of the model exhibited was, of course, that with the 40,000 Prussians removed. It remained there for more than a century.

Siborne was never to see the final results of his great labours: over twenty years after the model was commissioned for display in the USM, after a long and twisting route that led from Dublin to London, all around Britain and then back to Ireland, it finally arrived in the institution for which it was originally designed – the United Service Museum.

14 *Humbugged?*

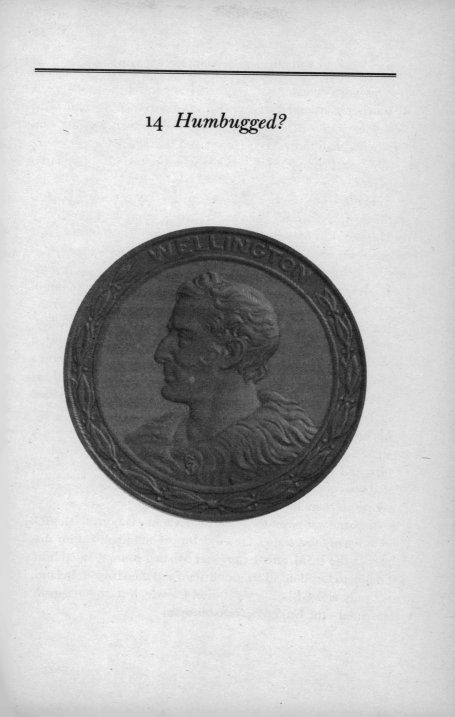

Wellington medallion

'Truth-lover was our English Duke,
'Who never sold the truth to serve the hour;
'Whatever record leap to light,
'He shall never be shamed.'
Tennyson's 'Ode on the Death of the Duke of Wellington', Stanza VII

As Wellington pondered over his *Waterloo Despatch* the morning after the battle, a great deal must have been going through his mind. The affair had certainly been a near-run thing, and there had been several crucial moments when the balance could have tipped in the other direction. One of these was his reaction, or lack of it, to the arrival of the news of the outbreak of hostilities on the morning of 15 June 1815. The Duke must have considered very carefully what he should say about that moment. He had, after all, made various promises to his Prussian allies in the days and hours before this event, promises he had largely failed to keep. Crucially, it was the Allied strategy in this campaign to defend Brussels to the fore. Militarily, this was a highly risky matter as it involved concentrating to the fore in the face of an offensive from the most brilliant captain of the era, rather than the safe bet of falling back in the face of an advance by Napoleon's experienced troops. Strategically, that would have meant abandoning the city of Brussels to Napoleon. Politically, that was unacceptable as the loss of this city would have destabilized the newly founded Kingdom of the Netherlands and the uncomfortable and forced union of what is modern-day Belgium with the Netherlands. A victory to Napoleon could have upset the balance of power so carefully re-established at the Congress of Vienna.

It has often been said that Napoleon's offensive took the Allies by surprise. The Emperor thought this and later claimed so in his accounts of the Hundred Days. As with all myths, there is an element of truth in this story. The Allies were, however, far from surprised and were aware of Napoleon's every move. In the days leading up to the outbreak of hostilities, there had been various reports of the build-up of French forces on the northern border of France. Officially, war had not been declared, so the border between France and the Kingdom of the Netherlands was open. Travellers and businessmen still crossed it, bringing with them information on the French concentration. The postal system was still operating, with news from Paris reaching Brussels quite normally. Spies and informants were operating behind the lines. Napoleon was aware of how openly information was moving and did his best to cover his movements and intentions by spreading disinformation.

The reports Wellington was getting were, however, largely accurate. He had two main sources: his informants in Paris and his listening post at Mons, close to the border. He had informants in the highest places in Napoleon's government, including the Ministry of Police and Général Bertrand's cabinet. His agent in the Ministry of Police was no less a person than the minister himself, the double-dealing Joseph Fouché, who had placed bets on all eventualities. Bertrand was actually married to the niece of a serving British army officer, Colonel Henry Dillon, who used his family connections to obtain confidential information. Wellington was highly confident of the efficiency of his network of agents. Indeed, he boasted to

Müffling that 'Prince Blücher's espionage was badly organised, [but he] was very certain of his, and that he would hear immediately of everything in Paris that was on the march to the Netherlands.'[1]

Major-General von Dörnberg, a Hanoverian holding a command in the King's German Legion, was in charge of the listening post at Mons. Historians have often blamed him for failing to send on vital news to Wellington, but an examination of the record shows this not to be true. On most days leading up to the outbreak of hostilities, Dörnberg sent at least one, and often more, reports to Brussels. The record also shows that most of this information was reliable.

The Prussians were not idle and they had their own sources of information, conducting reconnaissances deep into France and gathering news from various spies. Wellington and Blücher regularly passed on reports to each other, and at the frontier, the Netherlanders and the Prussians exchanged all the intelligence they received. It seemed that all eventualities were covered.

As Siborne established, Wellington received the news of the outbreak of hostilities at 9 a.m., so why, then, did the Duke not react immediately? Napoleon was also aware of Wellington's informants, and it is most likely that Fouché provided the Emperor with information regarding them, so covering this particular bet. And Fouché was also doing his best to keep on the right side of the royalists, just in case they were to return to power. There is an account in his memoirs of how he claimed to have squared this particularly complex circle:

> In such a decisive moment, my situation was delicate and difficult; I did not want Napoleon any more, and knew that

if he were victorious in this campaign, I would continue to suffer his yoke along with the rest of France, as a victory would prolong his disastrous rule. I had also made commitments to Louis XVIII, which I was not only inclined to keep, but which prudence required me to guarantee. Furthermore, my agents had promised both Metternich and Wellington to move mountains. The generalissimo [Wellington] required that I at least obtain the plan of campaign for him . . . This is what I decided. I had certain knowledge that the unexpected invasion by Napoleon would most likely take place between 16 [June] and, at the latest, 18 [June]. Napoleon wanted to fight a battle with the English army on the 17th, separating it from the Prussians, after having pushed the latter back. He expected to be all the more successful with his plan, as Wellington, on the basis of false information, believed he would be able to put back the commencement of the campaign until 1 July. The success of Napoleon's undertaking thus depended on surprise. I made my moves accordingly; on the day of Napoleon's departure [from Paris to the front], I sent Madame D. with a message in cipher containing the plan of campaign. At the same time, I laid a number of obstacles at the place she would have to cross the border, so that she could only reach Wellington's headquarters after the event. This accounts for the inexplicable uncertainty of the generalissimo, which has surprised everybody and caused much speculation.[2]

Although there was a legal dispute over Fouché's memoirs at the time they were published in which their veracity was challenged, this story does have a ring of authenticity: can Wellington's delayed reaction to the news of the outbreak of hostilities be explained by him waiting for what he considered to be absolutely reliable information from Paris, information that never arrived? Was this how Napoleon humbugged Wellington? It is interesting to note that Wellington was livid when Alison repeated Fouché's account of this episode in his *History*.

If Wellington had admitted in his *Despatch* that he had failed to react to this news for hours, in circumstances that required immediate action and after having promised rapid support to his Prussian allies, he would have had a lot of explaining to do. Coming up with an excuse would have been all the more difficult, because after he realized he had made a major error of judgement, the Duke continued to give the Prussians the impression that all was running to plan. What would seem to have happened is that once he realized he had made this mistake, Wellington was on the horns of a dilemma. If he had admitted to the Prussians Napoleon had humbugged him, then the chances are they would have fallen back, leaving Wellington to bear the brunt of Napoleon's assault. Without Prussian support, Wellington would have suffered the first defeat of his career and Brussels fallen to the French. He could not allow that to happen. Keeping his cool in circumstances in which a lesser man would have gone to pieces, the Great Duke decided to bluff and muddle his way through, hoping that things would work out in the end.

At 7 p.m., just after having issued his first orders, Wellington had Müffling write a letter to Blücher. This letter contained the words, 'As soon as the moon comes out, the Reserve will march off, and, if the enemy does not attack at Nivelles immediately, then the Duke will be at Nivelles with his entire force tomorrow to support Your Highness, or, in the event of the enemy having already attacked, after consultations with you, will move on either his flank or rear.'[3] This document survived the ravages of the Second World War and can still be viewed in the Prussian Archives in Berlin. When the German Waterloo historian Julius von Pflugk-Harttung examined it at the beginning of the twentieth century, it still had a British wax seal on its cover, was marked 'immediate' and bore three crosses, which was the British system for indicating it had to be given absolute priority. A British courier must have carried it and not one of Müffling's aides. British horseflesh was said to be the finest in Europe at this time, and as the greatest haste was required, a red-coated dragoon was sent bearing the news. Though Wellington was clearly the source of this information, he had issued no such orders and was not in a position to get his entire forces to Nivelles the next day. He was using Müffling as a dupe to provide Blücher with false information, information that would cause the Prussians to hold their positions in expectation of support from Wellington.

After having received further information from the front, particularly confirmation from Blücher that he was indeed holding his positions, Wellington issued a second set of orders at 10 p.m., the 'After Orders'. While the movements ordered would go some way towards closing the gap between Wellington's forces and Blücher's, the Duke had yet to commit himself to a particular course of action. That is, however, not what he had Müffling tell his headquarters. Around midnight on 15 June,

Müffling sent a further report to Blücher indicating that Wellington's army would be concentrated within twelve hours, and that he would have 20,000 men at Quatre Bras by 10 a.m. on 16 June. Wellington knew that was simply not possible. However, this information confirmed his earlier assurances to the Prussians. Indeed, on the morning of 15 June, Müffling had reported to Blücher on behalf of Wellington that 'The Anglo-Batavian army is, according to the enclosed order-of-battle, deployed in such a way that Lord Hill and the Prince of Orange, in positions from Enghien via Braine le Comte to Nivelle[s], can be concentrated in a short time.'[4]

Wellington's deception of the Prussians did not stop there. At 10.30 a.m. on 16 June, he sent Blücher a letter from Frasnes, a village just south of Quatre Bras, in which he presented the concentration of his army as much more advanced than he knew it to be. It is noteworthy that this letter was the one and only communication sent from his headquarters in the entire campaign that was in the Duke's own hand. Müffling, who would have been aware that his master was being sent false information, was for once not asked to write out this document. Wellington must have been very concerned that the Prussians might include a copy of this letter in one of the parcels they sent to Siborne, and fear of its publication in the third edition of the *History* might go some way to explain the Duke's determination to damage Siborne's credibility.[5]

Wellington had lost the initiative to Napoleon and was in danger of leaving the Prussians out on a limb. His lack of action had severely endangered the security of Brussels and the success of the war. He decided to use the Prussians to hold up Napoleon and buy the time needed for him to find a way through. Of course, he never told them, and should this ever have become public knowledge at the time, the consequences could well have been severe. By raising this issue and refuting parts of the Duke's *Despatch*, Siborne was threatening to undermine one of the pillars of the British establishment.

Not only did Siborne draw attention to the implausibility of Wellington's account of the timing of the outbreak of hostilities, he also challenged the Duke's position on the effectiveness of the Prussian intervention at the Battle of Waterloo. Why was it the Duke did not want to give his ally full credit for its role in the battle? It was just not a question of promoting an over-inflated ego, an act of glory grabbing when there was enough to go around for all. Wellington was not merely pursuing fame and fortune to a greater extent than he already possessed. He was fearful of Prussia's territorial ambitions and the effect this would have on the balance of power in Europe. It was not in Britain's best interests for him to say anything that would give weight to the claims of 'mine enemy', as the Duke once described the Prussians.

Siborne was scornful of the charge made by Wellington's supporters that Zieten had neglected to inform the Duke of the events at the front early on the morning of 15 June 1815. In the third edition of his *History*, he commented,

> I have already shown that Zieten forwarded reports to his Grace on the 13th and 14th (either directly or through General Müffling), of the actual state of affairs in his front, and that these were found to be perfectly consistent with those which had been received from other quarters. Such was

their tendency that in a letter, still extant, written by General Müffling on the morning of the 15th, to General Count Gneisenau, the chief of the Prussian staff, it appears that at the Duke's head-quarters it had been considered very probable that the enemy would have attacked even on the 14th. He had thus fully prepared the Duke for that which there was abundant reason to expect would very shortly take place.[6]

Referring to Gleig, Siborne continued that he did 'very much regret that any English writer should have cast so severe a censure of negligence upon our gallant Prussian allies for not having communicated to the British head-quarters earlier intelligence of the events upon the Sambre on the morning of the 15th of June'.[7] Sadly, despite Siborne's refutation of the charges against Zieten, historians today continue to repeat them.

Not only is the Wellingtonian version of the outbreak of hostilities questionable. Other accounts of the events at the Duchess of Richmond's ball in Brussels on 15 June conflict with the received wisdom. Once Wellington had issued his 'After Orders', he prepared to go to the ball. Just after he arrived, the festivities were interrupted. Around midnight, Lt Henry Webster of the 9th Light Dragoons (and not Müffling) reached Brussels after riding from the front at breakneck speed with urgent news. Some years later, Webster told the story. Although a little inaccurate in places, his account of the scene is most informative:

At ten o'clock _____ [name omitted[8]], the minister came to me, telling me that the advanced guard of the Prussians had been driven in at Ligny [in fact Charleroi]; and ordering me, without a moment's delay, to convey the despatch he put in my hand to the Prince of Orange. 'A horse ready-saddled awaits you at the door,' he said, 'and another has been sent on, half an hour ago, to a half-way house, to help you on the faster. Gallop every yard! You will find your chief at the Duchess of Richmond's ball. [It is more likely that Webster was told to go to Wellington's headquarters because he could not know what time the Prince of Orange was going to leave Wellington's headquarters to go to the ball.] Stand on no ceremony; but insist on seeing the Prince at once.' I was in my saddle without a second's delay; and thanks to a fine moon and two capital horses, had covered the ten miles [actually nearer twenty miles] I had to go within the hour! [He needed more like two hours.] The Place at Brussels was all ablaze with light; and such was the crowd of carriages, that I could not well make way through them on horseback; so I abandoned my steed to the first man I could get hold of, and made my way on foot to the porter's lodge.[9]

An officer of Picton's 5th Division witnessed Webster's arrival: '. . . An orderly dragoon [Webster], covered with dust and foam, arrived at the hotel of the Commanding General, bearing despatches from the front, and earnestly inquired of the Duke of Wellington. He was taken to the house of the Duke of Richmond . . .'[10]

Webster continued,

On my telling the Suisse [a servant] I had despatches of moment for the Prince, he civilly asked me if I would wait for five minutes; 'for,' said he, 'the Duchess has just given orders for the band to go upstairs, and the party are now about the rise. If you were to burst in suddenly, it might alarm the ladies.' On that consideration I consented to wait. I peeped in between the folding doors and saw the Duchess of Richmond taking the Prince of Orange's arm, and Lady Charlotte Greville the Duke's, on their way to the ball-room. The moment they had reached the foot of the stairs, I hastened to the Prince's side and gave him the despatch. Without looking at it, he handed it behind him to the Duke, who quietly deposited it in his coat-pocket.

The Prince of Orange claimed he opened the note and informed Wellington of its contents, which the Duke did not want to believe. This seems more likely, as the despatch was addressed to the Prince and not the Duke. Webster concluded,

The Prince made me a sign to remain in the hall. I did so. All the company passed by me, while I hid myself in a recess from observation for fear of being asked awkward questions. As soon as the last couple had mounted the *première étage*, the Duke of Wellington descended, and espying me, beckoned me to him, and said, in a low voice, 'Webster! Four horses instantly to the Prince of Orange's carriage for Waterloo!'[11]

In fact, the Prince returned to his headquarters in Braine-le-Comte and did so in such a hurry that he forgot to take his sword. Webster was awarded a sabre of honour with a gold hilt for his services that evening.

The crucial sentence of the message read, 'At this instant,

Captain Baron de Gagern has just arrived from Nivelles with a report that the enemy has already pushed as far as Quatre Bras.'[112] A lesser man than Wellington might well have been crushed by this news. Quatre Bras was a vital crossroads on the highway from Brussels to Namur. The main line of communication between the Duke's and Blücher's headquarters ran along this road. Wellington's army was too weak in numbers to face Napoleon alone, so the support of the Prussians was vital. With communications cut, coordination of their actions would now be impaired and the success of the campaign thrown into jeopardy. Furthermore, in his first orders Wellington had instructed the only troops he had at that point to move elsewhere, abandoning Quatre Bras to the French. With this mistake, Wellington had played right into Napoleon's hands.

The Duke did not panic. Aware that it was too late to accelerate the long process of sending orders to his furthest detachments, he merely ordered his troops in the Brussels area, particularly Picton's division, to be prepared to start their march from Brussels the next morning earlier than originally planned. An officer of that division related, 'Whatever these despatches [as carried by Webster] contained, the arrival of which would soon be whispered around the room, and create a sensation, no further change was made in the chief's arrangements as concerned us, than altering the hour of departure in the morning from four to two o'clock.'[113] This division would be the first to leave the city that morning, forming the head of the column marching down the highway from Brussels to the important road junction just south of the then almost unknown village of Waterloo and onwards.

Between 2 a.m. and 3 a.m., Wellington left the ball to snatch a couple of hours sleep. The scene was now set for the unfolding of the remainder of this drama.

The victor writes the history. Rarely has this old adage been more apposite than when applied to Wellington and Waterloo. While an objective analysis of Wellington's role and achievements in this campaign show it not to have been his finest hour, history normally regards Waterloo as being his greatest victory.[14] There are several reasons for this. Wellington was well aware of the need to promote his image. Personal and national interests often coincided and overlapped. Being aware that he symbolized Britain's standing in Europe, he carefully projected and protected that picture. The Duke's role in the Peninsular War, where his constant victories over the French made him famous, gave much of Europe hope that Napoleon would eventually be deposed. It would be easy for Wellington to persuade public opinion that what he said and did was always right. The European states then were dependent on British loans and subsidies to finance the war against France, so there was also a case of he who pays the piper. Furthermore, during the campaign in the Low Countries in 1815, certain of the Allied states, particularly the Netherlanders and smaller German states, were constantly looking over their shoulders at Prussia, whose territorial ambitions caused them considerable concern. Britain and Prussia had come close to going to war in January 1815 with each other over the spoils of post-Napoleonic Europe, so these states looked towards Britain for protection, a role Wellington gladly took up. It is little wonder that public opinion in these countries favoured the history that presented

Wellington as the victor of Waterloo, rather than the Prussians. Had the Duke given the Prussians full credit for their role in the battle, it would probably have led to them making even louder demands for further territorial aggrandisement, upsetting the balance of power so laboriously established at the Congress of Vienna. Wellington's version prevailed.

Waterloo generated a large amount of coverage in the weeks and months following the Battle. Virtually without exception, these accounts and histories toed Wellington's line, particularly when it came to the time at which Wellington first heard the news of the outbreak of hostilities and the role of the Prussian army at Waterloo. It is interesting to note that while Napoleon's official reports on his battles gave rise to the saying 'to lie like a bulletin', challenging the veracity of parts of Wellington's *Waterloo Despatch* caused Siborne considerable problems.

Siborne started this affair as a bright, enthusiastic, hard-working but somewhat naive lieutenant. He must have been overjoyed when, on that fateful day early in 1830, Lord Hill commissioned him to make the Large Model. A man of great talents, both as an artist and as a cartographer, this was the chance of a lifetime for him to prove himself. Fame and fortune beckoned, but fate had chosen another, more tortuous path for him. Of course, Siborne unquestionably accepted the word of two great generals of the British army, Hill and Hardinge, and acted accordingly. How could he have possibly imagined that Hardinge's memory of their agreement would fade after a change of government and that he would later claim so implausibly that he had not agreed to finance the model until it was finished?

The time spent at La Haye Sainte must have been like paradise on earth for Siborne. The documentation he produced of the battlefield was exhaustive, unique and a great historical treasure. If that was not enough, the voluminous archive of eyewitness accounts provides the student of the campaign with material that would never have come to light were it not for Siborne. The models, particularly the Large Model, are monumental, in all senses of the word, allowing future generations to understand the significance of Waterloo as well as Victorian Britain's perception of its importance.

Any one of the setbacks Siborne suffered would have caused most men to give up. For Siborne, though, no obstacle was too high to overcome. First there was a parsimonious Whig government, one hostile to Wellington. Siborne, honour-bound to meet his obligations to his tradesmen, raised money on his own account, a heavy burden that was to accompany him for much of the rest of his life. Then came Wellington's great hostility when he realized that Siborne had uncovered the truth. It took quite some time for Siborne to realize what was going on. At first, he must have been a little incredulous, but when it became clear what he was up against, Siborne fought back as hard as he could. Our David did not fell this Goliath, but he did give him serious trouble. Siborne's personal courage in taking on such a formidable adversary – one of the most powerful men in the world at the time – and his determination to bring to light historical truth, is admirable.

Apsley House treated Siborne most unfairly. He never got the promotion he was promised. Funding was not made available until after his death. He was accused of making the model when on duty, when in fact he devoted years of his own time to it. The claim that Siborne had never contacted the Commander-in-Chief or his senior officers was not true, and Wellington demonstrably knew that. Nevertheless, this rumour was spread for years. The assertion that Siborne's apparent pro-Prussian stance was due to his German origins was equally without foundation. The malicious tale that the model was a confused mess of no historical value was put about to damage his reputation. In case there are those who would argue that Siborne's problems were exacerbated by overenthusiastic advisors acting on Wellington's behalf, it should be remembered that the paper trail can be traced back to the Duke himself and that there are eyewitnesses who recorded certain of the malicious statements he made about Siborne at public gatherings. There can be no doubt as to his involvement.

Every time Siborne suffered a knock, he picked himself up and worked towards the next opportunity of ending his plight. Every time it looked like he was going to achieve that, Wellington was waiting with the next blow. The negative review of his *History* inspired by the Duke was published to coincide with the exhibition of the models on the thirtieth anniversary of the battle, when it would cause the most damage. The mass-market version of the *History* would have brought Siborne several hundred pounds and done much to ensure that historical truth would have reached a broader public. A certain high authority thwarted that; Gleig's *Story* prevailed and continues to do so today. Wellington's manipulation of the record has been highly successful.

Siborne's slightly myopic quest for the historical truth must have worried Wellington. Siborne's correspondence with the Prussian General Staff and his access to their archives was the one matter the Duke feared most, as his deception of his allies in 1815 could well have come to light. Wellington was, however, spared that ignominy in his lifetime. The Duke's anger against this junior officer was not motivated by vanity alone. His image was more than a projection of his ego; Wellington symbolized the struggle against Napoleon. His success reflected the standing of Britain in the world. His disgrace – and Siborne could well have destroyed Wellington's reputation – would have damaged Britain.

One could with considerable justification charge Wellington with gross abuse of his power – and, even at the time, there were those that did. Equally, one could charge Siborne with a considerable degree of obstinacy. Had he simply done what he had been told, he could well have become a wealthy man. However, Siborne placed historical accuracy above financial gain and, to my mind, one must respect him for that.

Siborne's story has now been told. Although there is the occasional gap in the record, a wealth of material is available from which to draw. His attempts to ensure that history was not rewritten were valiant, but eventually cost him his health. By the time of his death, the personal financial problems the model caused him were now more or less resolved. He ended the affair with his integrity largely intact, albeit at great cost to his person. This makes it all the more deplorable that rather than follow his example of conducting critical research from corroborated primary sources, many Waterloo historians prefer to toe the Wellingtonian line on various points, despite its obvious inconsistencies. It is time that justice was done for Siborne, and hopefully the record is at last straight: the visitor to the National Army Museum can now understand what great efforts went into producing the Large Waterloo Model.

Siborne's brother officers appreciated his labours and their obituary to him read,

We regret to state that our esteemed friend Captain William Siborne, died on the 13th instant, at his residence, the Royal Military Asylum at Chelsea, of which institution he was the Military Secretary and Adjutant. It is with pain we add, that this excellent officer and very amiable man succumbed to a lingering illness, which was originally produced by nine years of close application to his well known and splendid model of the Battle of Waterloo, and further exasperated by repeated disappointments as to its destination.

This unequalled model was, in the first instance, undertaken at the behest of the Government, but became neglected and ultimately abandoned by them, to the bitter mortification and loss of the ingenious Captain; who also wrote an accurate and detailed history of the war in France and Belgium in 1815, to illustrate his laborious and elaborate work. The task was both onerous and expensive; and what ought to have been a sure means of preferment and profit, proved only the fruitful source of vexation and illness. Indeed, when we recollect how many officers have been placed on the Staff for having merely been able to copy a military plan, we think of Siborne, and grieve!

There can be no doubt that Strathfieldsaye [sic] would be the proper location for this extraordinary and historic model; but in default of that measure, we hope it will rest where the Captain was desirous it should do, namely, in the United Service Institution.[15]

Fortunately, the models survived the test of time. The Large Model remained on display in its prestigious location in Whitehall for more than a century, and the *Guide* went into several reprints, as did the *History*. Nevertheless, Siborne's achievements could well have faded into the mists of time, for in 1963 the Large Model was taken from public display and put into storage. It could have been forgotten or even destroyed, but thanks to a small group of enlightened and determined people, it was saved for posterity. This great work of art is again on public display, in the National Army Museum in London, the route it took there being almost as twisted and tortuous as that in Siborne's days. Due to the lack of space in its current venue, only one side of this enormous object can be viewed directly. Nevertheless, it is still possible to see the village of Plancenoit in the top left-hand corner, now cleared of most of the Prussian soldiers that were once positioned around it.

Although history has been distorted, the model remains a great work of art, a wonderful achievement that required so much sacrifice and resulted in the premature death of its constructor. It is a monument not only to the bravery of the soldiers of all the participating nations, but also to the great talents and the determination of William Siborne. It is also a record of the pettiness of a great man's ego and of a battle about history, one that began within hours of the final shot, and shows no sign of abating two centuries later.

Ultimately, Wellington achieved what Napoleon could not do: he removed the Prussians from the field of Waterloo. It was, however, his smallest victory.

Acknowledgements

Nobody has ever looked at Siborne's story in detail before. Assembling all the known archive material on the subject has proved to be very time-consuming. I would like to say this account was exhaustive, but hope that the documentation needed to close the one or two minor gaps might some day be located.

As the writing of this book started at the Public Record Office in London, it would be appropriate to start by thanking Dr Keith Bartlett and Hilary Jones for the preliminary work they did for me by locating much of the material in their collection that refers to William Siborne. Jane Crompton and Karen Grannum kindly assisted me in obtaining a copy of his will there. Three other institutions that gave me considerable assistance, thanks to the connection to Siborne, were the National Army Museum in London, now home to the Large Model – Julian Humphrys, Michael Ball, Emma Brown, Jo Woolley and Keith Miller were particularly helpful in locating material in their collection; the Royal United Service Institution, the former home to the Large Model – the librarian John Montgomery gave me access to archive material never before used; and the Royal Armouries in Leeds, where Martin Pegler and Philip Abbott kindly provided me with a copy of their documentation on the New Model.

Many other archives, museums and institutions provided

me with invaluable assistance. Life would have been much more difficult without regular use of the facilities of the British Library in London, where Dr Christopher Wright, custodian of Siborne's *Waterloo Correspondence* was particularly helpful, as was Dr Barry Taylor. Dr Christopher Woolgar and other members of the staff at the Hartley Library, University of Southampton, home of the *Wellington Papers*, kindly assisted me on several occasions during the course of my research. Dr Iain G. Brown at the National Library of Scotland kindly provided me with copies of the *Murray Papers* and advice on other manuscripts. St Catherine's House supplied a copy of Siborne's death certificate. The Guildhall Library, the Society of Genealogy, the Family Records Centre and the London Probate Index and the London Metropolitan Archives endeavoured to locate a copy of Siborne's will and other documents on the Siborne family. My thanks go to Bridget Howlett of the Joint Archive Service of the Corporation of London for locating his baptism record. Dr B. Woelderink and his staff at the Koniglijk Huis Archief in 'S Gravenhage located the correspondence referring to Siborne's use of the *Prince of Orange's Papers*, helping me to put an end to one of the false accusations against Siborne. Virginia Murray of John Murray Ltd. provided me with copies of the documents referring to Gleig's *Story* and other material. Ute Dietsch at the Geheimes Staatsarchiv preussischer Kulturbesitz in Berlin was, as always, most helpful with my enquiries. Alexander Fiebig of the Zeitungsabteilung der Staatsbibliothek in Berlin located newspaper clippings on the Exhibition of the New Model there in 1846. Thomas Bantle, Managing Director of E. S. Mittler & Sohn in Hamburg, kindly answered my enquiry. Colonel Donal

O'Carroll and Dr Kenneth Ferguson of the Military History Society of Ireland supported my attempts to locate the records of Armit & Borough and aided my researches in Dublin. Gregory O'Connor of the National Archive of Ireland answered my questions on that collection of papers, while Elizabeth Kirwan at the National Library of Ireland, Manuscripts Department, kindly allowed me access to the Kilmainham Papers. The Library itself also supplied me with useful material. Mary Clarke, Dublin City Archives kindly assisted me with other enquiries. Dr A. P. W. Malcomson of the Public Record Office of Northern Ireland, Belfast, also aided my attempts to locate the records of Armit & Borough. Rachel Watson of the Northamptonshire County Record Office kindly answered my enquiry, as did Sarah Davis of Shropshire Records and Research Service, Mark Ballard and Helen Orme of the Centre for Kentish Studies and Helen E Roberts of the Brynmor Jones Library at the University of Hull. Karen Sampson of Lloyds TSB Group Archives was particularly helpful, providing me with copies of some of Siborne's financial records. Philip Winterbottom of the Royal Bank of Scotland Group Archives kindly attempted to locate the USI's accounts of the purchase of the Model for me. Dr Peter J Thwaites of the Sandhurst Collection provided me with details of Siborne's early years. The Royal Engineer's Museum and the Royal Hospital Chelsea endeavoured to locate material for me. Dr Richard Gassan, Instructor, University of Massachusetts at Amherst, Massachusetts pointed me in the direction of Sarah Friedman and Leslie Hunt of the Historical Society of Pennsylvania, who researched the records of Siborne's American publisher on my behalf. Annette Fern of The Harvard Theatre Collection,

Houghton Library at the Harvard University, Cambridge, Massachusetts, kindly helped me locate various papers on the history of the panorama. Ngadi W. Kponou of the Beinecke Rare Book and Manuscript Library at Yale University, New Haven, Connecticut, responded to my enquiry on the papers of George Lackington. Dr Richard Virr, Curator of Manuscripts of the Rare Books and Special Collections Division of McGill University Libraries in Montreal kindly searched his collection for a copy of the missing War Office Authority of 15 May 1830, sight of which would have answered several questions. Robyn Myers of the Worshipful Company of Stationers and Simon Eliot of the Centre for Writing, Publishing and Printing History at the University of Reading supported my attempts to locate the records of Siborne's publisher in London. Adam Freeman of News International assisted my enquiries into back issues of *The Times*.

I am of course particularly grateful to my editor, Julian Loose, at Faber and Faber, London. It was entirely his idea of turning part of the vast amount of material I have collected on the Waterloo Campaign and its historiography into this book and I greatly appreciate all the support he has give me. My thanks also go to Angus Cargill for his suggestions for improvements to the manuscript.

Many individuals kindly supported my research, giving me their time and knowledge. Brian Siborne and Jennifer Taggart, both descendents of William, pointed me in the right direction on several occasions. The Duke of Wellington graciously answered my enquiries. The Marquess of Anglesey was kind enough to allow me access to the *Paget Papers* on several occasions. Dr David Chandler gave me much useful information on the events leading to the restoration of the Large Model. James

Opie and William Carman shared their expert knowledge on model soldiers with me, providing me with several useful leads. The Reverend Cooney and Glenn Thompson of the Old Dublin Society gave me information on Siborne's time in Dublin. Dr Mark Nicholls provided me with continuous support, both in his capacity as Hon. Editor of the *Journal of the Society of Army Historical Research* and as Librarian at St John's, Cambridge. Dr John Houlding, Derek S. Mill and Lars-Holger Thümmler gallantly aided my attempts to transcribe ever more of Siborne's *Waterloo Correspondence*.

Other individuals that kindly assisted me included Colonels John Hughes-Wilson and Gerald Napier, Harry Hanson, Arthur Harman, Dallas Gavan, Mike MacGillivray, Andrew Uffindell, David Hollins, Stephen Wood, Mark Urban, Geert van Uythoven, Andrew Roberts, Dr Neville Thompson, Professor Hew Strachan, Stuart Reid, Dr Michael Occleshaw, Andrew McCormack, Allan Mountford, John Cook, Stephen Maison, Bruno Naeckerts, Rod McArthur, Ron McGuigan, Yves Martin, Bill Leeson, Geoff Holland, Tim Hicks, Dr Paddy Griffith, Pierre de Wit, Richard Dodman, Jacques Logie, David Pinder, Philippe de Spoelberch, Guy Dempsey, and last but certainly not least, a special thank you to Tom Holmberg, whose access to various databases greatly facilitated my researches. I would also like to thank Gareth Glover, Derek S. Mill, John Montgomery, John Wood and Stephen Wood for notifying me of errors in the text.

I only hope I have not left anybody out of this long list. Although I could not have written this book without the kind assistance of the people mentioned above, I am, of course, solely responsible for any errors there might be in this text.

Bibliography

Manuscript Sources

Archives of John Murray Ltd, London

Exhibitions of mechanical and other works of ingenuity, British Library, London (BL)

Gneisenau Papers, Rep 92, Geheimes Staatsarchiv preussischer Kulturbesitz, Berlin (GStA)

Kilmainham Papers, MSS 1001–1390, National Library of Ireland, Manuscripts Dept, Dublin (KP)

Minutes of the Council of the United Service Institute

Murray Papers, National Library of Scotland, Edinburgh (NLS)

Records of Lea & Febiger, Historical Society of Pennsylvania

Treasury Papers, Public Record Office, London (PRO TI)

War Office Papers, Public Record Office, London (PRO WO)

Waterloo Correspondence, BL Add MSS 34,704–8, British Library, London (BL)

Waterloo Model Papers, National Army Museum, London (NAM)

Printed Sources

NEWSPAPERS

The Atlas; A general newspaper and journal of literature, London, James Whiting, 1826–62.

The Courier, London, J. Stamp, 1792–1842.

Court Gazette and Fashionable Guide, London, 1838–46.

Court Journal: gazette of the fashionable world, literature, music, and the fine arts, London, William Thomas, 1829–56.

Illustrated London News, London, William Little, 1842 – present.

John Bull, London, R. T. Weaver, 1820–56.

Königlich Berlinische privilegirte Staats- und gelehrte Zeitung, (Vossische Zeitung), Berlin, Vossischer Erben, 1785–1911.

Morning Post, London, J. Nott, 1803–1937.

Naval & Military Gazette and Weekly Chronicle of the United Service, London 1833–86.

The Times, London, 1788 – present.

United Service Gazette, and Naval and Military Chronicle, London, C. I. Coltson, 1833–1921.

PERIODICALS

Blackwood's Magazine, Edinburgh, William Blackwood & Sons, 1817–1980

Colburn's United Service Magazine, London, Henry Colburn, 1844–90 (USM)

Dublin University Magazine, Dublin, William Curry, Jun. and Co., 1833–77

Fraser's Magazine, London, J. Fraser, 1830–82.

Notes & Queries, London, Spottiswoode, 1849–date

Quarterly Review, London, John Murray, 1809–1967

United Service Journal & Naval & Military Magazine, London, Henry Colburn & Richard Bentley, 1829–41 (USJ)

United Service Magazine & Naval & Military Magazine, London, Henry Colburn, 1842–3 (USM)

United States Magazine and Democratic Review, New Series, New York, J. L. O'Sullivan and O. C. Gardiner, 1841–51

GUIDES

Guide to the Model of the Battle of Waterloo now Exhibited at the Egyptian Hall, Piccadilly, London, P. Dixon Hardy, 1838

Guide to Captain Siborne's New Waterloo Model Representing the Splendid Charge between One and Two O'Clock by the British Heavy Cavalry under

The Marquess of Anglesey and by the British Infantry under Sir Thomas Picton, London, 1844

Guide to Captain Siborne's Original Large Waterloo Model Representing the Entire Field with the Whole of the Armies Engaged when the Duke of Wellington, with the British Troops, Repulsed Napoleon's Imperial Guard, and Gained the Glorious Victory of Waterloo, London, 1845

Explanatory Notes of the Positions of the Allied and French Armies in the Battle of Waterloo, June 18th, 1815, at the Period Represented on the Model Constructed by the late Captain Siborne, and now in the Possession of the Royal United Service Institution, Whitehall Yard, 2nd edition, London, W. Mitchell & Co., 1872

Description of the Model Constructed by Capt. William Siborne (Late of the 9th and 47th Regiments), of the Battle of Waterloo now in the Museum of the Royal United Service Institution, London, 1896

Royal United Service Museum, *The Battle of Waterloo Being a Description of the Large Model Constructed by the Historian Captain William Siborne and Exhibited in the Museum*, London, 1909

BOOKS

Altick, Richard D., *The Shows of London*, Cambridge, Massachusetts, Belknap, 1978

Anglesey, Marquess of, *One-Leg: The Life and Letters of Henry William Paget*, London, Jonathan Cape, 1961

Anon, *An Account of the Battle of Waterloo, Fought on the 18th of June 1815*, London, James Ridgway, 1815

Anon, *A Description of the Defeat of the French Army under the Command of Napoleon Bonaparte*, London, 1816

Anon, *A Description of Marshall's Grand Historical Peristrephic Panorama of the Ever-Memorable Battles of Ligny, Les Quatre Bras and Waterloo*, Bristol, T. J. Manchee, no date

Anon, *Description of the Field of Battle and Disposition of the Troops Engaged in the Action, Fought on the 18th of June 1815, near Waterloo*, Quebec, L. Bedard, 1817

Anon, *The Battle of Waterloo Containing the Series of Accounts published by Authority*, 8th edn, London & Edinburgh, John Booth, T. Egerton & J. Fairbarn, 1816

Anon, *Who Was Who, 1897–1916*, London, A. & C. Black Ltd., 1920

Army lists, various years

Aspinal, A., *The Correspondence of Charles Arbuthnot*, London, Royal Historical Society, 1941

Astley, Philip, *The Battle of Waterloo*, London, 1815

Bamford, Francis and Wellington, (7th) Duke of, *The Journal of Mrs. Arbuthnot 1820–1832*, 2 vols, London, Macmillan & Co, 1950

Barker, Henry Aston, *A Description of the Defeat of the French Army . . . Now Exhibiting in Barker's Panorama*, London, 1816

Baring, Georg, *Erzählung der Theilnahme des 2. leichten Bataillons der königlich deutschen Legion an der Schlacht von Waterloo*, in the *Hannoversches militärisches Journal*, Hanover, 1831

Colby, Reginald, *The Waterloo Despatch*, London, HMSO, 1965

Comment, Bernard, *The Panorama*, London, Reaktion Books, 1999

Cotton, Edward, *A Voice from Waterloo*, London, 1849

Craan, W. B., *An Historical Account of the Battle of Waterloo*, London, Samuel Leigh, 1817

Dallas, Gregor, *1815 – The Roads to Waterloo*, London, Richard Cohen Books, 1996

Dalton, Charles, *Waterloo Roll Call*, 2nd edn, London and New York, Arms & Armour Press/Hippocrene, 1978

De Bas, F., *Prins Frederik der Nederlanden en Zijn Tijd*, 4 vols, Schiedam, H. A. M. Roelants, 1887–1913

De Bas, F. and De T'Serclaes de Wommersom, J., *La Campagne de 1815 aux Pays-Bas*, 3 vols, Brussels, Albert Dewit, 1908

Eaton, Charlotte Anne, *The Battle of Waterloo*, London, Booth & Egerton, 1815

Fitzpatrick, W. J., *The Life of Charles Lever*, 2 vols, London, Chapman & Hall, 1879

Fouché, Joseph, *Mémoires de Joseph Fouché, duc d'Otrante*, Paris, France-Éditions, 1944

Fraser, William, *Words on Wellington: The Duke – Waterloo – The Ball*, London, John C. Nimmo, 1889

Gawler, J. C., *George Gawler, K. H., 52nd Light Infantry: A Life Sketch*, Derby & London, Bemrose & Sons, 1900

Gleig, George Robert, *The Life of Arthur, Duke of Wellington*, London, New York, Longmans, Green & Co, 1891

Gleig, George Robert, *The Story of the Battle of Waterloo*, London, John Murray, 1847

Gleig, Mary E. (ed.), *Personal Reminiscences of the First Duke of Wellington*, Edinburgh & London, William Blackwood & Sons, 1904

Gurwood, John (ed.), *The Dispatches of Field Marshal The Duke of Wellington*, 12 vols, London, John Murray, 1837–8 (WD)

Gurwood, John (ed.), *The Dispatches of Field Marshal The Duke of Wellington*, 8 vols, London, Parker, Furnivall & Parker, 2nd edn, 1844–7

Guy, Alan J. (ed.), *The Road to Waterloo*, London, Alan Sutton, 1990

Hanson, Harry, *The Coaching Life*, Manchester, Manchester University Press, 1983

Harris, James, Earl of Malmesbury, *A Series of Letters of the First Earl of Malmesbury, his Family and Friends from 1745 to 1820*, 2 vols, London, R. Bentley, 1870

Henegan, Richard, *Seven Years' Campaigning in the Peninsula and the Netherlands from 1808 to 1815*, 2 vols, London, 1846

Hofschröer, Peter, *1815 – The Waterloo Campaign*, 2 vols, London, Greenhill Books, 1998–9

Hornby, Sir Edmund, *An Autobiography*, London, Constable & Co., 1929

Houssaye, Henry, *1815*, Paris, Didier Perrin, 4th edn, 1898

Hughson, David, *Walks through London Including Westminster and the Borough of Southwark*, London, Sherwood, Neely, and Jones, 1817

Jackson, Basil, *Notes and Reminiscences of a Staff Officer*, London, Harrison & Sons, 1877

Jennings, Louis J. (ed.), *The Croker Papers*, 3 vols, London, John Murray, 1884

Logie, Jacques, *Waterloo – l'évitable défaite*, Paris-Gembloux, Éditions Duculot, 1984

Madelin, Louis, *Fouché 1759–1820*, 2 vols, Paris, Librairie Plon, 1903

Maxwell, Herbert, *The Life of Wellington*, 2 vols, 2nd edn, London, Sampson Low, Marston & Co, 1900

Maxwell, Herbert (ed.), *The Creevey Papers*, 2 vols, London, John Murray, 1904

Mercer, Cavalié, *Journal of the Waterloo Campaign kept throughout the Campaign of 1815*, Edinburgh and London, William Blackwood, 1870

Miller, David, *Lady De Lancey at Waterloo*, Staplehurst, Spellmount, 2000

Müffling, Carl von, *Aus Meinem Leben*, Berlin, E. S. Mittler und Sohn, 1851

Müffling, Carl von, *History of the Campaign of the British, Dutch, Hanoverian and Brunswick Armies*, London, T. Egerton, 1816

Oettermann, Stephan, *The Panorama – History of a Mass Medium*, New York, Zone Books, 1997

Owen, Edward (ed.), *The Waterloo Papers*, Tavistock, AQ & DJ Publications, 1998

Pflugk-Harttung, Julius von, *Vorgeschichte der Schlacht bei Belle-Alliance*, Berlin, Richard Schröder, 1903

Pilbeam, Pamela, *Madame Tussaud and the History of Waxworks*, Hambledon & London, 2003

Plotho, Carl von, *Der Krieg des verbündeten Europa gegen Frankreich im Jahre 1815*, Berlin, Carl Friedrich Amelang, 1818

Pückler-Muskau, Hermann Ludwig Heinrich, *Tour in England, Ireland, and France, in the Years 1826, 1827, 1828 and 1829*, Philadelphia, 1833

Reeve, Henry (ed.), *The Greville Memoirs*, 8 vols, London & New York, Longmans, Green & Co., 1888

Reid, Stuart, *Redcoat Officer 1740–1815*, Oxford, Osprey Publishing, 2002

Robertson, D., *The Journal of Sergeant D. Robertson, Late 92d Foot*, Perth, 1842

Russell, Gillian, *The Theatres of War – Performance, Politics, and Society 1793–1815*, London, Oxford University Press, 1995

Scott, John, *Paris Revisited in 1815, by Way of Brussels: Including a Walk over the Field of Battle at Waterloo*, 2nd edn, London, Longman, Hurst, Rees, Orme and Brown, 1816.

Seaton, R. C. (ed.), *Notes and Reminiscences of a Staff Officer*, London, John Murray, 1903

Siborn, William, *A Practical Treatise on Topographical Surveying and Drawing*, London, C. & J. Rivington, 1827

Siborne, Herbert (ed.), *Waterloo Letters*, London, Paris & Melbourne, Cassel & Co., 1891

Siborne, William, *History of the War in France and Belgium in 1815*, 2 vols and atlas, London, T. & W. Boone, 1844

Siborne, William, *History of the War in France and Belgium in 1815*, 3rd edn, London, T. & W. Boone, 1848

Sidney, Edwin, *The Life of Lord Hill*, London, John Murray, 1845

Six, Georges, *Dictionnaire Biographique des Généraux & Amiraux Français de la Révolution et de l'Empire (1792–1814)*, 2 vols, Paris, Georges Saffroy, 1934

Smith, E. A., *Wellington and the Arbuthnots*, Stroud, Alan Sutton, 1994

Spiers, Edward M., *Radical General – Sir George De Lacy Evans 1787–1870*, Manchester, Manchester University Press, 1983

Stanhope, 5th Earl, *Notes of Conversations with the Duke of Wellington 1831–1851*, London, Oxford University Press, 1938

Strachan, Hew, *From Waterloo to Balaclava*, Cambridge, Cambridge University Press, 1985

Strachan, Hew, *Wellington's Legacy – The Reform of the British Army 1830–54*, Manchester, Manchester University Press, 1984

Strafford, Alice Countess of, *Personal Reminiscences of the Duke of Wellington by Francis, The First Earl of Ellesmere*, London, John Murray, 1903

Sydow, Anna von (ed.), *Gabriele von Bülow*, Berlin, E. S. Mittler & Sohn, 1929

Thomas, Hugh, *The Story of Sandhurst*, London, Hutchinson, 1961

Thompson, Neville, *Earl Bathurst and the British Empire 1762–1834*, Barnsley, Leo Cooper, 1999

Thompson, Neville, *Wellington after Waterloo*, London and New York, Routledge & Kegan Paul, 1986

Thoumine, R. H., *Scientific Soldier – A Life of General Le Marchant, 1766–1812*, London, Oxford University Press, 1968

Tulard, Jean, *Joseph Fouché*, Paris, Fayard, 1998

Wagner, August, *Plane der Schlachten und Treffen, welche von der preussischen Armee in den Feldzügen der Jahre 1813, 14 und 15 geliefert worden*, 4 vols, Berlin, Prussian General Staff, 1821–5

Ward, B. R., *A Week at Waterloo in 1815 – Lady De Lancey's Narrative*, London, John Murray, 1906

Wellington, 2nd Duke of, *Supplementary Despatches and Memoranda of Field Marshal Arthur Duke of Wellington*, 15 vols, London, John Murray, 1858–72 (WSD)

Wellington, 7th Duke of, *Wellington and His Friends*, London & New York, Macmillan & Co., 1965

Wellington, 7th Duke of, *The Conversations of the First Duke of Wellington with George William Chad*, Cambridge, Saint Nicolas Press, 1956

Young, Julian Charles, *A Memoir of Charles Mayne Young*, London & New York, Macmillan & Co., 1871

Notes

2 A Nation of Show-Keepers

1 This document is reproduced in full in the Appendices.
2 Percy was a grandson of the first Duke of Northumberland and son of the Earl of Beverley. He had been appointed ADC to Wellington only a few weeks before the battle. His scarlet and gold coatee is among the Waterloo relics kept in the State Dining Room of Alnwick Castle, the ancestral seat of his family in Northumberland. Another relic is a handkerchief sachet made of deep purple velvet that an admirer gave Percy as he left the Duchess of Richmond's celebrated ball in Brussels during the night of 15/16 June 1815 for the front. Percy thrust this memento into his pocket, not noticing it again until after the great battle. The *Despatch*, folded into two, fitted neatly into the sachet.
3 *A Description of the Defeat of the French Army . . . Now Exhibiting in Barker's Panorama, Strand, Near Surry-Street* (London, 1816), 9.
4 *Ibid.*, 3.
5 Altick, *The Shows of London*, 201 fn.
6 *The Times*, 22 March 1842, 6.
7 *USM*, New Series, i, 61.
8 Scott, *Paris Revisited*, 205.
9 *Notes & Queries*, 19 July 1862, 52.
10 Scott, *op. cit.*, 206–7.
11 Cotton was born around 1792 on the Isle of Wight. At Waterloo, he served in the 7th Hussars and distinguished himself by rescuing a

comrade, Trooper Gilmoure, from beneath his wounded horse and carrying him to safety before the next French advance. He also served as orderly to Sir Hussey Vivian, who commanded a cavalry brigade at Waterloo and later befriended Siborne. In 1835, after retiring from the army, Cotton went to live in the village of Mont St Jean. Here, he became a guide to the battlefield and set up a museum of Waterloo relics and memorabilia at the base of the Lion Mound. He died on 1 July 1849 and was buried in the garden of Hougoumont. However, his remains, along with the remains of sixteen officers, were later reinterred in the crypt of the Waterloo Memorial at Evere Cemetery near Brussels, unveiled by the Duke of Cambridge on 26 August 1890.

12 Cotton, *A Voice from Waterloo*, 3rd edn, 1849, Preface, vii.

13 *Ibid.*

14 Astley, *The Battle of Waterloo* (London, 1815). It went into several editions. Philip Astley Senior (1792–1814), a veteran of the Seven Years War (1756–63), opened his Amphitheatre in London in 1770. Considered to be the first modern circus ring, it provided significant competition to the theatres in Covent Garden and Drury Lane. Originally a sergeant in the 15th Dragoons, Astley Senior was at first the sole performer, specializing in riding with one foot on the saddle and one on the horse's head while brandishing a sword. He gradually included other equestrians, acrobats, rope-dancers, aerialists, clowns, and the first recorded circus freak show. In 1794, it was renamed the Royal Amphitheatre of Arts and came under the patronage of both the Prince of Wales and the Duke of York.

15 Pückler-Muskau, 157.

16 Wellington to Sir John Sinclair, 12 April 1816, *WSD*, x, 507.

17 Wellington to Sir John Sinclair, 28 April 1816, *WSD*, x, 507.

18 Wellington to William Mudford, 8 June 1816, *WSD*, x, 509.

19 *Illustrated London News*, 13 November 1852, 407.

3 Fame and Fortune

1 The *USJ* went through several incarnations. From its founding in 1829 until 1841, it was known as the *United Service Journal and Naval & Military Magazine*. In 1842–3, it was renamed the *United Service Magazine and Naval & Military Magazine*. From 1844 to 1890, it was known as *Colburn's United Service Magazine*, before being renamed simply the *United Service Magazine*. It ceased publication in June 1920.

2 Clerke was a Peninsula veteran. His right leg had been amputated after being in combat at Redinha on 12 March 1811. He became a popular editor of the *USJ*, respected for his fairness.

3 *USJ*, 1829, i, 239.

4 Douglas had had a varied military career, including time in the Peninsular War and in Canada. He had also been on the supreme board of the Royal Military College at the time Siborne was a Gentleman Cadet.

5 Lt-General Sir Herbert Taylor (1775–1839) had a highly successful career in the military and politics. In April 1793, he joined the headquarters of the Duke of York's army in the Netherlands, where he saw action on several occasions. In March 1794, he was commissioned as cornet in the 2nd Dragoon Guards, being promoted to Lieutenant in July. In September 1795, he returned to England as a captain and soon afterwards was nominated Assistant Military Secretary to the Commander-in-Chief. In July 1798 Taylor accompanied Lord Cornwallis to Ireland on his appointment as Lord-Lieutenant as his Aide-de-Camp, Military Secretary and Private Secretary. He returned to England in February 1799 to take over the duties of Private Secretary to the Duke of York. In January 1801, Taylor was promoted to major in the 2nd Dragoon Guards, and that December to lt-colonel in the 9th West India Regiment. On 13 June 1805, he was appointed Private Secretary to George III and continued in that office during the Regency. He was promoted to be Brevet Colonel in July 1810, and to be Major-General in June 1813. He resumed the duties of Private Secretary to Queen Charlotte on his return from his mission to the Crown Prince of Sweden, and continued

in this office until her death in November 1818. In March 1820, Taylor was appointed Military Secretary at the Horse Guards. In May 1825, he was promoted to Lt-General. On the death of the Duke of York in January 1827, he was appointed Military Secretary to the new Commander-in-Chief, the Duke of Wellington. When the Duke resigned from that post in July 1827, Lord Palmerston, then Secretary at War, nominated Taylor as deputy. George IV made him his first and principal Aide-de-Camp in May 1827. In March 1828, Taylor was appointed Master Surveyor and Surveyor-General of the Ordnance. It may have been in this capacity that he first met Siborne. In August 1828, he became Adjutant-General of the army, an appointment he held until the accession of William IV in 1830, when he became the new king's Private Secretary. He retired on William IV's death in 1837.

6 *USJ*, 1830, i, 367.

7 The exact date in 1830 when Siborne was approached in this regard is not certain. However, there is a gap in his correspondence from February 1830 to February 1831, indicating he was away from his desk for much of that time. We know that the decision to found the United Service Museum was made public in March 1830. The War Office memorandum mentioned May as the month when Hill contacted it, so the decision had been made by then. We also know that Siborne spent eight months conducting his survey at La Haye Sainte and that he returned before the end of the year. That being the case, he must have left Dublin in early in May, so Hill most probably approached him in April.

8 PRO WO43/538, fols 192–5.

9 See, for instance, PRO WO43/538, fol. 187.

10 Fitzpatrick, *Life of Charles Lever*, ii, 408. The name of the writer of this passage was bowdlerized in the original text, but was most likely to have been Davis.

11 Benjamin Siborn obtained his captaincy on 5 November 1807; served with the 2nd Battalion in Moore's Spanish Campaign, 1808/9; fought under Lord Chatham at Walcheran in 1809; in the Peninsula in 1810; was gravely wounded at the Battle of Nivelle, 10 November 1813, these

wounds ultimately leading to his death; served with Packenham in North America; transferred to the 1st Battalion on his return to Europe in 1815; died on 14 July 1819 on St Vincent in the West Indies 'from the after effects of his wounds'.

12 Officers of the artillery and engineers, who were promoted by seniority and not by purchase, needed formal instruction in mathematics and related subjects, and since 1721, they had been taught at the Royal Military Academy in Woolwich, London.

13 This system had its benefits as the value of the commission took the place of any provision for retirement pensions; officers who found themselves unsuited to military life could sell up and realize the cash, rather than 'soldier on' in a profession they disliked merely to provide for their future.

14 Général François Jarry (1733–1807) was a rather eccentric Frenchman; small, lean, with pinched features and scanty grey hair. Active service and several wounds made him appear older than he already was. According to his own story, he had even served under Frederick the Great, supposedly as head of the Prussian Military Academy, until the Great King's death in 1786, although no record of this is known to exist. Jarry then commanded a French division under Général Dumouriez in 1792, the year of the Cannonade at Valmy, the turning point in the Revolutionary Wars. Incurring the displeasure of the French government at a time when heads rolled for such offences, Jarry fled to Britain, where he sought to make his living by teaching military theory to aspiring officer cadets. As he gave his classes in French, the teenagers he taught had a double benefit, although one suspects that only the highly motivated learned anything from him. Jarry had suggested the founding of a military academy for all officers to Lord Auckland, father of Amelia Eden, for whom the Prime Minister, William Pitt, had formed an attachment. Auckland brought Jarry to the attention of Henry Dundas (1742–1811), then the Secretary of War. However, Jarry lacked the influence and the perseverance to get very far. It would take a British officer to achieve that.

15 John Gaspard Le Marchant (1766–1812) was a pensive man. He was not, as his name suggests, a Frenchman, but hailed from the Channel Islands. He was mortally wounded in the Peninsular War leading a cavalry charge at the Battle of Salamanca in 1812. He had made a name for himself by introducing a system of cavalry sword drill, which in turn had led to the adopting of a newly designed sword. He also considered setting up courses of instruction in other regiments, but he knew there were few commanding officers with either the knowledge or the inclination to try. Le Marchant was riding the mail coach to Guildford one autumn day in 1798, pondering how he might extend and improve his regimental school for officers. The solution, as he saw it, was to found a national establishment. A determined man, he was not deterred by setbacks and opposition from vested interests, and he did not need long to get his way.

16 Sébastian le Prestre de Vauban was a French military engineer who revolutionized the art of siege craft and defensive fortifications. He fought in all of France's wars during Louis XIV's reign (1643–1715).

17 PRO WO76/186, fol. 29. Ensign was the equivalent to a second lieutenant today.

18 PRO TS/11 113, Report of Lieut. Siborn.

19 Lehmann had been a major of the Saxon infantry and Director of the Depot for Military Maps and Plans. His work on topography, *Die Lehre der Situationszeichnung oder Anweisung zum richtigen Erkennen und genauen Abbilden der Erdoberfläche in topographischen Charten und Situationsplänen*, had first been published in Dresden in 1812. It became a standard text and was reprinted several times in the nineteenth century. That being the case, it is not certain which edition Siborne read. The first is likely to have been available to him at Sandhurst. The third, improved edition was published in 1820, about the time Siborne was working on this topic. Lehmann was the first man to develop a system of marking gradients on maps. After he left General von Langenau's regiment in 1793, he devoted himself to cartography. With a redesigned drawing table, he mapped the hilly regions of Saxony,

inventing a new way of showing gradients. He established that the cosine of the angle of light falling vertically on a plane is proportional to that of the horizontal plane. The steeper the gradient, the darker it was shaded. Black and white lines of proportional thickness were used to represent every slope. As we shall see later, Siborne adapted and developed this system further. In 1806, Lehmann saw active service on the French side in the sieges of Danzig and Graudenz which so affected his health that he later died. It was his friend Professor G. A. Fischer that had his work published.

20 Herbert Taylor Siborne (1826–1902) was also an army officer and a historian. He joined the Royal Engineers, fighting in the Kaffir Wars and in the Crimea. He was posted to the War Office in 1860, where he spent the next thirteen years designing defences for the naval bases in the Thames and Medway estuaries. In 1891, he published a selection of the Waterloo correspondence his father had collected under the title *Waterloo Letters*. He did this on the suggestion of a distant cousin in Dublin, E. Percival Wright, M. D. In November 1893, Herbert attempted to sell this valuable and unique collection of documents at Sotheby's, London. A mere £29 was bid, so he withdrew the item. A year later Wright approached the British Museum on his behalf, offering the manuscripts for sale, having already sent part of the collection as a sample. On 15 November 1894, Herbert accepted £50 in payment. The Waterloo correspondence can today be viewed in the Manuscripts Department of the British Library. Thanks to Herbert, scholars can still appreciate the full extent of William's research.

21 See Nedderbury to the Deputy Adjutant General, 10 February 1826, NLI, Kilmainham Papers, MS 1157, fol. 107; Nedderbury to Gregory, 10 February 1826, MS 1046, fol. 255. James Butler, Duke of Ormonde and Viceroy to Charles II, founded the Royal Hospital in 1684. It was not a medical institution in the strictest sense, but rather a home for old soldiers, just like the Royal Military Asylum (RMA) in Chelsea, London. The building, which today houses the Irish Museum of Modern Art, was completed two years before the RMA and was used for its original

purpose for almost 250 years. It is a magnificent building, one styled on Les Invalides in Paris, with a formal façade and a large, elegant courtyard.

22 Much of Siborne's daily routine can be reconstructed by reference to the Chief Secretary's Office Registered Papers in the National Archive of Ireland.

4 The Field of Waterloo

1 The earliest history of the farm is a little vague, but it seems a wealthy family of farmers named Moitomont from Braine l'Alleud, then a nearby village, founded the estate in about 1536. In 1618, they sold it to Jean Glibert, the Gliberts being an important family in the area. Jean was evicted in 1659 for not paying the interest on his mortgage, and the farm was sold. A certain Henry Glibert, probably a close relative, bought it, together with his son-in-law François Boucquéau, who also farmed the neighbouring Mont St Jean estate. Henry died in 1664 and the farm remained in the family's possession until 1687. The incessant wars at the end of that century devastated the countryside and ruined the farmers, with La Haye Sainte being destroyed in 1696. Boucquéau signed over the farm to his son, who was also named François. Under François junior, both the farm and family prospered, and the farmhouse was rebuilt. In 1696, he purchased le Caillou, the house that Napoleon later used as his headquarters in the battle. In 1720, the estate passed on to François' son Jean-Baptiste. On his death in 1775, his heirs sold the farm to Count Charles-Henri Boot de Velthem, a chamberlain of the Emperor of Austria, for the then considerable sum of 27,000 florins. Much of modern Belgium was at this time under the rule of the Austrian Habsburgs and included in the Holy Roman Empire, as the German Confederation was then known. On Velthem's death in 1829, Spoelberch bought the estate. Velthem was not actually present on the day of the battle; he had rented the farm to a certain Pierre Moreau. See: Logie, *Waterloo – l'évitable défaite*, 119.

2 Eaton, *The Battle of Waterloo*, i–iii.

3 *Ibid.*

4 *Ibid.*

5 *Ibid.*, iv.

6 *Journal of Sergeant D. Robertson*, 144–5.

7 Scott, *Paris Revisited*, 208–9.

8 'Erzählung der Theilnahme des 2. leichten Bataillons der königlich deutschen Legion an der Schlacht von Waterloo', in the *Hannoversches militärisches Journal* (Hanover, 1831), 69–90.

9 *Ibid.*, 73–4.

10 *Ibid.*, 74–5.

11 Scott, *Paris Revisited*, 211–12.

12 BL Add MS 34,707, fols 215-7.

13 *Ibid.*

14 *Ibid.*

15 Scott, *Paris Revisited*, 212–3.

16 Colby's office was in the old Mountjoy Barracks, which was across town from the Royal Hospital. He brought with him his vast experience of surveying from Britain, from which he had developed some experimental measuring devices, including the 'compensation bar'. This instrument was constructed with a dual arrangement of brass and iron designed to limit the contractions caused by changes of temperature, and had an ingenious arrangement of connecting microscopes. Colby's compensation bar has been used ever since in base measurements around the world. He also used a zenith sector constructed by the famous Jesse Ramsden, who was one of the great instrument makers of the latter half of the eighteenth century. Although there is no written record of this, it is most likely that Siborne and Colby were well acquainted. Sir Herbert Taylor, as Surveyor-General of the Ordnance, may have introduced them.

17 Siborne, *History of the War in France and Belgium in 1815* (3rd edn), 203.

18 *Notes and Queries*, 3rd S. ii, 19 July 1862, 51–2.

19 See BL Add MS 34,704, 128. See also *Waterloo Letters*, 263.

20 Siborne, *History of the War in France and Belgium in 1815* (3rd edn), 212 fn.

5 The Model of the Battle

1 Minutes of the Council of the USI, 6 January 1851.
2 *USJ*, 1833, ii, 239–40.

6 Money Matters

1 Lindsay to Siborne, 4 April 1833, BL Add MS 34,703, fol. 129. Frederick Henry Lindsay (1791?-1854) was a clerk in the commander-in-chief's office at the Horse Guards. He probably started work there in 1806 as 'Foreign Clerk'. Around 1822, he became one of the 'First Clerks' and was 'Chief Clerk' from 1829-41, when he was elevated to the rank of 'Assistant'. He died in Bad Kreuznach, Germany, aged 63, and his obituary gives his position as 'First Assistant to the Military Secretary at the Horse Guards'.
2 Memorandum by William Siborne of 20 August 1833, BL Add MS 34,703, fols 130–131.
3 Sulivan to Sir James Stewart, 21 September 1833, PRO TI/3388.
4 BL Add MS 34,707, fols 290–3.
5 PRO WO43/538, fol. 192v.
6 *USJ*, 1831, ii, 225.
7 PRO WO43/538, fols 164–5.
8 Memorandum by William Siborne of 20 August 1833, BL Add MS 34,703, fols 130–1.
9 PRO WO43/538, fol. 159.
10 *Ibid.*
11 Sulivan to Stewart, 21 September 1833, PRO TI/3388.
12 Stewart to Ellice, 30 September 1833, PRO WO43/538, fol. 157.
13 Siborne's Circular, 26 October 1833, PRO TI/3388.
14 PRO TI/3388.
15 Cuyler to Siborne, 13 November 1833, BL Add MS 34,703, fols 142–3.

16 PRO WO43/538, fol. 168, includes the following account:

	£	s	d
Moulding, Casting, and colouring of Figures required in the representation of the Troops	800	··	··
Engraving of Large Plan on Stone, and printing of Copies, for the purpose of obtaining necessary and authentic information as to positions, movements, &c	120	··	··
Carpenters' work, including Packing-Cases &c	100	··	··
Plaster of Paris	10	··	··
Oil, Colors [sic], &c	15	··	··
Materials required in the representation of country	60	··	··
Working Tools &c	10	··	··
Assistant	85	··	··
Conveyance to London, Travelling Expenses, &c	110	··	··
Sundries	30	··	··
	£ 1340	··	··

17 BL Add MS 34,703, fols 140–1.

18 PRO WO43/538, fol. 174.

19 Ellice to Stewart, 16 December 1833, PRO WO43/538, fol. 179.

20 BL Add MS 34,703, fol. 152.

21 BL Add MS 34,703, fols 147–8.

22 BL Add MS 34,703, fols 149–51.

23 BL Add MS 34,706, fols 193–6.

24 BL Add MS 34,703, fols 171–3.

25 BL Add MS 34,705, fols 269–70.

26 It was Siborne's view that the attack by the Imperial Guard was undertaken in two columns, and certainly this is how eyewitnesses in Wellington's army perceived it. Siborne's attempts to get corroboration from French eyewitnesses were unsuccessful, but since the publication of Siborne's third edition in 1848, various French authorities have written on the subject, particularly Houssaye. This material indicates that the French assault may well have been undertaken in three, and not two, columns. The first wave, consisting of the 1/3rd and 4th Grenadiers, attacked the Nassau, the Brunswick and Halkett's brigades, van der Smissen's battery and Detmer's brigade, and was repulsed by their

counter-attacks. The second wave, consisting of the 1 and 2/3rd Chasseurs was blasted away by Maitland's Guards. The third wave, consisting of the 1 and 2/4th Chasseurs, was driven off by Adam's flank attack, consisting chiefly of the 52nd Light Infantry. The French are likely to have advanced in a hollow square formation, three ranks deep, as they had no cavalry support.

27 BL Add MS 34,703, fols 153–6.
28 BL Add MS 34,703, fol. 192.
29 *Ibid.*
30 BL Add MS 34,703, fols 193–4.
31 BL Add MS 34,703, fols 194–5.
32 BL Add MS 34,703, fol. 233.
33 *The Atlas*, 6 October 1838, 635.
34 *Guide to the Model of the Battle of Waterloo now exhibited at the Egyptian Hall, Piccadilly*, 1-2.

7 Finding the Facts

1 Mercer had in fact kept such extensive notes of the campaign that his son published them in 1870 as a *Journal of the Waterloo Campaign*. This work soon became a classic and is still in print today.
2 BL Add MS 34,708, fols 376–8.
3 *Waterloo Letter* No. 121.
4 *Waterloo Letter* No. 122.
5 BL Add MS 34,708, fols 191–4.
6 Georges Mouton, Count Lobau (1770–1838) volunteered for the Revolutionary Army, becoming a general under Napoleon. He was appointed to the rank of marshal in 1831.
7 See BL Add MS 34,703, fols 180–1, for Siborne's enquiry, and fols 217–8 for Lobau's initial response.
8 Nicolas-Jean de Dieu Soult, Duke of Dalmatia (1769–1851) rose through the ranks of the Revolutionary Army to become Napoleon's Chief-of-Staff in 1815. Charles-Auguste-Josephe Count Flahaut de la Billarderie

(1785–1870) was an ADC to Napoleon in 1815 and very much a Bona-
partist. Rémy-Joseph-Isidore Exelmans (1775–1852) also rose through
the ranks of the Revolutionary Army and commanded a cavalry division
in 1815.

9 BL Add MS 34,705, fols 281–2.
10 BL Add MS 34,705, fols 362–5.
11 *Ibid.*
12 BL Add MS 34,704, fols 161–2.
13 BL Add MS 34,706, fols 118–21. De Bas, Frederik, iii, 1208, has the tran-
script, and the Netherlands Royal Archives have a record of the documents sent.
14 *Waterloo Letters* No. 130.
15 *Ibid.*
16 BL Add MS 34,706, fols 443–4.
17 BL Add MS 34,706, fol. 459.
18 *Ibid.*
19 *WD*, xii, 474 fn.

8 Father Blücher's Children

1 George William Chad (1784–1849), a career diplomat, was the second
son of Sir George Chad of Thursford Hall, Norfolk.
2 General Sir Henry Clinton (1771–1829) commanded the 3rd Division at
Waterloo.
3 Wellington, 7th Duke of, *Conversations with the First Duke of Wellington*, 4.
4 *Ibid.*, 7.
5 BL Add MS 34,705, fols 350–1.
6 BL Add MS 34,706, fols 153–4.
7 *WSD*, x, 513.
8 It first came to light in 1863 when the second Duke published the tenth
volume of a selection of his father's papers known as the *Supplementary
Dispatches*. By then both Siborne and the Great Duke were dead.

Wellington was certainly very careful in his lifetime about which of his papers should be published and which should not be. This memorandum was evidently one of those he did not wish to be published.

9 BL Add MS 34,706, fols 163–4.

10 BL Add MS 34,706, fol 165.

11 BL Add MS 34,706, fol 166.

12 On 20 January 1829, Wellington succeeded Liverpool as Lord Warden of the Cinque Ports. Walmer Castle was the official residence of the Lord Warden, and from then, Wellington spent much of his time there.

13 BL Add MS 34,706, fols 173–6.

14 *Ibid.*

15 BL Add MS 34,706, fols 238–9.

16 BL Add MS 34,706, fols 250–1.

17 BL Add MS 34,706, fols 271–5.

18 *Ibid.*

19 BL Add MS 34,706, fols 280–1.

20 BL Add MS 34,706, fols 312–3.

21 BL Add MS 34,706, fols 326–7.

22 BL Add MS 34,706, fols 352–3.

23 *WSD*, x, 476.

24 Stanhope, 108–9.

25 Maxwell, ii, 19–20.

26 Seaton, 95.

27 *USJ*, ii, 1839, 203.

9 Finding the Money

1 NAM 6807-453.

2 NAM 6807-453.

3 BL Add MS 34,706, fols 193–6.

4 PRO WO43/538, fols 183–6.

5 PRO WO43/538, fol. 187.

6 PRO WO43/538, fol. 182.

7 BL Add MS 34,706, fol. 199.

8 We know the model cost around £3,000 to produce. In December 1830, Siborne's expenses of £62 6s 7d for his trip to La Haye Sainte were refunded. In February 1832, he received a refund of £120 13s 3d. In April 1833, he received £200 of the £217 12s 6d he had spent the previous year. In January 1834, the First Subscription was raised, but we do not know how much money this produced for Siborne. It could not have been much, because in September 1834, he took out a private loan of £1,500 secured against his life. In 1836, he got a couple of hundred pounds as an advance against royalties for the *History*. That brought him roughly £1,800 or so in total, leaving a debt of around £1,200. Early in 1837, three generals loaned him £100 each. Exactly when and how he was to repay that is not clear. Siborne's share of the receipts from the First Exhibition in 1838 amounted to £800. Assuming he repaid the three generals at that stage, that left him with a debt of around £500, excluding the bank loan. We know that a creditor to whom he owed £500 threatened to seize the model in December 1841, yet that did not happen. We also know that at some stage somebody took out a mortgage of £800 on the model. It is likely these two events were linked. We know that the model was repainted after the First Exhibition, incurring costs, which the extra £300 from the mortgage may well have covered. It would seem that Siborne was no longer under pressing financial difficulties by this stage and only had the one creditor to satisfy. It is probable that his promotion to captain in 1840 was by purchase. This is likely to have cost £1,100, an indication of an improvement in Siborne's financial position. As the pay he received as Secretary of the Royal Military Asylum, Chelsea, from 1843 was only £182, substantially less than his salary in Dublin, then it seems no longer had the bank loan to finance. We can assume that the loan of £1,500 had been cleared, and having paid £1,100 for his promotion, it seems that Siborne had a surplus of £2,600. We are not sure if Siborne financed the New Model from his own pocket or if it was the Marquess of Anglesey, but Siborne's records of this time no longer carry the urgent pleas for cash that they did ear-

lier. In 1845, he had an income from the second exhibition and the American edition of the *History*, although we do not know how much. In 1846, Siborne received revenues from both the Berlin Exhibition of the New Model and the German edition of the *History*. The 1846 subscription raised £847 13s 5d. A further subscription was started by the USI in 1848. That year, the third edition of the *History* was published, although there is no record of how much Siborne was paid for that. On his death in 1849, it seems unlikely that Siborne had any personal debts, although somebody owned a share of the Large Model. The 1850 subscription raised a further £280 5s 0d and in 1851, the USI paid £2,062 for the model. One assumes the mortgagee's demands were satisfied and the balance went to Siborne's heir, his wife.

9 Contingent Accounts for 22 December 1835, NLI, KP, MS 1345.

10 See *Waterloo Letter* No. 12.

11 See *Waterloo Letter* No. 109.

10 The First Exhibition

1 *Morning Post*, 5 October 1838.

2 *The Times*, 5 October 1838, 4.

3 USG, 6 October 1838, 8.

4 *John Bull*, 7 October 1838, 475.

5 *John Bull*, 14 October 1838, 487–8.

6 BL Add MS 34,707, fols 193–4.

7 *The Atlas*, 6 October 1838, 635.

8 Wellington, Seventh Duke of, *Wellington and His Friends*, 133–4.

9 Gawler claimed to have assisted him with the compilation of the *Guide*, but other than Gawler's statement, there is no direct evidence of this. Siborne's records do show a considerable amount of correspondence from Gawler that no doubt aided his researches, but Gawler was far from being the only contributor. (See: *Gawler, A Life Sketch*, 33.)

10 *Guide* (1st edn), 1–2.

11 BL Add MS 34,708, fols 232–3.

12 *USJ*, 1839, ii, 203.

13 *USJ*, 1844, ii, 3.

14 Siborne to Hardman, 10 September 1841, BL Add MS 34,707, fols 288–9.

15 See: PRO WO43/538 fols 196-8; copy in BL Add MS 34,707 fol 312.

16 BL Add MS 34,707, fol. 147.

17 *Exhibitions of Mechanical Works*, 93.

18 Minutes of the Council of the USI, 4 December 1839.

19 PRO WO76/186.

20 PRO WO31/806.

21 BL Add MS 34,707, fols 177–8. The Vivian family owned estates near Truro, Cornwall.

22 BL Add MS 34,707, fols 288–9.

23 PRO WO43/538.

24 PRO WO43/538, fols 196–8; copy in BL Add MS 34,707, fol. 312.

25 *Ibid.*

26 *Ibid.*

27 PRO WO43/538 fols, 192–5.

28 Wellington, Seventh Duke of, *Wellington and His Friends*, 133–4.

29 Mowbray, Sir John R., 'Seventy Years at Westminster', in *Blackwood's Edinburgh Magazine*, vol. clxiv, no. dccccxciii, July 1898, 13–14. It is interesting to note that when this memoir was published, a barrister by the name of T. W. Brogden wrote to Herbert Siborne on 2 July 1898 asking him if he was aware of Wellington's view of the model. Herbert did not keep a copy of his reply of 7 July, but Brogden's response to that, dated 12 July, is on record. From that, it is evident that Herbert was aware the Duke had never seen the model. Brogden, incidentally, very much a Waterloo buff, found Wellington's comments objectionable.

30 Strafford, 211.

31 See PRO WO43/538, fols 190–1, for the text.

32 Siborne's original can be found in BL Add MS 34,707, fol. 314. The copy he sent to Murray can be found in NLS Adv MS 46.9.12.

33 NLS Adv MS 46.8.21, fols 200–2.

34 The original can be found in BL Add MS 34,707, fols 314–5. The entry
    in Murray's letter book is in NLS Adv MS 46.9.12, fols 137–8.

35 The final ink copy can be found in BL Add MS 34,707, fol. 312, the pen-
    cil draft copy is fol. 316.

36 BL Add MS 34,707, fols 320–1.

37 BL Add MS 34,707, fols 322–3.

38 BL Add MS 34,707, fols 324–5.

39 BL Add MS 34,707, fols 317–9.

40 BL Add MS 34,707, fols 328–9.

11 The *History*

1 BL Add MS 34,707, fols 432–3.

2 *Ibid.*

3 WP2/94/103.

4 Records of Lea & Febiger, Collection 227B, Cost Book 1838–53, fol. 81.

5 *United States Magazine*, xvii, 318–9.

6 The most extreme example of this is Major-General William Napier's
   story, sent to Siborne on 28 November 1842. According to Napier, Müffling took thirty hours to ride thirty miles from the front with the news.
   Such a story could never be true, as Müffling was based in Brussels and
   had a party of dispatch riders at his disposal. Furthermore, simple
   mathematics reveals the impossibility of Napier's account. Müffling, he
   claimed, arrived in Brussels shortly before 11 p.m. The Prussian outposts first clashed with the invading French at about 4 a.m. That is a
   difference of nineteen hours, not thirty. One suspects that the
   inscrutable Napier, never a friend of Wellington's, might well have been
   making mischief, drawing attention to the inconsistencies in Wellington's accounts by means of a canard. While several accounts of the campaign give credence to what so obviously cannot be true, more fittingly,
   this myth forms the basis for a scene in Bernard Cornwell's fictional
   Sharpe's Waterloo.

7 Siborne, *History of the War in France and Belgium in 1815* (1st edn), i, 76–7.

8 *USJ*, 1841, ii, 172.

9 Siborne, *History of the War in France and Belgium in 1815* (2nd edn), i, 76–7.

10 Siborne's footnote is reproduced in full in the Appendices.

11 BL Add MS 34,703, fols 199–200.

12 BL Add MS 34,705, fols 303–4.

13 BL Add MS 34,706, fols 280–1.

14 Siborne to W. F. Wakeman, Dublin, 28 November 1836, NAM 6807-453.

15 Siborne to Murray, 14 February 1843. NLS Adv. MS 46.9.5, fol. 165. In this letter, Siborne also requested Murray to use his influence to help place his son Herbert, who had been educated in Germany. Interestingly, one of the allegations made against both the Sibornes is that neither had any knowledge of the German language. Reference to William's papers, and the history of Herbert's education, show how unfounded such accusations are.

16 *USG*, 8 June 1844, 3.

17 *Dublin University Magazine*, xxiv, cxl, July 1844, 126.

18 *The Times*, 27 January 1845, 8–9.

19 *USM*, May 1844, ii, 3.

20 *Ibid.*

21 The family disputed the authenticity of these memoirs when they were published and attempted to stop their distribution by recourse to law. While the details of the account given can be disputed, such an explanation for Wellington's hesitation at the beginning of the campaign is plausible. Fouché's biographer, Louis Madelin, considered the memoirs to be authentic. For a further discussion, see my *1815 – The Waterloo Campaign: Wellington, his German Allies and the Battles of Ligny and Quatre Bras*, especially 332–3.

22 *USM*, May 1844, ii, 11, fn.

23 *The Quarterly Review*, lxxvi, 224.

24 *Ibid.*; 233–40 deals with Alison and Fouché; 244 covers Grolman.

25 Strafford, 191.

26 Strafford, 204–5.

27 Strafford, 206.

28 Strafford, 210.

29 *USM*, October 1847, 183.

30 Strafford, 211.

31 *The Quarterly Review*, lxxvi, 218.

32 BL Add MS 34,708, fols 202–3.

33 BL Add MS 34,708, fols 208–9.

34 Siborne, *History of the War in France and Belgium in 1815* (3rd edn), xiii, fn.

12 The Prussians and The *Story*

1 *Militair-Wochenblatt*, xxix, i, 4 January 1845, 3.

2 *Ibid.*

3 See BL Add MS 34,703, fols 199–200.

4 Unfortunately, Mittler's records were destroyed by allied bombing in 1945, so it is no longer possible to check the details.

5 BL Add MS 34,708, fols 265–8.

6 *WD*, xii, 473.

7 BL Add MS 34,708, fols 273–4.

8 BL Add MS 34,708, fol 281.

9 Siborne, *History of the War in France and Belgium in 1815* (3rd edn), 36 fn.

10 Croker, i, 345.

11 Gleig, *Personal Reminiscences*, 23.

12 *Ibid.*, 23–25.

13 *Ibid.*, 27.

14 Sir William Augustus Fraser (1826-1898), fourth baronet, was the eldest son of Colonel Sir James John Fraser (d. 1834), third baronet, of the 7th Hussars, who was on the staff at Waterloo. He was gazetted a cornet in the 1st Life Guards in 1847, but he left the army in 1852. A staunch conservative, he became a familiar figure at the Carlton Club, where he was known pre-eminently as a raconteur of stories about Wellington and

Waterloo. He became a considerable authority on Wellington, publishing *Words on Wellington* in 1889 and *The Waterloo Ball* in 1897.

15 Fraser, *Words on Wellington*, 148–9.

16 John Murray to Gleig, 30 May 1846, archives of John Murray Ltd.

17 *USM*, November 1846, 436.

18 *The Spectator*, 5 June 1847, 551.

19 *USM*, August 1847, 602–3.

20 Siborne, *History of the War in France and Belgium in 1815* (3rd edn), xiii.

21 Gleig, *The Story of the Battle of Waterloo*, 49.

22 Siborne, *History of the War in France and Belgium in 1815* (3rd edn), xiv.

23 *Ibid.*, xxiv.

24 See *The Times*, 27 August 1847, 7.

25 Receipt dated 15 March 1847, archives of John Murray Ltd.

26 WP2/135/96-8.

27 See the 3rd edn, 11: 'By some unaccountable neglect Wellington was not informed of the attack until after three o'clock in the afternoon.'

13 Charge!

1 Siborne to Lt.-Colonel Marten, 16 July 1840, Brynmor Jones Library, University of Hull, DDMM/28/8.

2 Lt James Hope to Siborne, 3 September 1840, BL Add MS 34,707, fols 193–4.

3 BL Add MS 34,707, fols 412–5.

4 *Waterloo Letter* No. 18.

5 Henry William Paget, later the Marquess of Anglesey, was born in 1768 to a family of great landowners. In 1794, he raised a regiment from his father's tenantry that joined the Duke of York in Flanders. He participated in the expedition to Holland in 1799 at the head of the 7th Light Dragoons. He served briefly in the Iberian Peninsula under Sir John Moore before participating in the ill-fated Walcheran expedition of

1809. On his father's death in 1812, he became the Earl of Uxbridge. In 1815, he returned to Flanders to command Wellington's cavalry. At Waterloo, he had driven back d'Erlon's Corps as it was making Napoleon's first attempt at pushing through Wellington's centre. This assault came close to penetrating the Duke's positions and it was Uxbridge's charge that saved the day. Towards the end of the battle, he lost a leg and had it buried in a nearby garden. Paget was created the Marquess of Anglesey on 4 July 1815. After Waterloo, he held various posts, particularly as the Lord Lieutenant of Ireland from 1828–9 and then from 1830–3. It is probable he met Siborne then.

6 *Waterloo Letter* No. 3.

7 Commissioner's Minutes 1833–1846, PRO WO143/10, fol. 521.

8 Siborne to Brown, 9 October 1843, NLS Adv MS 2843, fol. 110.

9 *Army List 1845*, 315.

10 *Guide* (1844), 3–4.

11 *Court Journal*, 28 December 1844, 842.

12 *Illustrated London News*, 14 June 1845, 382.

13 *Court Gazette*, 21 June 1845, 1238.

14 *USG*, 28 June 1845, 6.

15 *The Times*, 6 July 1850, 2, gives details.

16 BL Add MS 34,708, fols 232–3.

17 Colonel Bowles to Siborne, 16 March 1846, BL Add MS 34,708, fols 237–8; Earl Howe to Siborne, 23 March 1846, BL Add MS 34,708, fols 239–40; Lord Strafford to Siborne, 9 April 1846; Peel to Siborne 13 April 1846, BL Add MS 34,708, fols 243–4; Fox Maude to Siborne, 15 July 1846, BL Add MS 34,708, fols 256–7.

18 BL Add MS 34,708, fols 251–2.

19 BL Add MS 34,708, fol. 252.

20 BL Add MS 34,708, fols 273–4.

21 *The Times*, 6 July 1850, 2.

22 *Vossische Zeitung* No. 291, 12 December 1846, No. 296, 18 December 1846, 3. Beilage.

23 BL Add MS 34,708, fols 263–4.

24 United Service Institution (USI), Minutes of Council, 6 December 1847.

25 USI, Minutes of Council, 6 December 1847.

26 See Minutes of RMA of 19 July 1848 in PRO WO143/11, fol. 168.
    Siborne was granted five weeks' sick leave. It is not known if he ever
    recovered and returned to his duties.

27 See his Death Certificate.

28 PRO PROB 11/2144.

29 USI, Minutes of Council, 13 April 1850.

30 Nineteenth Annual Report of the Council of the United Service Institu-
    tion, 10.

31 USI, Minutes of Council, 15 July 1850.

32 Twentieth Annual Report of the Council of the United Service Institu-
    tion, 10–11.

33 USI, Minutes of the Council, 17 July 1851.

34 USI, Minutes of the Council, 4 August and 17 November 1851.

14 Humbugged?

1 Müffling, *Leben*, 221.

2 Fouché, ii, 341–2.

3 GStA, Rep 92, Gneisenau, A 48, fol. 93.

4 Pflugk-Harttung, *Vorgeschichte*, 47.

5 The Frasnes Letter, as this document has subsequently become known,
   has been the subject of considerable controversy since General von
   Ollech included a facsimile of it in his *History of the Waterloo Campaign* published in 1876. Indisputably in Wellington's hand, the Duke's
   apologists consider that his staff gave him incorrect information which
   he unwittingly passed on to the Prussians. However, as the information
   he gave his allies conflicted with his orders, the reports he had been sent
   and what he saw of his troops with his own eyes, this defence is entirely
   implausible and was discredited some years ago.

6 Siborne, *History of the War in France and Belgium in 1815* (3rd edn), 36 fn.

7 *Ibid.*, 37 fn.

8　It was common practice in nineteenth-century texts to delete names of living persons from published texts.

9　Young, 307–8.

10　*USJ*, 1841, ii, 173.

11　Young, 307–8.

12　De Bas & T'Serclaes de Wommersom, i, 409.

13　*USJ*, 1841, ii, 173.

14　For a corrective to nearly two centuries of unquestioning acceptance of Wellington's version of these events, see my *1815 – The Waterloo Campaign*, 2 vols, Greenhill Books, 1998–9.

15　*Colburn's USM*, February 1849, i, 308.

Index

All military units are British unless otherwise denoted.
References to illustrations appear in **bold** type.